THE GENTLEMAN
FROM MASSACHUSETTS:

HENRY CABOT LODGE

The Gentleman
from Massachusetts:

Henry Cabot Lodge

By
KARL SCHRIFTGIESSER

AN ATLANTIC MONTHLY PRESS BOOK

LITTLE, BROWN AND COMPANY · BOSTON

1944

Published September 1944
Reprinted September 1944
Reprinted October 1944

ATLANTIC–LITTLE, BROWN BOOKS
ARE PUBLISHED BY
LITTLE, BROWN AND COMPANY
IN ASSOCIATION WITH
THE ATLANTIC MONTHLY PRESS

PRINTED IN THE UNITED STATES OF AMERICA

FOR MY MOTHER

A Word of Thanks

I SHOULD like to thank several persons who have aided me in writing this book. First a word of appreciation to Charles W. Morton, Jr., associate editor of the *Atlantic Monthly*, who was the first to share my belief that a biography of Henry Cabot Lodge was worth doing. Mr. Ellery Sedgwick also deserves a special word, as does Claude Moore Fuess of Phillips Academy, Andover, Massachusetts, who gave me much valuable advice and assistance. Others who were extremely generous of their time were Mr. J. Frank Mahaney of the *Lynn Item* and Mr. Alfred Clark of the *New York Times*. The Messrs. Frank Buxton, Edward J. Dunn, and Laurence Winship allowed me to prowl unmolested through the files of the *Boston Herald*, the *Boston Post*, and the *Boston Globe*, respectively; and Thomas Bracken, head librarian of the *New York Times*, and his entire staff, particularly on the night side, were more helpful than they know. Others who in one way or another aided me in gathering material, or in preparing the manuscript, were Senator Robert A. Taft, former Senator George Moses, Oswald Garrison Villard, Clarence S. Brigham of the American Antiquarian Society, Robert Whitney of Washington, Henry H. Crapo of New Bedford, Miss Sally McCaslin, Mrs. Mary W. Morris, June Kavanagh Maher, and several nameless public servants in the Boston and New York Public Libraries. And to Stanley Salmen, for his patience and his skill, a heartfelt word of appreciation. My wife and daughter, too, deserve more than this inadequate bow.

K. S.

Acknowledgments

I am indebted to Charles Scribner's Sons for permission to quote from *Selections from the Correspondence of Theodore Roosevelt and Henry Cabot Lodge*, from Lodge's *Early Memories* and *The Senate and the League of Nations*; to Houghton Mifflin Company for permission to quote from *The Letters of Henry Adams*, edited by Worthington Chauncey Ford, from *The Education of Henry Adams*, from *The Life of George Cabot Lodge*, by Henry Adams, from *Portrait of an Independent*, by M. A. DeW. Howe, and from *Beveridge and the Progressive Era*, by Claude G. Bowers; and to Harper & Brothers for permission to quote from *Henry White — Thirty Years of American Diplomacy*, by Allan Nevins. I also wish to thank the authors and publishers of all the books and articles listed in the bibliography, and particularly Denna F. Fleming, author of *The United States and the League of Nations, 1918–1920*.

K. S.

Contents

Contents

THE GENTLEMAN
FROM MASSACHUSETTS:

HENRY CABOT LODGE

I

The Seed of Essex

MANY a Yankee ancestry stretched further back into the history of New England than did that of Henry Cabot Lodge. The first Cabot did not arrive on these shores until 1700, and the first Lodge did not set foot in Boston until nearly a century later. It was wealth and intellect rather than priority of residence that had placed the Cabots on that particular eminence where they could afford to snub the Lowells and speak only to God. That they stood there, cold and aloof and sufficient unto themselves, none could deny. It seemed they had stood there always, that they were older than Plymouth Rock.

To a true Bostonian the peculiar superiority attached to the name of Cabot needed no explanation. Elsewhere, the mystery had to be dispelled. The first book which Henry Cabot Lodge wrote was undertaken for this purpose. With all America to choose from, the young man had selected his own great-grandfather as the subject of his youthful bid for fame. Indeed, of all his ancestors — and they were many — George Cabot was the only one to whom the budding Harvard historian could point with any degree of intellectual pride. This great gentleman had singlehandedly lifted the rich and ancient Cabot family above the commercial commonplace in which it had been comfortably settled before the American Revolution.

No other Cabot, and certainly no Lodge, had done anything to deserve the immortality of print. But anyone might see that George Cabot — friend of Washington, adviser of Hamilton, United States Senator from Massachusetts, and, according to the querulous John Adams, would-be President of New England — anyone might see that he had truly been a great man. Had not a whole generation known of him as the Federalist Sage? Were not the letters sent from his Brookline study documents of abiding worth, gems of political philosophy even one hundred years later? All his life Henry Cabot Lodge was to look to him with admiration, for George Cabot was the very embodiment of those solid virtues that had sprung from the cold Essex soil and flowered in the great port of Boston when the Republic was being born.

John Cabot was only twenty years old when he arrived from the Isle of Jersey at the seaport of Salem, then, next to Boston, the busiest and wealthiest center in New England. Very little is known about him, or about his social or financial standing at the time of his immigration. He appears to have been a personable young man, quite acceptable to the well-to-do and established families of the town. Within two years he married Anna Orne, whose family had been merchants in Salem for many years.

By his own initiative and the aid of her dowry he soon became a solid citizen as an importer and exporter of general merchandise. He and Anna Orne Cabot had nine children. Seven of them married into what the family historian has described as "the wealthiest and most distinguished of the old Puritan families of Salem." The oldest son is memorable as the first of forty-three Cabots to attend Harvard College within the next century and a half. He was a doctor by profession.

Esther Cabot, the second-oldest girl of the family, is also memorable in the Cabot genealogy because she made the first of numerous alliances between the Cabots and the Higginsons, one of the most dignified and prolific of the early

4

Puritan families settled on the North Shore of Massachusetts Bay.

The immigrant John Cabot, whose business was mostly trading in rum and molasses, became a rich man. He built a "mansion house," a warehouse and a wharf, and he supported pews in two churches. When he died, in the summer of 1742, he left an estate consisting of £4000 in silver currency, 410 gallons of rum, nearly 5000 gallons of undistilled molasses, his harborside real estate, and two schooners. Most of his tangible assets passed to two of his sons, Francis and Joseph Cabot, who also inherited his business shrewdness, perhaps an even greater heritage.

During the Seven Years' War their privateers brought them a measurable fortune from preying on French commerce. Joseph, the younger but more able of the brothers, used his new wealth to send for an English architect to design and build a fine Georgian mansion. Not only was his home physically one of the most gracious in the town, but the hospitality dispensed therein was famous in its day. His business and his social life absorbed him and he had no time for politics or civil affairs, although many of his friends and his wife's relatives, the Higginsons, held public office and were active in the conduct of the town and Colony.

Joseph Cabot lived to be only forty-seven years old and when he died his widow soon sold the Salem house and moved to one she had built in the less crowded town of Beverly. Her sons, John and Andrew Cabot, also moved to that port. They were daring young businessmen. Their fleet of vessels were continually on the run between Massachusetts, the southern colonies, and Spain, their holds crowded with molasses, rum, salt codfish, and iron.

Able sailors, shrewd merchants, and tight-fisted shipowners, these third-generation Cabots laid the solid foundations on which was built that "salt-fish aristocracy" which soon was to determine the economic and political future of New England. In this they were greatly aided by their younger and somewhat wayward brother, George, who had been born in the Salem mansion on January 16, 1752. It was he who was to give the family lasting distinction.

George Cabot was sent to Harvard College and was placed seventeenth in a class of forty-two boys, a standing which had nothing to do with his intellect but which signified where the father stood financially and socially among the North Shore and Boston families. Indeed, George Cabot was a singularly casual scholar. During his freshman year he joined in a brisk student rebellion against the bad butter served in commons, and two years later he suddenly left Cambridge barely in time to escape public reprimand for his "idle behavior" and "great neglect of his studies."

The restless youngster was at once sent to sea by his brothers under one of their strictest captains. The sea change did him good, so much so that on his eighteenth birthday his brothers rewarded him by giving him command of a small schooner, which he sailed from Beverly to Bilbao, Spain, with a load of codfish. Within a year he was placed in command of the larger schooner *Premium*, the newest addition to the growing Cabot fleet. He took her to the James River with a cargo of rum and cider, sold that and bought a cargo of wheat.

In the meantime he had fallen in love with his double first cousin, Elizabeth Higginson, an energetic and strong-willed young lady. For a wedding present he was given a one-sixth interest in the Cabot Brothers' business and the control of several of the firm's best ships. Under his bride's guidance he soon became a hard-driving and domineering trader. When he was twenty-three years old, the Revolution against the British King broke. Instead of having a disastrous effect upon the brothers Cabot, the Revolution was a boon. Their

6

forty-four busy privateers and letters-of-marque ships brought them a fortune which they safely stored in a private bank in Bilbao until peace was restored.

It was of these three brothers that Judge Curwen, a Loyalist who had fled to London, wrote in 1779: "Those who five years ago were the meaner people are now, by a strange revolution, become almost the only men of power, riches, and influence. The Cabots of Beverly who . . . had but five years ago a very moderate share of property are now said to be by far the most wealthy in New England."

As the wealth, power, and influence of these North Shore families increased it was only natural that they should take political means to guard them. They knew that they must take control of the new government lest those who had listened too attentively to Sam Adams and Tom Paine should attempt to carry into effect the principles for which they had fought the British. It was not love of politics that drew young George Cabot into the arena. It was the necessity of economic self-interest.

The very year that Judge Curwen was commenting upon New England's *nouveaux riches* George Cabot traveled to Concord to argue against the proposal of the Boston merchants to fix prices in order to thwart the depreciation of currency. Thereafter he was to be more and more involved in Massachusetts and federal politics.

Among men of his class and standing one question was foremost at this time: the framing of a constitution for the Commonwealth. The document which was finally adopted was mainly the work of John Adams, that irascible little man who believed in a government of laws and not of men and who secretly longed for the establishment of an American monarchy. While it met with the approval of the North Shore merchants, who had formed a political group which became known as the Essex Junto, there were others who

7

were afraid of it. The Baptists despised it because it set up Congregationalism as a state religion; the farmers were sure it gave the "marchantile towns" over-representation; the inland centers saw themselves doomed by the power given the seaports. Property qualifications for voters were doubled over the old Charter — a gratuitous insult, so many said, to the unpropertied. Well, these matters could be thrashed out at meeting, where each town had the right to accept or reject each clause before sending its final ballots to be counted.

And so they were thrashed out and the people thought they would get the kind of constitution they desired. But they failed to reckon with the Convention, of which George Cabot was a prominent member. He was one of the group entrusted with the counting of the ballots. The associates met behind locked doors. At the town meetings the people had understood that a two-thirds vote was required for the passage of each clause. Cabot and his colleagues decided otherwise: the vote should be applied to the paper as a whole. At least two of the articles, and perhaps more, failed to receive approval of the voters, yet the committee deliberately juggled the returns to make it appear that they had. And so the Convention ruled that the people had accepted as a whole a constitution they wanted only in part. George Cabot returned to his Beverly mansion convinced that he had done a good day's work.

With the coming of peace the Essex Junto became increasingly important. By virtue of his wealth and his political acumen George Cabot was recognized as one of its most potent leaders. In 1783 he served a term as State Senator under the constitution he had helped put over. As an ardent disciple of Alexander Hamilton he became known beyond the boundaries of the Commonwealth. At the Massachusetts ratifying convention, to which he was a delegate, he worked closely with the Federalists in bringing into existence the Federal Constitution which Fisher Ames, his close friend, always insisted was "dictated by commercial necessity more than any other cause."

Long before he was forty years old George Cabot was considered a leading citizen. In 1789 George Washington was pleased to be his guest at Beverly. Two years later he was made a Senator from Massachusetts. He was, at this time, a dignified gentleman of commanding stature, gracious manner, and an excellent conversationalist. He was an effective member of the Senate, then a small body which always met in closed session. No advocate of the rights of man, he introduced the Fugitive Slave Act which passed both houses of Congress in 1793.

George Cabot's business ventures were extensive. Primarily he was an importer and exporter and the owner of a large fleet of sailing vessels, but in the 1780's he became a foremost promoter of cotton manufacturing. He was an investor in the Essex Bridge, one of the first American corporations. With Joseph Lee, his brother-in-law, he formed a general business partnership in 1785 and was so successful that seven years later he was able to retire with what was known as a "reasonable and sufficient fortune." He was a director of the first bank in Massachusetts and president of the Boston branch of Mr. Hamilton's United States Bank.

Most of the men of Essex came rushing to Boston after the Revolution, snapping up the abandoned mansions of the Tories who had fled the war and setting themselves up as the new aristocracy of the town. George Cabot, too, left Beverly. For a time he lived in splendor on a large estate in Brookline, which was recognized as the unofficial headquarters of New England Federalism. While living there he spent much of his time writing long letters of political advice. When his old friend Hamilton — whose adviser he had been (as Daniel Webster said) on "everything that belonged to the commercial system of the United States" — was killed, he dedicated his life to keeping the Federalist Party from foundering.

Wearied of active politics George Cabot resigned from the Senate in 1796 and two years later refused to accept the Secretaryship of the Navy to which he had been appointed by President Adams. He was content to bask in his reputation as the Federalist Sage. He moved to Boston, where he was now a director of the Suffolk and the Boston Marine insurance companies. In his eyes Thomas Jefferson was an "anarchist." When news reached him of Mr. Jefferson's purchase of Louisiana he was convinced that the acquisition of the new territory meant the perpetual subjection of New England to the South and West.

It was George Cabot's old friend, Timothy Pickering, who first suggested secession. Secretly he approached other members of the Junto — crusty Fisher Ames, Theophilus Parsons, the cold and calculating North Shore philosopher, and Mr. Higginson, the powerful shipmaster. They looked with sympathy upon the idea. But they were afraid to carry it into action. George Cabot expressed their views when he said: "The thing proposed is obvious and natural; but it would now be thought too bold, and would be fatal to its advocates as public men; yet the time *may* soon come when it will be demanded of the North and East, and then it will unavoidably take place."

Pickering's "plot" came to nothing and was forgotten, by those who were aware of it, until the War of 1812 deeply hurt the pocketbooks of the New England shippers. It was not far from the minds of a little group of "cautious and elderly men, who detested democracy, but disliked enthusiasm as much," who met at Hartford on December 15, 1814. At the head of this group, although "dragged in like a conscript to the duty of delegate," was George Cabot, now sixty-two years old. They locked the doors behind them and to this day it is not known exactly what took place. Among the demands approved by the delegates were one barring from federal office any but native-born Americans, another limiting Presidential office to one term, and a third prohibiting successive Presidents from being chosen from the same state. That angry words were spoken against the United States Government and that talk of secession was openly raised are undoubtedly true.

The war ended before the demands of the Hartford Convention could materialize into an active program. When old John Adams, grown stout and cranky, heard about the goings-on, he cackled: "George Cabot's close-buttoned ambition has broke out at last; he wants to be president of New England, sir."

George Cabot himself was growing old, and sunk deep in pessimism. He said one day to his old friend Pickering, "Why can't you and I let the world ruin itself in its own way?"

The Federalist Party died with the end of the War of 1812 and age and disillusionment soon broke up, as a political power, the little group of Massachusetts conservatives who had risen to eminence from that cold and narrow strip of the North Shore. But their philosophy and creed were never to die in Massachusetts. Their sons and grandsons were to see to that.

George Cabot's son, Henry, was born in Beverly in 1783, while his father was serving in the Massachusetts Senate. He was sent to Harvard at the age of thirteen but, like his father, was forced for disciplinary reasons to withdraw before graduation. For the next few years he studied law in the office of one of his father's friends and in 1804 he started practice. It is doubtful if he cared much for his profession or if he was a great success at it, for he soon gave it up and through his father's influence entered the insurance business.

His wife was Anna Blake, daughter of a family long connected with the merchant aristocracy of Boston and a descendant of the Admiral Blake who had once sunk a Spanish fleet at Santa Cruz. They took a house on fashionable High Street, but when George Cabot died they moved into the Summer Street mansion where the Sage had lived during the later years of his life. After his father's death Henry Cabot retired from business and lived the life of a Boston gentleman.

When Henry Cabot was eight years old, a young stranger named Giles Lodge arrived by accident in Boston. He was just twenty-one years old at the time, tall, blond, and of Huguenot descent. He also was a member of the Ellerton family which had boasted residence in England since the days of William the Conqueror. His home was in Liverpool, where his two brothers conducted an importing business. As their agent he had been sent to Santo Domingo in 1791, arriving there in time to find himself in the midst of a bloody uprising and massacre of the native Negroes. He fled for his life on the first vessel he could board and eventually found himself disembarking at Boston. He liked the city and his brothers set him up there as their American agent.

Hardly more than a year after his arrival Giles Lodge fell in love with a Boston girl named Mary Langdon and they were married. Mrs. Lodge's father was a cousin of President Samuel Langdon of Harvard, who is remembered for the prayer he uttered for the Continental soldiers on the eve of Bunker Hill. Her maternal grandfather, John Walley, had been a major general in an expedition against Canada, and later served as a member of the Governor's Council. Their only son, John Ellerton Lodge, was born in Boston on November 26, 1807. Twenty-five years later he married Henry Cabot's daughter, Anna Sophia, who, on May 12, 1850, bore him a son. They named him Henry Cabot Lodge.

II

Boston Incarnate

IN THE first springtime of the nineteenth century's decline, Grandfather Henry Cabot's smooth granite house sat in cool and isolated splendor behind the thick foliage of what is now Boston's dilapidated Winthrop Square. On the Sunday morning of Henry Cabot Lodge's birth the pear trees, whose fruit next autumn would bring accustomed prizes at the Horticultural Society, were dropping their petals over the marble nymph in the garden at the rear. Close by on Summer Street the horse-chestnut trees were already preparing for their summer duty of shutting out the gaze of the curious from the homes of solid Boston gentlemen who lived in this center of respectability. Peace and quiet dignity lay over the snug eighteenth-century remnant of the busy port.

To most of Boston's 133,000 inhabitants the event that had just occurred upstairs in Mr. Cabot's house meant nothing. But in that little island between Washington Street and Commercial Wharf, and along the harbor side of Beacon Hill, the news created a ripple of pleasant excitement. As John Ellerton Lodge could proudly announce, when in the morning he walked briskly off to his countinghouse in the granite block on the Wharf, he now had a son as well as a seven-year-old daughter. To the child's grandfather, still tall and erect, it meant the arrival of another Cabot, a descendant in the third generation of Senator George Cabot of Beverly, Brookline, and Boston, under whose magnificent shadow the family still dwelt. His friends and neighbors —

those families whose wealth and genealogical prestige gave meaning and personality to the old city — would understand his glow of pride.

The infant Henry Cabot Lodge was one of their breed. With a gesture of welcome they signified their approval almost at once by dropping his first name and calling him Cabot thenceforward to the end of his life. That he was to be their century's personification of his great-grandfather these Bostonians could not know. He was a Cabot born in Boston and that was enough. Many years later Henry Adams, whose understanding of stratospheric Boston society was profound, with that lightly cynical touch of which he was the master, called Henry Cabot Lodge "Boston incarnate — the child of his local parentage."

Henry Cabot Lodge was born in the heart of a little world bounded by a city. In such isolation he was to grow to maturity and long after he had known New York and Washington, London, Berlin, Paris and Rome, he was still to bear the marks of its insularity. "Oh, you bigoted New Englander!" Theodore Roosevelt used to chide his "dear old boy" when they were playing at statesmen together under President Harrison's mildly disapproving eye. In deportment, manner, accent, and thought he never escaped the influence not of the accident but of the fact of his birthplace. And that was Boston: not the teeming city of docks and slums but the clean, calm, cultured little world within the city, a world aloof, untouched, and inhabited by an impeccable elite over whom the Cabots reigned supreme.

The Cabots did not boast of their leadership. They assumed that it was understood and accepted by all. "My boy," Henry Cabot used to say to his grandson, "we do not talk of family in this country. It is enough for you to know that your grandfather is an honest man." Thus, with singular aptness, was blended the old Puritanism with an ineffable Yankee distaste for England and its ways which had lasted in Boston since 1776. And yet, paradoxically, Boston was English in so many ways: in its silent acceptance of an aristocracy, in its literary tastes, in its architecture, in its speech. It might call itself the Athens of America but it thought of itself as another London, its houses almost as old, its streets as crooked, and the blood of its best families as free from alien strains as that of those who attended Queen Victoria's court.

Boston was still a potent city. Its society had not grown soft. The age of trusteeship had not fully arrived with its attendant weakening of the will to achieve. State Street meant as much as Wall Street, and probably more, in the great financial centers of the world. The true Bostonian was an active and expansive man, no matter how cold and narrow he might seem while seated at his desk. His lines of communication did not stop at Worcester, but at Canton. His canvas whitened the rich harbors of the world; his voice gave orders in the Deep South and the Far West; it was his steel against which the hammers of the expanding nation rang. It was his money, everywhere, that got things done. And if his home was filled with books and paintings, the sound of music and good talk, were not these the things worth striving for?

Henry Cabot Lodge's father was as busy a man as could be found in any Boston warehouse or along any Boston wharf. His family and friends often worried because he drove himself so much. If Bostonians ever allowed themselves to talk about such things they would say he was a rich man. But since they were rich, it was not considered in good taste to mention the matter except, of course, in some cozy moment at the Temple Club or over the teacups in a Summer Street parlor. His friends, and they were many, lived like himself, sumptuously in old mansions; they were ad-

15

mired for their philanthropy, their patronage of the arts, and sometimes for their eccentricities. They traveled, collected *objets d'art* and good books. Many of them were scholars. Almost all of them had gone to Harvard and would send their sons there. The pattern of their life was formed.

There was still an oligarchy, and a caste. It consisted of fifteen, perhaps twenty, families, many of whom, like the Cabots, stemmed from the Essex seed, and for all their patrician benevolence they ruled with a hand of iron. Nearly one quarter of all the nation's cotton spindlage was owned by them and they controlled at least half of the huge insurance capital of Massachusetts and 40 per cent of Boston's extensive banking resources. Their money was secure. It had been since the establishment of the Boston Manufacturing Company in 1813, since the founding of the Massachusetts Hospital Life Insurance Company five years later.

Known as the Boston Associates, these gentlemen controlled the very flow of the Merrimack and the Connecticut Rivers. Mill owners paid the rates they set. Manufacturers paid them for the use of the machines on which they held patents. The canals and the new railroads were under their ownership or control throughout the entire state. Their textile domain extended from Maine and New Hampshire to Rhode Island. They were the builders of cities, some of which, like Lowell and Lawrence, bore their names. They controlled the press and pulpit and politics of Massachusetts. It was they who had sent the great Daniel Webster to the Senate: Webster, the corporation lawyer who had assumed Hamilton's toga when he said, "The great object of government is protection of property at home, respect and renown abroad." Above all men of their time he was their hero, sound on the tariff and the interests of Massachusetts, for the preservation of which he "preached union — and surrendered the fugitive slave."

John Ellerton Lodge was a shipowner and trader, with his vessels on constant trek to the Orient; by instinct and through marriage he was a member of this close society. His father, Giles Lodge, had been an early investor in the cotton factories of New England and John had spent his early youth as a cotton factor in New Orleans. At the head of the household, however, was Henry Cabot, who divided his time between the Temple Club on West Street, his own library, and the theater, for all of which he had an equal passion. He had known Dan'l Webster for many years, admiring him as a politician, but preferring him as a fishing companion. It was only when the great Daniel made his Seventh of March speech upholding the Compromise of 1850 that old Henry Cabot, in both sorrow and anger, turned his back on his friend. There having been no more Federalists when he came of age in 1804, or none to speak of, he had grown up as a Whig; then he had become a Free Soiler; in a few years he would join the new Republican Party and vote for Frémont. Now in his old age he was an object of awe and respect: as a child had he not hidden under a sideboard and seen and heard George Washington when the President had visited his father?

Even more Bostonian, in thought and deed, was Henry Cabot's sister, Elizabeth Cabot Kirkland. She was opinionated and, some said, sharp-tongued, but after all, as a Cabot and the widow of John Thornton Kirkland, Harvard's indifferent and liberal President, had she not a right to her own mind? A widely traveled lady, she liked to bask in her reputation as the first American woman to ascend the Great Pyramid. When her grandnephew was born, she ordered him brought to her rooms on Summer Street every day. And every day, for the last two years of her life, she doted over the blond little boy, perhaps feeling that through her presence he would grow up to be a true Cabot, a true Bostonian.

Against this background and among these people Cabot Lodge the child grew up. His earliest years were spent in his grandfather's large house. The great lawyer Rufus Choate, hurrying his "ignominious, but convenient" way through the alley beside the Cabot stable, could see him playing in the garden under the watchful eye of the Cabot footman. When the heat of summer steamed the Boston streets he and his sister, Elizabeth Cabot Lodge, would be hurried off to their grandfather's "villa" at Nahant, that almost-island off Lynn which always reminded Henry Adams of a ship just stranded on the rocky coast of Cape Ann. Thus, winter and summer, the child was kept from contact with the world.

In Boston there were the sons of Bostonians to play with; in Nahant there were the same. Not until he was past his twentieth year was Cabot Lodge to be aware of any life except that which he and the other sons of the Boston oligarchy lived. His father may have read in the newspapers that half of Boston's ten thousand children in the primary schools were of foreign parentage, and mostly Irish, but Cabot Lodge was to know of this part of the other Boston only because the "muckers," as he called them, pelted him with snowballs when he went coasting on the Common. Of that city of "indescribably loathesome slums," which Dr. Josiah Curtis exposed in 1849, he was to know nothing. Winthrop Place and Half Moon Place were as far apart as two worlds.

When he was five years old he was placed in the genteel hands of Mrs. Parkman, a brilliant friend of his mother who, Boston-like, had started a small and select school for her own children and those of her friends. As a descendant of John Eliot, the Apostle to the Indians, who had founded the Roxbury Latin School in 1645, her motto was, "Use your mind. I don't care what you answer if only you use your mind." The boy learned easily to read in English and French and formed a dislike for mathematics which lasted all his life. Mrs. Parkman's was a school of great refinement where, as Cabot Lodge said in his old age, "the boys were picked." He was always to remember the soft rich voice of Fanny Kemble, the actress-idol of all the Boston ladies, who came there one afternoon to read poems to the little boys.

The year 1857 saw a financial panic sweep the country. Many friends of John Ellerton Lodge were affected, although he managed to ride the storm without appreciable loss. Among those who foundered was Samuel Eliot, who had entered business late in life after a distinguished career which had led him to Washington as a Whig member of Congress. He was forced to sell his fine home at 31 Beacon Street, not far from the red-brick Bulfinch State House and next door to the magnificent mansion and famous gardens once occupied by John Hancock, the first Governor of Massachusetts, who was known to many of his contemporaries as that "empty barrell" but who, as Cabot Lodge was once to write, stood out "with a fine show of lace and velvet and dramatic gout, a real aristocrat, shining and resplendent" against the drabness of the town.

Because "trade" was already encroaching upon the region where the Cabots had lived so long, and because the city was about to cut the newly ordered Devonshire Street across the site of Henry Cabot's home and garden in Winthrop Place, Mr. Lodge decided to move. For $50,000 he bought Mr. Eliot's home, which he completely remodeled and into which, in due time, he moved his family. Beacon Hill was also a part of that little world within the city beyond whose mythical boundary no Cabot ever stepped.

By now the boy had outgrown Mrs. Parkman's parlor school and education was to be continued in the basement of the Park Street Church where Mr. Thomas Russell Sullivan ministered to the intellectual needs of the "young Heathens and little Gallios" of the neighborhood. Young Cabot Lodge's healthy and well-fed companions were, for the most part, neighbors or kinsmen: Sturgis Bigelow, Henry Parkman, Henry Lee, Sam Cabot, George Lyman, Russell Gray — youngsters who were headed for Harvard and local fame as doctors, inventors, politicians, and judges. In this company Cabot Lodge worked hard and kept near the head of his classes.

In all respects his was a happy childhood. Although his father had been past thirty when he married and past forty when his only son was born, young Cabot Lodge found him an understanding companion. They spent all the time that could be spared from school or countinghouse together, driving to the elder Lodge's shipyard in Medford, or down to Nahant to tend the gardens in the spring. Long afternoons were passed at Commercial Wharf, where Mr. Lodge's ships — *Argonaut, Don Quixote, Sancho Panza, Kremlin, Storm King, Cossack, Magnet,* and *Sarah H. Snow* — tied up on their visits to the home port. The spicy-salty air, the sweet molasses kegs, the captains and the sailors, the postage stamps to be collected from returning friends, all added to the joy of boyhood and gave Cabot Lodge memories that were to remain as fresh as the east wind always.

So it was to be, also, with Nahant — the sea, the rocks, the breaking surf, and the boundless expanse of ocean. There were boats to row and sail; there was swimming with his friends; later there was a Morgan horse named "Pip" to ride. His was a quiet, orderly, healthy youth. Mr. Lodge was a man of considerable taste whose father, although absorbed in business, had owned to a passion for the "poet's poet," Spenser. His own interests ran more to Shakespeare and Pope, both of whom he would endlessly recite on his journeys with the boy to Medford and Nahant. His home was filled with books. No wonder that by the time he was ten, Cabot Lodge had read all the *Waverley Novels* and was on his way to a similar record in the works of Charles Dickens, Jacob Abbott, and Maria Edgeworth.

Mr. Lodge loved the companionship of intellectuals. Charles Sumner, the abolitionist, often dined with him when in the city. John Lothrop Motley, historian of the Dutch Republic, was so close a friend that he was "Uncle John" and Mrs. Motley was "Aunt Mary" to the boy. Mr. Agassiz was always on hand at Nahant to identify any strange fish Cabot might catch. That kindly, black-haired necromancer, Benjamin Peirce, was never so absorbed in mathematical abstractions that he did not have time to invent a new game for Cabot or Elizabeth to play. Tall and startling Rufus Choate, the lawyer, was their neighbor and frequent guest.

After four years of Mr. Sullivan's instruction, Cabot and most of his classmates were transplanted to the care of Mr. Dixwell, the stern and puritanic proprietor of a private Latin school where the classes were small and the boys once again were "picked." Mr. Dixwell's mission was to prepare his young charges for the four years of Harvard to which they inevitably were to be subjected. For this purpose his years as a master of the Boston Latin School, which had been doing just this since 1635, had given him excellent training. Under his watchful eye, Cabot Lodge studied Greek and Latin, French and German, English, mathematics, and history. He did his work satisfactorily, but without distinction.

Shortly after the opening of the school term in September 1862, tragedy entered the Lodge home. Early one evening, while Cabot was having his supper, his father came in for his customary chat with the boy. Although he was tired and drawn he joked for a while and then went up to his room to rest before dinner. There was a sudden crash and when

21

the servants reached him they found he had fallen on the floor, dead from a heart attack. The twelve-year-old boy was overwhelmed with shock and grief, and he was soon sent to a friend's house to spend the trying days before the funeral. The service was held at the Brattle Street Church and was widely attended, for Mr. Lodge's acquaintances in the city were many. Years later Cabot Lodge's most vivid memory of the sad occasion was the large number of poor people to whom his father had been charitable who crowded into the rear of the church.

Although he was to be deeply aware of a void in his life for a long time after his father's death, the healthiness of his mind and body and the serenity of his surroundings quickly dissipated any morbid feelings he may have possessed.

As might have been expected in a household in which Charles Sumner was a frequent guest, the Lodges were strong Unionists. Abraham Lincoln was their hero from the beginning. The Civil War was a holy cause. Immediately after President Lincoln's call for volunteers in the early spring of 1861, Mr. Lodge had wanted to raise a cavalry outfit for the Union Army, but an injury received in a riding accident disqualified him for service. Unable to serve actively he had to content himself with helping to enlist other volunteers and with raising money for the Sanitary Commission. His patriotism was intense and he followed carefully the despatches in the newspapers.

Although Cabot's immediate family was personally untouched by the conflict, the young men whom Cabot had seen at his sister's parties went off to fight. Huntington Wolcott, older brother of Cabot's friend Roger Wolcott, came home fever-ridden and died at the age of seventeen. Cabot attended his funeral. He heard young Captain Oliver Wendell Holmes tell of his experiences. The casualty lists in the newspapers listed among the dead and wounded many young men whose families were intimate friends of his own. At school the progress of the war was freely discussed and before Lee's surrender the young boys were being given military drill.

Cabot saw young Robert Gould Shaw lead his Negro regiment off to war. All the passions and prejudices of the North swept around him and formed in his mind impressions and opinions that were not wiped out in a lifetime. He was never to forget how as a boy he hated the Indiana conspirators and the draft rioters of New York; nor was he ever able to forgive those Northern Copperheads who were openly or secretly "assailing the government, seeking to cripple it and proclaiming their sympathy with its enemies." They were, he wrote in 1913, "utterly disloyal and deserve to be spoken of in history in proper terms as among the worst foes of the country."

At this time also, his inborn Yankee disinclination towards Great Britain received a lasting impetus. When he read in the English newspapers and in *Blackwood's Magazine* British criticism of the Northern cause he trembled with "impotent rage." In his mind, then and thereafter, the issue was simple. "The war was fought to save the Union," he wrote in his old age, when recalling his youth, "but it was slavery which had put the Union in peril." One morning he was aroused very early by a servant and told of the assassination of Abraham Lincoln. The crime which ended the great President's life raised him in Cabot Lodge's eyes "to the proportions of a demi-god."

Thus to the distant sound of fife and drum Cabot Lodge grew up. He learned then, he said, and never forgot, the lesson that there can be but two sides to any question: right and wrong. In this instance, the North was right and the South was wrong. Nothing could alter that. Fully as much as his own economic predilections, the Civil War, as seen through the eyes of a Boston childhood, determined the future course of his intellectual life.

The summer after Cabot's sixteenth birthday was marked by a journey abroad, the first Mrs. Lodge had taken since, as a girl, she and her father had posted in a carriage to all the fashionable places on the Continent. Although Cabot had spent some weeks with his mother at the St. Nicholas Hotel in New York three years before, and during the following summer had visited Niagara Falls, this was his first extended trip away from Boston. Besides Mrs. Lodge and Cabot there were Elizabeth and her husband and Constant Davis, who went along as a companion and tutor for Cabot.

The trip led the group first to England and then to Paris, Rome, Naples, Venice, and Vienna. Of vastly more importance in Cabot's life than the countries visited, the cathedrals examined, or the sites seen, was the presence of the frail young tutor, already ill of tuberculosis beyond the hope of recovery. Constant Davis was several years older than Cabot, having been graduated from Harvard in 1864. His father was Rear Admiral Charles Henry Davis of the United States Navy and his mother was Mrs. Lodge's second cousin as well as her lifelong and most intimate friend. He was one of those happy scholars who made Virgil and Homer interesting, who could extract the oratorical essence from Cicero and make the poets in Felton's *Greek Reader* glow far beyond their grammatical construction. The beauties and humors of Shakespeare came alive on his tongue. He was an ideal companion for a young man soon to enter Harvard. Without pedantry he made the European tour an important chapter in the education of Cabot Lodge.

The Lodges left America in June 1866 and did not return until the following spring. On the first day of July, Cabot began his examinations for entrance to Harvard. For three days he was subjected to oral inquisition. When he returned to the "villa" he found his family gathered on the veranda. With downcast eyes he approached them, muttering something about having received "four conditions." There was a deep silence, for that meant a summer of study if he were to pass them off in the fall. Then Colonel O. W. Holmes, Jr., who was a guest, gave the boy a sharp look and exclaimed, "The young villain! He is without conditions." He was. As a reward he was allowed to spend the summer fishing and hunting with his cousin in Canada and the Adirondacks.

When Cabot Lodge entered Harvard College in the autumn of 1867, Dr. Thomas Hill was in the last year of his presidency. The courses were generally stiff, inelastic and unimaginative. It was not until the beginning of his junior year that young Dr. Charles William Eliot was to take charge, shake up the ancient institution, introduce the system of "electives" and make Harvard into a modern college. But even in Cabot's freshman year the old educational habits were changing and reform was in the air. He entered with one of the largest classes in the history of the college, a class which was to send forth 158 graduates in 1871.

Cabot Lodge, freshman, was a tall, slender youngster with blond curly hair, who dressed well and fashionably. Among his classmates he was noted for his rather caustic wit. He traveled, of course, in the most select company and experienced no difficulty in being elected to Hasty Pudding and Porcellian. As a student he was without distinction. He was no athlete, although he liked rowing on the Charles River and sparring in the gymnasium. In a more democratic institution he would have been considered a dude and a snob. In Harvard he was just another rich young man from Boston with no aim in life beyond receiving a gentleman's "C" and having a good time. In later years he was to say that he had detested school but that he enjoyed college, where he spent "four very happy years."

Cabot Lodge's father had been of that group of Boston gentlemen who in 1854 had founded and subsidized the Boston theater which for many years was managed by Junius Brutus Booth. Henry Cabot had taken his grandson to the Howard Athenaeum to see *Julius Caesar*. Later the boy became a devotee of William Warren's stock company at the Boston Museum. On his first visit to New York he and his closest friend, Sturgis Bigelow, had spent most of their time going to the theater. In Europe he had heard all the good operas of the day. Now, at Harvard, he took part in the college theatricals put on by Hasty Pudding and he attended every new play in Boston. Whenever the Boston Opera needed a "supe" to carry a spear, Cabot would be on hand.

Between classes and the theater and the mild social affairs of Cambridge, Beacon Hill, and Brookline, the time passed quickly. At least until his senior year he drifted through his courses, a rather snobbish young man — when he heard Charles Dickens lecture he was "haunted by a suspicion" that the English author whose books he had devoured "was not quite a gentleman" — faintly amused by the literary dissertations of Professor James Russell Lowell, but otherwise intellectually unmoved. Then he fell under the spell of a strange and cynical young man, twelve years his senior, who the year before had decided to talk to boys at Cambridge instead of dancing with girls in Washington, and had come on, at President Eliot's suggestion, to teach medieval history, a subject about which he knew nothing.

The friendship with Henry Adams, established in the autumn of 1870 when Cabot Lodge stumbled into his classroom, was felicitous. It marked a turning point in the aimless life of the wealthy young Boston gentleman. The teacher and pupil had much in common. Like Cabot Lodge, Henry Adams had wandered through life until this period without any clear idea of the direction he was taking. A descendant of the second and sixth Presidents of the United States, wealthy enough so that he did not have to earn his own living, he had served as secretary to his father, Charles Francis Adams, when that gentleman was Ambassador to the Court of St. James's. Somewhat vaguely he dreamed of becoming a great man, worthy of his overwhelming ancestry. At thirty-one, however, he had done nothing notable and his family urged him to accept President Eliot's invitation to become an Assistant Professor of History in the department headed by his future brother-in-law, Ephraim W. Gurney. Having no valid excuse not to do so, Adams had come to Cambridge where he lived with his younger and brilliant brother, the shy and introspective Brooks Adams, in the home of his aunt, Mrs. Edward Everett.

His informality as a teacher — he used no textbooks and was quite willing to confess his ignorance publicly — and his obviously brilliant mind made him liked by the few pupils who attended his classes. With the exception of Constant Davis, he was the first mature person among Cabot Lodge's acquaintances with a capacity for imparting knowledge joyfully, and so, almost at once, he occupied an important part in Cabot's life. Henry Adams was to stay at Harvard for seven years. During all that time Cabot was his particular protégé. Adams planned his life for him and for many years led him along the path of his choosing. When, in later years, Cabot branched out on his own road, away from the goal indicated by Henry Adams, the two men remained the closest of friends.

Adams, however, did not introduce Cabot to Nannie Davis. Cabot probably could not remember the time when he had not known this attractive sister of Constant whose full name was Anna Cabot Mills Davis. They had played games together as children at Nahant, they attended the same parties in Boston when they were growing up. There was nothing but approval expressed when they became engaged in Cabot's junior year.

Cabot considered Rear Admiral Davis to be one of the most wonderful men he had ever known. His grandfather, Daniel Davis of Barnstable, had been Solicitor General of Massachusetts at the beginning of the nineteenth century and had married Lois Freeman, daughter of the Unitarian pastor of Boston's King's Chapel. They were the parents of thirteen children. The oldest, Louisa, had married William Minot, who was, in Henry Adams's phrase, "of a family more thoroughly Boston, if possible, than all the rest." The youngest child of this union was born in Boston in 1807 and in 1823 left Harvard College to become midshipman on the frigate *United States* under Commodore Isaac Hull. Although during the Civil War he had been engaged in several of the more decisive naval battles, particularly as Admiral du Pont's fleet captain at Port Royal and as commander of the Upper Mississippi gunboat flotilla, it was as a seagoing scholar that he was best known. He had made the first thorough study of the dangerous waters around Nantucket Island and he had helped establish the *American Ephemeris and Nautical Almanac.*

The mother of Cabot's fiancée was the daughter of United States Senator Elijah Hunt Mills of Northampton, Massachusetts. Her sister had married Benjamin Peirce, Harvard's famous professor of mathematics, and whenever the admiral was not at sea, he made Cambridge his home. It was there that Nannie had grown up. She had played on the Harvard grounds as a girl and from infancy was closely associated with Harvard scholars and professors. As might be expected, she was a precocious young lady, an omnivorous reader, who could quote classics at will. But she was also lively and fond of fun, with sparkling violet eyes and blonde hair setting off her small and excellent figure.

As June 1871 approached, Cabot was more taken up with plans for his approaching marriage than he was with plans for Commencement. No scholastic honors were coming his way. In spite of Henry Adams, he was able only to stand near the middle of his class.

III

The Literary Life

ON JUNE 24 Cabot Lodge filed past President Eliot and received his degree of Bachelor of Arts. The following day he and Nannie were married in Christ Church, the eighteenth-century Protestant Episcopal edifice which faces Harvard Yard and Cambridge Common. After a honeymoon of nearly a month, Cabot Lodge and his bride and his bride's sister, Evelyn, sailed for Europe. They were to be gone for a year.

Cabot Lodge was neither imaginative nor adventurous. His year abroad was spent following much-trodden paths among familiar places. The trio might have stepped from the pages of a novel by Henry James as they sedately moved about in polite English circles, to which they had entree through his mother's friends, with whom they stopped. Because Cabot wished that his ladies might see what he had seen before, he took them over almost the same route which he had traveled as a schoolboy with his mother. They visited Munich, the Passion Play at Oberammergau (which was then becoming fashionable), and Switzerland. In September they reached Paris, where the remnants of the barricades against the Paris Commune still lingered. In that grim city, where the "Bois de Boulogne was a treeless plain and the palace of Saint Cloud had perished," Cabot saw a Communard dragged screaming to jail; from his friends he heard grisly tales of violence of that fateful year. His sympathies were not with the Commune; indeed, he disapproved

30

of all French politics, mainly because of the French attitude toward the United States during the Civil War. It was not until many years later that he was to understand and confess that the "miserable imperial government and not the French people" was to blame for the turmoil and desolation which he witnessed in the late summer of 1871.

From Paris the little group went to Germany, where they were happy visitors in Dresden and Berlin, solid cities without mobs. After a stay in Vienna, they moved on to Italy and southward to Rome. In that city, so beloved in the nineteenth century by the Boston intellectuals, they spent the winter, but as April approached they hurried again to Paris. There, on April 6, their first child was born, a daughter whom they named Constance.

The aimless European jaunt, however, was not yet completed. They had no compelling reason to return to Boston. School was over. No business beckoned them. But, although he had yet had no occasion to use it, Cabot Lodge owned a mind which had been faintly stirred by Henry Adams and even by James Russell Lowell, and all his twenty-two years he had been surrounded by doers and thinkers. It was inevitable that he should not be content with idleness.

On his travels he discovered an interest in art and architecture. Although he read avidly and without direction, he studied every book on these subjects he could find. A born sightseer, he missed no picture gallery or cathedral on his way from London to Rome. Indeed, he was considered quite a bore on this account by the young Bostonians whom he met while they too were fashionably taking in the sights of the Old World.

Nannie, of course, could not accompany Cabot on his intellectual forays because of the birth of Constance. By a stroke of good fortune, however, he was to run across his classmate, Michael Henry Simpson, when they got to Rome.

This young Boston gentleman, the son of a rich manufacturer, had gained quite a reputation at Harvard as a student. Cabot and he had become most friendly in Henry Adams's history class. Of strict Congregational antecedents, Simpson had revolted against the stern Calvinist creed and, after a bitter struggle with his soul, had become an agnostic. Although he was outwardly full of fun, he saw "neither intelligence nor pleasure in an idle, self-indulgent life." He had dreamed of devoting his career to "literature and public service," but after another struggle with his Yankee soul, he had decided to enter at once into business and to aid in carrying on "the important industry which was part of his inheritance." As a businessman he intended to continue his reading and studying so that he might be well equipped to "take part in politics and make himself effectively useful."

The friends talked away many a serious hour in Rome, their topics ranging from the all-important one of Self and the Future to the almost as delightful busts of Caesar in the Capitoline Museum. Wandering over the Campagna and among the ruins of Ostia and Hadrian's Villa, these two young Boston gentlemen read Suetonius together and had an altogether enjoyable time. When they were not gazing rapturously at ruins, Simpson would expatiate upon the Republican party, in which he was a staunch believer and upon which he dreamed of exercising his influence and power in the years to come. His talk and his clearly defined ambitions made a deep impression upon Lodge. He, too, began to think, to try to reach some conclusion, and to find some way to make use of the opportunities he possessed. A life of "unoccupied leisure" no longer attracted him. In this dissatisfied mood Cabot said good-bye to his friend. Shortly after, he received the distressing news of Simpson's sudden death from malignant typhoid in Florence. He turned for solace and counsel to Henry Adams.

Cynical and indolent though the Professor of Medieval History at Harvard might be, he delighted in advising his younger friends nor did he ever lack the proper answer to their pleas. Cabot Lodge wrote him from Europe wondering if there were any sense in his going on with his studies, perhaps with the idea of someday becoming a writer. Henry Adams was flattered. On June 2, 1872, he sent off to Europe this pragmatic answer: —

. . . There is only one way to look at life and that is the practical way. Keep clear of mere sentiment whenever you have to decide a practical question. Sentiment is very attractive and I like it as well as most people, but nothing in the way of action is worth much which is not practically sound.

The question is whether the historico-literary line is practically worth following; not whether it will amuse or improve you. Can you make it *pay,* either in money, reputation, or any other solid value?

Now if you will think for a moment of the most respectable and respected products of our town of Boston, I think you will see at once that this profession does pay. No one has done better and won more in any business or pursuit than has been acquired by men like Prescott, Motley, Frank Parkman, Bancroft, and so on in historical writing; none of them men of extraordinary gifts, or who would have been likely to do very much in the world if they had chosen differently. What they did can be done by others.

Further there is a great opening here at this time. Boston is running dry of literary authorities. Anyone who has the ability can enthrone himself here as a species of literary lion with ease, for there is no rival to contest the throne. With it comes social dignity, European reputation and a foreign mission to close.

To do it requires patient study, long labor and perseverance that knows no limit. The Germans have these qualities beyond all other races. Learn to appreciate and to use the German historical *method* and your style can be elaborated at leisure. I should think you could do this here. . . .

The letter encouraged Lodge but it was still with "no definite plan, no taste, no aptitude, no mastering passion" that he returned with his family late in August and settled down in his mother's house at 31 Beacon Street. The winter that followed was dispiriting, for Cabot had chosen, as his first step toward the goal set by Henry Adams, the serious study of the early law of the Germanic tribes. He spent hours at the library, or in his own Beacon Street study, poring over dull books in German, seemingly going nowhere and achieving nothing. It was a lonely existence. Except for his immediate family he saw few people. But, as Adams had suggested, the long labor and perseverance was excellent training, for although he felt that he was working without object or purpose, he at least was learning to work. And this in itself was a new and exhilarating experience.

The late autumn of 1872, when he was hardly started on his researches, was enlivened by the great fire which swept away much of the old city in which he was born. During the aftermath of the holocaust he discovered that from which he had always been carefully sheltered: the "other city" of slums and poverty. When he helped distribute clothes and food to the homeless victims he was so moved by their wretchedness that for the next two years he willingly acted as an occasional district visitor for the Provident Association, one of the several charities in which his father had been interested. His social conscience was awakened by the flames.

When President Eliot had invited Henry Adams to teach at Harvard one of the inducements was that he should help Professor Lowell edit the *North American Review*. Now Lowell had resigned and gone abroad, leaving the magazine wholly in the hands of young Adams. After a European jaunt Adams settled down, in the summer of 1873, to the serious drudgery of his duties. The magazine had a maximum of literary reputation but a minimum of circulation — not more than 400 copies an issue. Besides, it was running a deficit. Had not Adams considered it a "sacred relic" — members of his family had contributed to its pages almost since the first issue in 1815 — he might not have taken the trouble with it that he did. He found the work a dismal chore — at times — and needed someone to help him with the dull routine.

When Adams accepted Lodge's invitation to luncheon at Nahant he found the younger man all that their contact at Harvard had led him to expect. Their talk ranged over a variety of subjects — Harvard, young Simpson, Europe — and they had a delightful time. In the afternoon, as they were walking down the road to the "wagon" that would take Adams over the causeway to the railroad at Lynn, Adams turned to his host and invited him to become Assistant Editor of the *Review*.

Cabot Lodge was pleased and flattered at the offer and, although he had no clear idea of what his editorial duties would be, he accepted at once. In his own mind he had pretty well determined to follow Adams's advice to strive for politico-literary glory. This was the ideal way to begin. Helping to edit a quarterly magazine, of course, did not take up all his time, so without really intending ever to practise law he entered the Harvard Law School, to be graduated, again without distinction, in the spring of 1874. Had it not been for Adams he might perhaps have set himself up as a lawyer and spent a dull, if distinguished, lifetime in the Massachusetts courts. Indeed, for a few months before he was admitted to the bar in April 1875 he clerked in the law office of Ropes & Gray, but quite obviously his mind was not upon his work.

The fastidious Adams was no easy taskmaster. He expected much of his pupil. He prided himself on being a perfectionist and took an almost sadistic delight in making Cabot do over and over again the work set before him. Even the brief book notices which he allowed Cabot to contribute to the "sacred relic" had to be rewritten many times before they gained the Master's approval. His first published writing — a one-page review of Baxman's *History of the Popes* — was written eight times before Adams would send it to the printer. Acidulous were the notes of advice Adams sent to his protégé, but all were aimed at forcing him to give his writing more variety and greater freedom, and to overcome his tendency to use superfluous words.

Under Adams's editorship the *Review* flourished. During the three years that he and Cabot labored over its pages its circulation grew to 1200 copies. As might be expected, their regime emphasized articles on history and politics. Dr. Lowell, who had imparted a literary flavor without much bite, remarked that Adams was making the old teakettle think it was a steam engine. Hardly an issue appeared without one of Henry's political essays; and his brother Charles Francis Adams, whose exposures of railroad corruption had previously appeared, continued his discussions of the contemporary scene. Charles F. Wingate wrote about Tammany Hall in scathing terms, Chauncey Wright discussed evolution, Simon Newcomb wrote about science, and such critics as William Dean Howells, Henry James, and H. H. Boyesen enlivened the pages.

Young Cabot might well have longed, and worked hard, to see his name and writing among those of such eminent contemporaries, and at last, after weeks of hard work, he finished an article that Adams thought was good enough to sign and print. This was a review of John T. Morse's *Life of Alexander Hamilton*.[1] During the composition of the re-

[1] In 1882 Morse, as editor of the American Statesman Series, was to bring out Lodge's own biography of Hamilton.

view Adams had continually to warn Lodge to make his essay "less objectionably patronizing to Morse" and to chide the young writer, who avowedly had made Dean Swift his prose master, for his youthful tendency to "sweeping and extreme statements." Such praise as he gave was grudging. Adams was obviously fond of his protégé, and even proud of him, but he found it difficult to tell him so. For this reason it was the greatest achievement of Cabot's life when the exacting master finally accepted Lodge's essay. "I wish I could again feel anything of the glow of pride which filled my being when the number containing it appeared," Lodge wrote in 1913.

To Henry Adams the task of getting out the *Review* was "hopeless drudgery," and he kept telling Cabot that he could see no future in it. "My terror is lest it should die on my hands or go to some Jew," he wrote. Another terror was James R. Osgood, the publisher. Mr. Osgood believed in giving the editor a free hand, but when Adams criticized Bayard Taylor's translation of *Faust*, which Mr. Osgood had published, the publisher was more than a little annoyed. It was over politics, however, that they came to grips. For the issue of October 1876, Adams and his brother Charles wrote an article entitled "The Independents in the Political Canvas," in which, characteristically, they urged the support of Tilden the Democrat over the Republican Blaine. The publisher did not see the article until the entire issue of the magazine had been printed. Unable then to rip it out he attached a disclaimer of responsibility for such a heretical view and announced that the editors had resigned. They had, Adams and Lodge together. Both editorially and politically, in 1876, they were independent young men.

Since the autumn of 1874 Cabot had been engaged on a serious and scholarly project — the study of the ancient Anglo-Saxon land laws. The forbidding subject was Adams's idea. He had several other graduate students at work, following the German system of research which he introduced to Harvard. Working with him were two other history students, Ernest Young and J. Laurence Laughlin, the latter of whom was to attain some distinction as a political economist. They all received their doctoral degrees at Commencement in 1876; Lodge's was the second ever awarded in History by the ancient college. Shortly before Lodge received this well-earned academic honor the master wrote him: —

Nothing since I came to Cambridge has given me so much and so unalloyed satisfaction as the completion of our baking this batch of doctors of philosophy. I am pleased with my scholars and I am proud of them. They have shown qualities which I believe to be of the first order.

Some months later Adams published the theses of Lodge, Young, and Laughlin in a scholarly-appearing tome, to which he supplied a foreword. Replete with footnotes and references, *Essays in Anglo-Saxon Law*, while repellent from a literary point of view, was so widely praised and used by legal scholars that it had to be reprinted in 1905. Adams showed his appreciation to Lodge in tangible form in the autumn of 1876 by arranging for the young lawyer-historian to be appointed to an instructorship in the History Department at Harvard.

Although it was Henry Adams's whimsy to insist through the years that his life was all a failure, his successful record as a teacher at Harvard disproves his facetious theory. He did as much for the high reputation of the college's History Department as any who ever had anything to do with it. Endowed with a sense of humor and of the fitness of things, Adams delighted in making Bostonians who were bred-in-the-bone Federalists support the Jeffersonian position in classroom discussions while he maneuvered those of the

Democratic tradition to defend what S. E. Morison has called "the most abhorred tenets of blue-light Federalism." It was his way of making education crackle.

On March 2, 1877, he carried his theory a step further. He wrote President Eliot, suggesting the establishment of a "rival course" to his, hoping in this way to "stimulate both instructors and students, and to counter-act, within its range, the inert atmosphere which now pervades the college." His choice for a rival was Henry Cabot Lodge, and with good reason, for, as he told Dr. Eliot, Lodge's views, "being federalist and conservative have as good a right to expression in the college as mine, which tend to democracy and radicalism." Dr. Eliot put the matter up to the Corporation, which quickly approved Adams's scheme for "increasing the interest in American history," although Lodge's salary was so low that Dr. Eliot, rather embarrassedly, later referred to his "almost gratuitous" services.

For the next two years Cabot taught history, inculcating his young students with sound Federalist ideology. Undoubtedly his indoctrination took, although in one instance it was successful in reverse. Edward Channing, who attended his course and later taught history at Harvard for many years, found that young Lodge and Hildreth's *History*, the standard textbook of the day, combined by reaction to make him a Jeffersonian. Although Lodge taught a general course, his specialty was the period of English colonization in America, a period when the Cabots were establishing themselves along the Essex shore and laying the foundations of the fortune that led them inevitably into the Federalist camp.

A young Bostonian, setting out consciously to become a great historian, could hardly have chosen a better time. There was, as Adams had shrewdly said, a place for him. Prescott, the great historian of Mexico and Peru, had been dead since Cabot was eight years old. Motley, who had wept when Cabot's father died, would himself die that year. Bancroft, at seventy-seven, was still tending his roses and exploring the history of the Constitution, but although he was to live to be ninety-one, he could afford to welcome a young competitor. Of all the great New Englanders, Parkman alone was comparatively young, just fifty-four, but even so his greatest work was done, the Oregon Trail had been covered. Cabot had known them all, had grown up under their benevolence. At twenty-seven he could not realize that New England's Indian summer had set in and that he, as much as anyone, would be the symbol of all that this autumnal season meant.

It was nothing against one of so insular a background that he should not step beyond his own family for the subject of his first book. All his life he had heard of George Cabot, but year by year he had seen the memory of that great man sink deeper and deeper into oblivion. With gusto the youthfully bearded scholar set about the exciting task of collecting his grandfather's letters and writing the story of his life.

Being a Cabot, he found the sources quickly opened to him, of course. He had just been elected a member of that select and sanctified institution, the Massachusetts Historical Society, where, a precocious child, he had been allowed to be seen and even sometimes heard by his elders. In addition to his distinguished colleagues he had the help and advice of Colonel Henry Lee, a kinsman, whose grandfather had once been George Cabot's business partner; the crusty gentleman, in the 1870's, was as "violent a Federalist" as though he had lived through the administrations of Washington, Adams, and Jefferson; he knew the family history in all its genealogical ramifications and was delighted to help the young man. Through family connections he gathered scores of George Cabot's revealing letters and in the archives of the Society he unearthed the forgotten papers of Timothy Pickering. Thus Cabot was able to work with new material and he could honestly feel that he was on the way to becoming the very Boston lion Adams had so glowingly described.

Of the fifty and more books he was to publish within the next forty-odd years only one or two stand on a par with the *Life and Letters of George Cabot.* Its originality and objectivity — virtues seldom associated with Henry Cabot Lodge — are still recognized by scholars. It was definitely his, and not Colonel Henry Lee's, book; and if it was pre-eminently sympathetic to its subject, Cabot suppressed nothing and mitigated nothing. Even such documents as placed his ancestor in an unfavorable light, particularly those that proved, so soon after the Civil War, that George Cabot had taken no strong stand against New England's proposed secession from the new Union, were offered without undue apology.

All during this period of his life Cabot had been taking an increasingly active interest in politics and had openly associated himself with a group of young reformers who were stirred by the maladministration of President Grant and affronted by the ambitions of James G. Blaine. Cabot had served, as we shall later see, openly with the so-called Liberal Republicans and Reformers, and if he was known at all to the general public it was through this connection. Writing at this time for the *New York Tribune* was an acid-tongued lady who used the pen name of Gail Hamilton, but who in reality was Abigail Dodge, cousin of candidate Blaine's wife. When Cabot's book appeared she attacked it, in a series of four scathing articles, in the *Tribune.* In his introduction Cabot had explained that he had written the book primarily to rescue his ancestor from oblivion, and Gail Hamilton, with a stroke of journalistic brilliance, headed her first article "Henry Cabot Lodge's Hand-to-Hand Fight with Oblivion." She pictured the young historian as a "very self-satisfied young man," a not too dishonest characterization, and then set out to destroy him. Cabot was quite annoyed.

One day, however, Colonel T. W. Higginson stopped him on the street and congratulated him on attracting so much attention.

"I wish she would assail one of my books that way," the *Atlantic's* popular essayist sighed, "for I have observed that the practical value of a critical notice is in proportion to its length and not in what is said."

The Colonel was right. The *Life and Letters of George Cabot* soon sold out and went into a second edition.

The five years that had passed since Cabot had returned from Europe had seen the addition of two sons to the family. The first had been born on October 10, 1873, and named George Cabot Lodge; the second son was born on August 10, 1878, and named John Ellerton Lodge.

During this period Cabot was torn between two ambitions: one was literary, the other was political. In the end the latter was to win, but before he immersed himself in politics he had two adventures which enhanced his growing reputation as a scholar. Shortly after his resignation from the Harvard faculty he was invited to deliver a series of lectures at Boston's famous Lowell Institute. He rewrote his Harvard lectures for this purpose. Published as they were in the *Evening Transcript*, they attracted attention beyond Boston and George William Curtis, that pale young reformer whom Lodge already knew through their association with the Mugwumps, induced Harper and Brothers to publish them. In later years Cabot Lodge was to regard the *Short History of the English Colonies in America* as "long and cumbrous" (a worthy criticism) but for several years they were a standard text in many colleges. When, a few years after their publication, Thomas Woodrow Wilson applied for admission for graduate work at Johns Hopkins University he cited his study of Dr. Lodge's book as one of the reasons why he felt competent to pass an examination in colonial history. Much to Cabot's surprise, however, the book was far from the popular success his biography of George Cabot had been. No Gail Hamilton reviewed it.

Since he had again gone to original sources, then not as deeply plowed as they are now, the history had its many good points. It is, however, mainly interesting today because it is the last of his books which reveal any fundamental historical originality or any pretense to it. Both this and his first book were written under the influence of Henry Adams at a time when Adams was still intending to make Cabot Lodge a professor at Harvard College.

The second adventure was less successful than the first. This, too, was in 1879, when Cabot's mind and time both were pretty much taken up with political ambitions. John Torrey Morse, Jr., had come across the moribund periodical the *International Review,* which was for sale. He called in Cabot and the young men, filled with enthusiasm, determined to make it into an influential organ of opinion. This they never did, although they tried hard. One of the first articles accepted was entitled "Cabinet Government of the United States" in which the author, a senior at Princeton, argued for open debate and against the undemocratic custom of deciding issues behind the closed doors of committee rooms. This essay was to form the basis of Woodrow Wilson's first book, *Congressional Government.* A second article from the same author was brusquely marked "R.R.R." (received, read, and rejected) by Editor Lodge.

Although the *International Review* was a failure, Cabot, at this time, found other outlets for his literary enthusiasms.

Through William Dean Howells, who had become editor of the *Atlantic Monthly* a few years before, and Thomas Bailey Aldrich, the jaunty little poet and editor who gathered about him all the writers of New England's twilight, he had access to the Contributors' Club and even the main pages of the *Atlantic Monthly*. As Claude M. Fuess once told the Massachusetts Historical Society, the young man had a "wit and urbanity and an air of omniscience which qualified him in an unusual degree for essay writing. He said clever things in a gentlemanly fashion, and carried with him the faint aroma of Harvard College so dear in those days to residents of Beacon Hill." Evanescent projects of a literary nature flitted through his mind: he edited a volume of ballads and lyrics for boys and girls between the ages of twelve and eighteen, he collected fairy tales for children of a younger age. His writing, and his occasional lectures, were bringing him, by the time he was thirty years old, an average income of $3000 a year. Not that he needed the money; he had inherited all that he could ever use, but it proved, to his Yankee conscience, that he could earn his living if it were necessary and that his life was no longer empty and purposeless. And yet, surrounded by his books and pallid busts in his Beacon Street study, and his roses (like Bancroft and Adams, he loved the "flower of the historians") in his sea-girt garden in Nahant, he was a restless and not quite happy man.

IV

Young Lodge of Boston

IN LATER years Henry Adams was to heap scorn on Cabot
Lodge for having become a politician, but it was Adams as
much as any man who bore the responsibility for it. In the
1870's and 1880's this descendant of politicians was deep
in the intrigues of the Reformers. Although professing no
personal ambition for public office, he dearly loved to
dabble in politics behind the scene.

Henry Adams knew a man he could use when he saw
one and he had spotted Cabot Lodge when he was very
young. For nearly a decade, beginning in 1874, they played
at politics together. In the course of their playing Lodge
met another man who was to have a profound influence at
this important period of his career. In background, education, temperament — indeed, in almost every way imaginable
— he was as different from Adams as any man could be.
While Adams shrank from the limelight, this tall, thin, red-
whiskered man with bushy hair and steel-rimmed glasses
was a familiar figure to all the readers of newspapers. He
was nearly twenty-two years older than Cabot. Since his
arrival in America in 1852, his career had been notable as
a soldier in the Civil War, as a politician devoted to reform,
as a fighter for lost causes, as the American Ambassador to
Spain. His name was Carl Schurz.

Cabot Lodge probably first met Carl Schurz at his
mother's home on April 29, 1874, where the liberal leader
was the guest of honor at a small dinner following his

45

memorable eulogy to the famous Civil War Senator from Massachusetts, Charles Sumner. It was fitting that the elder Mrs. Lodge should be Schurz's hostess for the great abolitionist had been a welcome visitor at the Lodge home at all times. At the dinner table, besides Mr. and Mrs. Schurz and their daughter, were Henry Wadsworth Longfellow, Ralph Waldo Emerson, and Oliver Wendell Holmes. It was, indeed, a truly Boston dinner party. Dr. Holmes, in his inimitable way, described a "dynamometer," or gadget designed to measure memory, a subject which, the mild Emerson said in a low voice, was "very disagreeable to me." Cabot, who had been enthralled that afternoon as Schurz had delivered one of the best addresses of his career, sat next to Mr. Longfellow. Mr. Longfellow was cold. He had not liked the eulogy and had told Cabot so in no uncertain terms, his Viking-blue eyes flashing, his white beard atremble. A year later, when Schurz's term as Senator had ended, Cabot went to Washington, at Adams's bidding, to attend a dinner given by Schurz's political friends. Soon thereafter Schurz was to take the young Bostonian under his wing and there he was to remain, docilely enough, until the great storm of 1884.

Cabot Lodge was not, of course, the only young Bostonian who felt the wind of political reform in the 1870's. In that circle of wealthy and ambitious young business, literary, and professional men where he, the cub lion, walked so airily, there were many who looked with disgust upon the degradation of the Republican Party. Moorfield Storey, who was five years Cabot's senior and who had been Sumner's secretary in Washington during President Johnson's impeachment, was one. Now returned to Boston, where he was a rising young lawyer, he was to be in the forefront of all movements towards political reform. Another was Brooks Adams, Henry's jealous, lonely, and erratic brother. A third was Charles Cabot Jackson, a kinsman of Lodge, and an energetic young broker of large acquaintance. A fourth was William E. Perkins, whose extracurricular interest was municipal politics. He went to the Common Council of Boston in 1871 for three years. All were old Bostonians, members of families prominent in the city for generations. There were others, of course, but these were the nucleus of a small group who gathered around Henry Cabot Lodge.

There were ample reasons why these gentlemen, all older than Cabot, should be attracted to him. For one thing he had a handsome house, a fine library, and the best-stocked wine cellar in town. His dinners were delightful both for the food and for the conversation that was passed around the mahogany board. Mrs. Lodge, too, was popular. Not only was she noted for her beauty, but she was amiable, attractive, possessed of charming manners and great social tact. So, when Lodge suggested to his friends that they "form an organization, non-partisan in character, for the purification of politics, and officered by men of such position that they would exercise great influence on public opinion," the group was quite willing to comply. Being men proud of Massachusetts, they called their proposed reform organization the Commonwealth Club. Many a delightful dinner at Lodge's house preceded the actual drawing-up of the charter. Although the rest of the city was completely unaware of its existence, its members were fully convinced that sooner or later it would exercise upon the electorate an influence as powerful as that of the Essex Junto just a century before.

In the early days of its existence the Commonwealth Club did little except sip Lodge's bewitching old Madeira, exchange pleasantries, and laugh at its leader's flashes of sharp Harvardian wit. They did a lot of deep thinking, and listened to Brooks Adams's mordant animadversions upon the

47

American scene as he pointed out to these young romanti- cists the follies of the time in which they lived. It was not until 1876 that they were impelled to action. In the mean- time, however, Cabot Lodge was being drawn closer and closer into the political web. At this period Henry Adams was not quite the dulcet creature he was to become. He had married in June 1872, and was woefully busy with his teach- ing, his editing, and his politics. He wanted no political post for himself, but he had visions of dictating policies through the press. In December 1874 he told Cabot, pri- vately and confidentially, that he and some others were negotiating for the purchase of the *Boston Daily Advertiser* at an estimated cost of $90,000, and asked his protégé to buy at least one of the eighteen available shares at $5000. The deal, however, fell through.

The following spring Carl Schurz, having shed his Sena- torial toga, went abroad hopeful that by the time next year's national campaigns started Charles Francis Adams, Sr., would accept the Republican Presidential nomination. Henry's father was, in the opinion of the traveler, the only Republican available who possessed "absolute independence of party dictation and entire absence of ulterior ambition." The elder Adams, then sixty-eight years old, may have been all that Schurz called him, but he still felt that the Presi- dency was within his reach.

With all this in the air which he breathed daily, Cabot Lodge willingly lent himself to Henry Adams's schemes. To be on the inside of national affairs even so slightly was pleasing to his youthful ego and a contrast to the dull routine of his historical studies. Besides, there was ever present in his mind the example of his own great-grandfather, with whose half-forgotten Federalist engineerings he was at this time deeply engaged. Throughout the summer he watched the national political scene closely. The greatest interest was centered in the gubernatorial campaign being waged in Ohio, where the Democrat, William Allen, was giving Rutherford B. Hayes many unhappy moments. Indeed, it looked as if Allen might win, and with this in mind Lodge was among those who sent pleading letters to the sojourning ex-Senator Schurz, urging him to rush back to the defense of Hayes. Reluctantly Schurz acquiesced. He stumped the state of Ohio for Hayes, whom he admired because of his interest in civil service reform. Thanks in great measure to Schurz's efforts Hayes won a decisive victory.

The Republicans were to meet in convention in June 1876, at Exposition Hall in Cincinnati. The Independents expected to be more influential by holding a separate meeting and Lodge wrote Schurz offering his services: "I feel guilty of great lack of modesty in making the request I am about to make, which is: are you willing I should come to your convention?" From that time on he was busy. He arranged for an article for the *North American Review* on the "Whiskey Ring" which Secretary Bristow had exposed, after it had defrauded the Treasury of $4,000,000 in two years, as being operated by a personal friend of President Grant with the assistance of the President's private secretary. By mid-February Adams was saying, "You are now plunged up to the ears in Washington intrigue," and was urging him to work hard for Bristow, whose chances of receiving the nomination, he felt gloomily, were one in one thousand.

Lodge spent much of the early winter of 1876 in Washington, writing almost daily letters to Adams on the state of political affairs. Adams, in turn, kept sending him advice. When Lodge wrote that he was certain Bristow would line up with the reformers Adams said: "You think he is ready to join us. If so . . . he should issue an indictment against the party that will show the people what we mean. If he is under the delusion that all this horrible corruption can be dealt with by any moderate language or with any blunt weapons, he is useless as a leader. We must have a man who cares nothing for party or he will betray us."

Back in Boston the "carefully selected and organized reformers," as Moorfield Storey called the members of the Commonwealth Club, were unanimously for Bristow. They met one evening at Lodge's home to lay their plans for his support when a strict constructionist among them arose, with a pained expression on his face, and called their attention to a provision in their constitution which forbade any partisan activities. "This came as a thunderbolt," according to Storey, who was present, "but proved harmless. The Commonwealth Club at once adjourned — and the assembled members on the spot organized the Bristow Club, which fought through the campaign. The Commonwealth Club never met again to my recollection."

Adams believed that the independents should not meet until after the Republicans but he eventually bowed to Schurz's determination to hold a convention in the early spring. Invitations therefore were sent out in late March, after Brooks Adams and Lodge had gone on to see Schurz and arrange the details. The notices were signed by William Cullen Bryant, the aged poet and editor of the *New York Evening Post*, President Theodore Dwight Woolsey of Yale College, Alexander E. Bullock, the reporter who had covered the Lincoln-Douglas campaign and who, a few years later, was to be Schurz's partner in ownership of the *Post*, and Schurz himself. Replies were to be sent to H. Cabot Lodge, 31 Beacon Street, Boston. Lodge saw that the invitations were sent out, the programs printed, and the other routine work done. From day to day he kept Schurz informed of acceptances and refusals. He acted as press agent for both the Boston and the New York newspapers.

On May 15, 1876, the reformers, nearly two hundred

strong and coming from seventeen states, met at the Fifth Avenue Hotel in New York. It was a distinguished gathering of some of the most brilliant minds in America who had emerged from their college studies, editorial sanctums, parsonages, and law offices, hopeful of effecting lasting reforms in the conduct of national affairs. President Woolsey presided and "young Lodge, of Boston" — as the *New York Times* referred to him — acted as secretary and read the roll call.

It was immediately apparent that the reformers had no program. Sentiment was strong against James Gillespie Blaine, who had already been accused, through the agency of the notorious "Mulligan letters," of taking money from the Union Pacific and other land-grant companies while Speaker of the House in 1871. It was obvious, too, that none present could stomach the other leading contenders for the Republican nomination, neither Roscoe Conkling, the vain, sensitive, and ruthless Senator with the "turkey-cock strut," from New York, nor the able and often idealistic Senator from Indiana, Oliver Morton. They were unwilling to come out in open support of Bristow. When the name of Charles Francis Adams, Sr., was presented, it was received with a chill — and was immediately withdrawn. At last the delegates declared unanimously that they would support no candidate "in whom the impulses of the party manager have shown themselves predominant over those of the reformer." They let it go at that, appointed Carl Schurz chairman of the permanent emergency committee, and disbanded.

It remained for a cynical Tammany chieftain to say what the meeting had accomplished: "Oh, they have re-enacted the moral law and the Ten Commandments for a platform," he told a reporter, "and have demanded an angel of light for President."

When the Republican National Convention convened, it

appeared for a while as if a deadlock might occur. Then a compromise candidate in the person of Governor Hayes of Ohio, the same man whom Schurz had hurried back from Europe to help elect, was placed before the convention. On the seventh ballot Bristow, who had polled only 113 votes on the first ballot, withdrew and Kentucky's 34 votes went to Hayes. Rather than see Blaine triumphant, Conkling and Morton followed suit and Rutherford Birchard Hayes of Ohio became the Republican standard bearer of 1876.

In the opinion of Carl Schurz the choice was acceptable. He went to Hayes and queried him on civil service reform and sound money, and when the Governor agreed to favor these planks, he promised him his support. Henry Adams, however, was shocked. Cabot Lodge was inclined to go along with Schurz and Hayes. Late that month Schurz came again to Boston, this time to receive an honorary degree of Doctor of Laws from Harvard College. Once more he was the guest of the Lodges. On that afternoon the Democrats nominated Samuel J. Tilden, corporation lawyer and former Governor of New York, who was known among the Republicans as "Slippery Sam."

Adams was closer to Lodge than Schurz was. And Adams swung to Tilden. "I can no more resist the pleasure of voting for Tilden than I could turn my back on a friend," he told Lodge late in June. The two men discussed the matter fully during the summer, sending notes back and forth to each other, Lodge from Nahant, Adams from Beverly Farms. To Adams's way of thinking, Tilden was the superior man primarily because he would "give the Democratic party some principles and some brains, and so force the Republicans to a higher level. . . . I think we had better go on talking Tilden," he urged, "I am unwilling to check latent virtue."

Against the onslaught of Adams and others among the young reformers Cabot wavered. In August he was writing

Schurz that he reserved the right "in voting for Hayes to give the fullest support to Tilden if he prove himself a real performer, which he never will." In September, with the election drawing nearer, Adams' began to suspect that their friend Schurz had sold out to Hayes in expectation of political reward. "I am not angry with him," he wrote Lodge, "but of course his leadership is at an end! Well! We know what he was! The leader who treats his followers in that way is a mere will-o'-the-wisp! I hope that he will get his cabinet office, and I hope that he will forget we ever worked to make him our leader, independent of party."

Like many another member of the Independent Party — "that rope of sand," as Adams called it — Lodge voted for Tilden in the November election. Shortly thereafter he wrote to Schurz: "I finally abandoned Mr. Hayes and voted for Mr. Tilden and I believe him to have been fairly elected. But I care very little for either candidate and a great deal for my country and its institutions."

It is, indeed, one of the ironies of history (as C. M. Fuess once pointed out) that, in 1876, Carl Schurz was an orthodox Republican and Henry Cabot Lodge cast his ballot for a Democrat. It was the last time the latter ever did so.

After the Hayes-Tilden contest Cabot was in a state of intellectual confusion. He knew that he wanted to get into the swing of things but he was not quite certain how to go about it, or with which party to take his chances. On July 15, 1878, he wrote to his old friend Roger Wolcott, whom he had known at Mr. Dixwell's Latin School and who was a year ahead of him at Harvard. Mr. Wolcott was later to become a Republican Governor of Massachusetts but at this time was one of the more active "young reformers" and a founder of the Young Men's Republican Club. The letter, although tinted with youthful cynicism, well expressed Cabot's own mental attitude of the period.

"Though my principles are not acceptable to the young reformers," Lodge wrote, evidently referring to his support of Tilden while most of them had advocated the election of Hayes, "I am not surprised to find they are liberal in regard to subscribers and I enclose you a small sum for the propagation of good doctrine. Broadsides are all very well, but as long as you tie yourself to the apron-string of one party you will never effect anything at such a juncture as the present. If you are not prepared to run an independent candidate or support a Democrat when the Republicans put up a bad man you will never in my opinion reach any practical result. You proclaim your intention of sticking to the party at all events and as long as you do that the party managers, and they are quite right, laugh at you and use you and do not care a rap about what you say or desire. I have no faith in reform within the church. It is true that to get anything done in politics you must work through the mediums of the great parties but you must be prepared to use one against the other and then you may do something and make them bid up instead of down. No other way can the young reformers be aught but a laughing stock." [1]

This letter, as it turned out, was a sort of prophecy in reverse. Roger Wolcott took Lodge's advice in 1884 and bolted the Republicans to support Grover Cleveland while Cabot Lodge (who should have been haunted by the existence of this document) nailed himself so fast to the Republican Party that nothing, not even his own conscience, could ever again rip them apart.

[1] Charles G. Washburn Collection, American Antiquarian Society, Worcester, Mass.

V

The Dude of Nahant

DURING the electoral fight Lodge was constantly in correspondence with Carl Schurz, but with consummate tact he managed to evade any serious political argument with his old friend. About a month before Hayes went to the White House Cabot and Henry Adams called upon Schurz in Washington. The older man, whom they found "as cordial and pleasant as ever," held no animosity toward the two defectors; indeed he had no reason to be otherwise than genial for, just as Adams had gloomily predicted, he was shortly to become Secretary of the newly created Department of the Interior in President Hayes's cabinet. Cabot could hardly have expected any reward for his pre-convention labors and probably did not ask directly for any. Several of his friends felt that the new Secretary of the Interior could well make use of him as an assistant. They failed, however, to press his case and he was passed over. Schurz, visiting Boston with President Hayes in June, spent a night at the Lodge home in Nahant. He may not have been aware of Lodge's "availability"; at least he did not offer him a post. Perhaps he suspected that Lodge's reforming zeal was but a passing phase in the young man's development, or he may have reasoned that he was not yet seasoned enough to make "lumber and Indians . . . his sole mental food," as they were soon to become in his own case. A month later Samuel Bowles of the *Springfield Republican* chided Schurz for not having given Lodge the job. "Nobody could have been better for you," he wrote. "With such a man at your right hand you would simply have doubled yourself. . . ."

Although he was shut off from the Washington scene Cabot by no means abandoned his interest in the political field. In 1877 Governor Rice appointed him to a three-year term on the State Board of Library Trustees and there he was to meet a man whose pragmatic influence upon his life was to be far greater than that of Henry Adams and Carl Schurz combined. The post itself was of minor consequence. The fact that he came to know Joseph Thomas Wilson intimately was all-important.

Mr. Wilson was a political power in what was then the Tenth Massachusetts District. In later years he was to be known as the "King of Nahant" — he was chairman of the Board of Selectmen for twenty-eight years and moderator of the Nahant Town Meeting for thirty-four. He had left a Maine farm and Maine fishing boats to become a North Shore cabinetmaker, and he was now one of the solid citizens of Essex, well-to-do if not wealthy, and a pillar of Republican respectability. The year before Cabot came to know him well he had risen to the judgeship of the Nahant Municipal Court.

With Schurz lost in his Indian reserves and Adams gone from Harvard, Cabot turned to Judge Wilson. He now decided to become the aggressor and earn his own political preferment the hard way. "When I came to the conclusion I would like to hold office," he later admitted, "I did not wait to be requested by friends, but I went out and told the men who had much to do with elections that I would like to run." In the Lynn district as good a man to see as any was shrewd Judge Wilson. Lodge saw him.

The advice of the boss was that the young man should start pretty near to the bottom of the ladder and work his way up. So that he might have all his time to further his

56

ambition Lodge resigned his Harvard instructorship at the end of the college year of 1879. Settling down in his Nahant mansion he told his neighbors that he would like to be offered the Republican nomination for state Representative. During the summer he worked on his editorial duties for the *International Review* and let himself be seen as much as possible in the district.

On the Fourth of July he traveled to Boston at the invitation of Mayor Frederick O. Prince to deliver the annual oration before the city fathers gathered in the Boston Theater. Since this was to be his first important public discourse, he had given it much thought and care. It was designed as a scholarly résumé of the history and achievements of the nation. After reviewing the struggles of the colonists, the framing of a constitution "adapted to the needs of the times," and the horrors of the Civil War, the young historian launched into an effective attack upon the dangers of paternalism and into a defense of individualism. Legislation, he said, can only assist human effort by giving security to all the citizens equally and by affording the best opportunities for great achievement.

"It ought to be our first care that the laboring classes shall have no just cause of complaint, but shall have reason to believe that peace and order can alone afford them the opportunity of permanently bettering their fortunes. . . . We must discourage strenuously the notion that legislation is all powerful. . . . We must recognize the limits of legislation and encourage individual independence."

In the ensuing years, when he had become one of the most vigorous supporters of a high tariff and of every form of Republican paternalism and centralization, this maiden speech was to be dragged out of its files by his opponents to show that, before he became a leader of the Republican Party, he had been an honest and liberal man.

Still there was no public clamor for his services and the first mention of his name was not made until October 29 when the *Lynn Item* casually remarked that "there is considerable talk in the Tenth Republican district of nominating George H. Chase, George C. Neal and Henry Cabot Lodge of Nahant."

The next day the Republicans of the Tenth District held their convention in Liberty Hall in Lynn. Twenty-four delegates, including Judge Wilson, who was also a member of the committee to count ballots, were in attendance. Two of the three candidates were quickly selected, and then a fight developed over who should be the third and final choice, with Judge Wilson holding out for Lodge. When the ballots were counted Henry Cabot Lodge received sixteen votes.

It was with some misgivings that the notification committee traveled to the Beacon Street home to inform him of the nomination. Although claiming residence at Nahant, he evidently had closed his house there for the season. This, however, did not bother the politicians as much as certain aspects of Lodge's character. They knew that as soon as he started campaigning the Democrats would attack him with all sorts of sarcastic personal abuse. They did. He was quickly labeled "the dude of Nahant," a "lah-de-dah" boy, "the silver-spoon young man," and "the gentleman rider of Nahant." The appellations, of course, fitted him. In Boston and Cambridge he was respected as a brilliant and rising young historian; in Lynn, a manufacturing city, all that was known about him was that he spent long summers at his Nahant estate, where he entertained rich friends and indulged in the aristocratic sport of horseback riding. (He was an excellent and even daring horseman in spite of his slight frame and appearance of scholarly frailness.)

"Lah-de-dah" Lodge took his nomination seriously. Although he failed to attend the huge and enthusiastic Republican rally in Lynn's Music Hall where it was decided to make "greenbackism" versus specie payment the major issue, he started his canvass the next day. From then until election day he worked unceasingly, speaking at every chance in all the public halls in the district. He won the reputation of being a dangerous opponent in debate. Far from being ashamed of his long Essex County ancestry or of his academic achievements he boasted of both. It was, however, neither of these advantages nor his ability as a campaigner that brought him victory. It was on the issue of Prohibition that the fight was actually waged.

Since 1855 the "liquor question" had been one of the foremost in Massachusetts. In 1874 a Democrat had been elected governor mainly on his promise to repeal the License Act which had restricted the sale of intoxicants to state agents, and to return control to the cities and towns. He had succeeded in doing this, but in 1878 the Prohibition members of the legislature had foisted the "Civil Damages Law" upon the people of the state. This stated that "every husband, wife, child, parent, guardian, employer, or other person who shall be injured in person or property, or means of support, by any intoxicated person" had the right to sue for damages not only the person who provided the means of intoxication but also the lessee or owner of the premises wherein it was provided.

At least two of Lodge's opponents had voted for the Civil Damages Law, and one of them was also the nominee of the Prohibitory Party. Both had such strong personal followings that the 150 liquor dealers of Lynn were alarmed by the prospect of the possible election of a prohibitionist. They held an emergency meeting and in the early morning hours decided to throw their weight to Lodge. When the polls opened the next morning, with a Republican sun brightly shining, the 150 liquor dealers and their friends were on hand to see that their candidate received the proper support.

More than 10,000 voters in the Tenth District went to the polls on November 4, 1879, but Lodge, who received 1652 votes, was the only Republican elected in the district. The other two victors were both workers in the Lynn shoe shops.

A week later, at a victory meeting in Saugus, Representative-elect Lodge made a pleasant little speech to the two hundred Republicans present. The *Lynn Item,* which had previously ascribed his victory to the all-out fight by the liquor interests, reported him as speaking "exultantly" of the "gallant fight" made by the Republicans. After thanking his friends for the confidence they had shown in him, he promised to do "his full duty as a Republican."

The Massachusetts General Court met at the State House on January 7, 1880, and the blond, blue-eyed freshman, with his neat and scholarly beard adorning his chubby face, was hopefully on hand. His first official task was to serve on the committee which drew the seats for the session. The first petition which he offered was on behalf of the Massachusetts Historical Society which sought "additional legislation for the better protection of ancient burying grounds." Shortly thereafter he was helping the trustees of the Boston Athenaeum, that select and bust-filled reading room where the Boston Brahmins had long dozed over their books and contemplated their ancestors who lay buried in the Old Granary beneath its windows, to obtain "authority to hold additional real and personal estate."

Between January 7 and April 24, when the House prorogued, the young innocent had ample opportunity to study practical politics at first hand. He was a member of two committees: a joint committee "on public service," which seems to have accomplished little if anything, and the workaday

Committee on Bills in Third Reading. As chairman of the latter he was a busy man. This was made up entirely of freshmen like himself. With them he was to have intimate contact with men of a type he had never before known. Jim Doherty, born forty-five years before in Donegal, Ireland, and now a Boston saloonkeeper; Silas Thayer, who kept a hotel and livery stable in Ashland; Bill Brown, a harness maker from Worcester County; Lorrin P. Keyes, a Berkshire farmer; Hugh Maxwell, a farmer from Heath, a small town up in Franklin County, and Seth Shepherd, the leading undertaker of the town of Mansfield. In the aggregate the legislature was a far cry from Harvard Yard.

On January 30, Representative Lodge set out to repay his outstanding political debt by introducing a bill to repeal the Civil Damages Law. The members from upstate, where sentiment for Prohibition was strongest, managed to block the bill almost at the outset by forcing the House Committee on Liquor Laws to report it "inexpedient to legislate." But, since it was a joint bill, the Senate was soon able to send it back to the House for further consideration. On every motion to delay action, and there were several, and whenever a weakening amendment was offered, the Representative from Nahant voted on the side of repeal. After several crippling amendments had been tacked on, Representative McGeough of Boston twice tried desperately to jam through an out-and-out repeal. Each time Lodge supported him. McGeough's second attempt lost by a vote of 129 to 88, but finally, after a hectic fight on the floor, in which Lodge evidently took no vocal part, the measure, although somewhat damaged, was sent to the Senate. In the end the prohibitionists managed to stave off repeal, but the act was so severely mutilated that it was not many years before it was defeated entirely and removed from the statute books. Lodge had the satisfaction of knowing that he voted consistently throughout on the one issue which was responsible for his election.

On the whole, throughout his first year of public service, Representative Lodge appears to have followed neither a reactionary nor a radical course. He voted against a bill ostensibly designed to protect the people of the Commonwealth against tramps and vagabonds but which was essentially an anti-labor bill. He was opposed to a bill described as being "for the better protection of insurance policy holders," as might be expected of one whose wealth in good measure was derived from owning stock in the oldest insurance companies in the state. He voted for the incorporation of the American Bell Telephone Company and introduced a bill increasing the salaries of Superior Court judges. A bill to restore the franchise to war veterans who had become paupers bore his support, as did another designed to bring about several much-needed reforms in the election law. In later years his enemies within the Republican Party were wont to chide him for his reckless "independence" while a member of the General Court. The record does not bear them out.

In one instance he set a precedent which he followed with stubborn consistency to the end of his life. He put his mind stiffly against woman suffrage in 1879 and never let it relax. In a way this was surprising for its foremost advocate in Massachusetts was his old friend, Colonel Higginson, the *Atlantic* essayist, and the only other "scholar in politics" in the General Court.[1] A great many people thought that the saber-scarred veteran of the Civil War, whose "Army Life in a Black Regiment" was one of the great documents of that grim struggle, was a "socialist" because of his determined advocacy of feminism. This, of course, was but one of his

[1] Colonel Higginson, author of a dozen books, listed his occupation in the House *Journal* as "author and journalist"; Henry Cabot Lodge, who had written only one book at this time, listed his as "Literature."

many interests: he also was a pacifist and he believed in freeing the Russian serfs. His friends admired him for his "moral sweep." His father had planted the elms in Harvard Yard, but that was long before the Colonel had become the town's leading dilettante and the founder, with Julia Ward Howe, of Newport's Town and Country Club. Neither he nor his advanced ideas were quite proper for an ambitious young politician to become associated with. When he tried to amend the Constitution to give women the right to vote and hold office young Lodge voted a decisive "NO!"

The General Court ended its labors on April 24 but Cabot Lodge did not hasten to his roses and his study at Nahant. There were more important things to do.

VI

Victory and Defeat

Towards the end of 1879 Representative-elect Lodge received a letter from his old friend Carl Schurz, who was never so busy with lumber and Indians that he forgot to watch his political fences. The Secretary of the Interior was well aware of the purpose of Ulysses S. Grant, now on the last stages of his memorable round-the-world tour, to seek a third term as President of the United States, but Schurz had no intention of letting this happen if in any way he could prevent it. And so he urged his former henchman, if he too were determined not to support Grant, to start at once speaking out "boldly and loudly." Lodge agreed. Always ready to call a conference at the slightest hint of a crisis, Schurz, after consultation with his friends, now arranged an informal meeting for May at St. Louis. There plans were laid for a larger caucus to be held after the Republican Convention should that body kowtow to the schemes of the stalwarts — the adherents of Conkling and the satellites of Blaine — and Grant thus become the party's choice.

Young Lodge returned from the refreshing meeting with his mind made up to attend the Chicago convention as a delegate from the Lynn-Nahant district of Massachusetts. As a member of the Republican State Committee he had a right to expect some support of his ambition but when he made known his wishes he was greeted with jeers and laughter. Everyone in Lynn knew that the party leaders had decided upon sending Amos F. Breed and to challenge that gentleman was unthinkable, especially when the challenger was a brash young man just turned thirty years old whose ultimate loyalty to Republican ideals had not yet been proved. Mr. Breed was a power, as a banker and as president of the Lynn Street Railway Company, and there were few daring enough to oppose him. But Cabot Lodge dared, and after a stormy session of the leaders, during which he had the support of Judge Wilson, he was elected delegate. Although this victory caused much consternation among the older Republicans it was hailed among the more progressive members of the party as a definite sign of Henry Cabot Lodge's growing prestige. As a reward he was chosen secretary of the Massachusetts delegation.

Had it not been widely known that Lodge was an anti-Grant Republican it is doubtful if he could have become a delegate. Throughout Massachusetts there was a wide and growing opposition to Grant's bid for a third term. In later years Lodge credited his success at the district convention to this feeling.

When they were gathered in the drafty Exposition Hall, a temporary affair of rough pine wood "tawdrily decorated with plaster busts and huge daubs of dead leaders of the Federated Whig and Republican Parties," as Lodge described it in a report prepared for Mr. Godkin of the *Nation*,[1] or in the Massachusetts headquarters at the Leland Hotel, Lodge had an excellent chance to observe the machinery of a great political party at work. He took full advantage of his opportunity.

The convention was little more than a bitter struggle for power between factions within the Republican Party. Even

[1] He was assigned to write an account of the convention but missed the deadline when it ran several days longer than had been expected. A copy of the report with later notes by H. C. Lodge is owned by C. M. Fuess.

to as innocent an observer as Cabot Lodge it seemed certain from the outset that there could be no reconciliation, no chance of union, between the Blaine and Grant camps, and that the balance of power was held by the unpledged and independent delegates: Wisconsin, with its twenty-two votes; Indiana with its thirty; and Massachusetts with its twenty-six. These were able at any moment to swing the nomination to either of the leading contenders, but unfortunately their strength, although their hearts were pure, was not sufficient to assure the defeat of both. And yet that is exactly what they did.

There were, of course, other hopefuls on hand. Massachusetts was backing the colorless but eminently honest Vermonter, Senator George F. Edmunds, who obviously hadn't a chance. James A. Garfield was there to offer the name of Senator John Sherman, brother of William "Tecumseh" Sherman, whose march through Georgia still brought cheers from all true Republican throats.

Cabot Lodge could hardly have had a better lesson in practical politics than he was now to witness. He described the scene, with eight to ten thousand sweating and noisy people milling about in the hall, as like the French Revolution "except there was nothing bloodthirsty about it," and he compared it to a hurricane.

Had Lodge got his account to the *Nation* in time for publication it would have been recognized as an outstanding piece of minor political reporting. Some of the sketches are keenly drawn: "'Long' John Wentworth lumbered out, hideous in face and repulsive in his old age . . . Logan favored the convention with bursts of roaring eloquence delivered in a stentorian and limitless voice and with a fine contempt for grammar," and after his defeat he "looked and acted as a half-savage man." Nor was his report without a touch of sharp wit: —

There was a general feeling that it would not be proper to carry the balloting into Sunday morning. Some one near the Illinois section said the Massachusetts men would object. "Yes," said Logan, "they're all a set of damned infidels in Massachusetts but they wouldn't think it proper to vote on Sunday."

Grant, it turned out, had more votes and Blaine fewer than most observers, including young Lodge of Boston, had anticipated.

On Tuesday morning the Massachusetts delegates, who hitherto had not been united but who had been mostly for Edmunds, turned solidly for Sherman. In quick order Wisconsin and Indiana

desperately left their candidate and united upon Garfield, who rose and protested and was ruled out of order. The break had come. On the next ballot amid intense excitement the anti-Grant men united for the final struggle and nominated the Ohio Senator. During this last ballot General Garfield sat immovable with a pained expression on his face. The situation was perhaps unequalled.

There can be few experiences more exciting than to sit in a Convention and see oneself nominated by a great and powerful party for one of the highest offices in the world. General Garfield bore the strain well. His whole appearance during the convention had been admirable in speech and action. All he said and did was broad, temperate and wise. That he is a strong candidate can hardly be questioned. He springs from the people and has a fine military record. He is an educated man and a scholar. There are two serious blemishes connected with the evil days of Grant's administration but he has done everything since that time to efface them. He is a man who has steadily grown and is still growing. He is a young man, comparatively, who holds broad, liberal and often independent views. He showed much courage in his position on the currency question in opposition to the popular sentiment in his own state and can stand fairly on a civil service platform. He is, moreover, the leader of his party in the popular branch and certainly the parliamentary leader of a party is entitled to attend at its head.

Cabot Lodge had less praise for Garfield's running mate, Chester A. Arthur, late of the New York Customhouse, who was nominated as a sop to the stalwarts. "That such a nomination on general principles is thoroughly bad and a direct insult to the present administration cannot be questioned," he lamented, "but that it is a strong one politically seems equally certain. No one will abandon Garfield on account of Arthur and in New York the defeated machine will instead of sulking be brought to full play under the direction of the shrewdest political manager in the country." Of this shrewdest political leader, Conkling, the secretary of the Massachusetts delegation had this to say: —

He disgusted every reasonable man by his arrogant and offensive manner and by his sharp and often mean sneers at his opponents, but every one confessed his force and strength as a leader. After Cameron and Logan had gone down to hopeless defeat he held his men together without a break or waver anywhere. His followers . . . never flinched or faltered . . . and on the last ballot Grant received two more votes than on the first. It was a splendid exhibition of political organization. It enabled Conkling to gain the Vice-Presidency from his victorious but disorganized opponents and put his mark indelibly upon the ticket. There is a certain devilish ingenuity about the nomination of Arthur. The liberal elements which fought so hard against Grant and won such a victory are bound in honor to support Garfield, but they are all denied the privilege of scratching Arthur, thanks to the Electoral System.

On one other score the convention was a success in the eyes of Lodge and that was the forcing of a civil service plank into the platform. Introduced into the committee by a colleague of Lodge's from Massachusetts, it had there received but four votes out of forty-seven, and so it was reintroduced from the floor as an amendment. "This produced a good deal of consternation among the delegates," Lodge reported, and a Mr. Flannigan of Texas "said that civil service reform was ridiculous and asked the delegates what they came to Chicago for if not for the offices." "What are we here for?" went all over the country, and became a political catchword in every campaign for years to come. After some debate the amendment was passed without dissent.

Four days after the convention came to a close. Lodge reported to the Republicans of his district. Cheered by the music of the National Band of Lynn and a fine display of fireworks, the Republicans marched to the old Methodist Church. The young orator was at his best that night.

"We have a candidate who will unite every Republican, stalwart or liberal. The convention was the most notable one since the Democratic Convention in 1860. Faction and feud ran high in both. Out of the Charleston convention came disunion and strife, but out of the Chicago convention came strength and life."

He then told the cheering crowd that Garfield stood to the Republican Party as Gladstone stood to the Liberals in England, "as the representative of all that is best in the party which is the party of freedom, of human rights, of reform and progress. It is needless to disguise the fact that if the Democrats select wisely we will have a hard contest. We must put up our best men in every district [he himself was about to seek re-election to the House] who will stand by the President and harmonize the party." Next he eulogized Blaine and Sherman and ended, amid cheers, by saying that if their example were emulated then "we can in November work the word 'Glory' in the gay and dancing threads of the banner on which we have inscribed the name of James A. Garfield for President of the United States!" His failure to mention Arthur was undoubtedly deliberate.

Although he later admitted he knew very little of the Congressional district in which he lived, Lodge, stimulated by his experiences at Chicago, let the word get around that he would like to go to Congress. This caused one newspaper to say that he had "all the *dis*advantages of character, education, independence, personal and political, wealth and social position." Wiser counsel among his friends prevailed and, although petulant, he withdrew his name from consideration.

In the Lynn-Nahant district, however, it was pretty well understood that he could have the nomination for re-election to the House in Boston if he wanted it. At one meeting where he was the principal speaker he received praise from an unexpected but welcome quarter when his colleague from Lynn, the candidate of the Workingmen's Party, said: "There was never a better representation of the genius of American institutions than is here represented in the person of Mr. Lodge, whose culture you all know, and myself, a poor workingman from the same district. When I took my seat in the House I had prejudices which my experiences dispelled. I found that the gentleman from Nahant was as humble a man as the poor shoemaker from Lynn."

At the district convention he was nominated by the unanimous vote of the twenty delegates present. The *Lynn Item* praised him as a "gentleman of education and literary accomplishments" and urged his re-election on the ground that politics would be improved by the attention of such a man. On November 2 he was re-elected, receiving 2095 votes. Throughout the state the Republicans were victorious. The next day there was a great parade, with firing of cannons, display of fireworks, and a banquet at Market Hall to celebrate what the *Item* called "the most successful campaign that Lynn has ever known."

There was less excitement in this second term than there had been the previous year. Colonel Higginson again brought up the distressing subject of woman suffrage and Representative Lodge again voted against all his measures, although he did graciously consent to introduce a bill which would allow married women to do business on their own account. Probably the most important matter considered was a bill which would have abolished the poll tax, payment of which was then a qualification to vote in Massachusetts. His old friend, Jim McGeough of Boston, fought hard and Cabot went down the line with him. They lost the battle, however, and the poll tax remained.

The winter of 1881 saw Cabot and John T. Morse, Jr., come reluctantly to the conclusion that they were not making a success of the *International Review*. Discouraging as this was it did not fill the young politico-historian with despair. Seated in an alcove at a round table covered with a checked red-and-white cloth, placed so he could look up at a statue of the Lydian Sybil carved by his friend Story, Lodge could work in utter peace on his new book — the life of George Cabot's great friend and his own political idol and historical mentor — Alexander Hamilton. Morse was to publish it the next year in his American Statesman Series and add to Lodge's reputation as the scholar in politics.

Even before the legislative session ended on Friday, May 13, Cabot Lodge opened his Nahant house. A new local campaign was in the near offing and it would do him no harm to be seen often in his district. Each day, when the legislature was meeting, he could be observed driving in his phaeton across the causeway to and from the Boston and Maine station in Lynn. Usually his nephew was waiting for him in the conspicuous vehicle when he arrived in Lynn in the late afternoon. Unfortunately for his political ambitions enough people did not see his brave display and on this account disaster faced him in the autumn of 1881.

Lodge easily won the nomination for State Senator from

the First Essex District, which comprised the city of Lynn and the towns of Swampscott, Saugus, and Nahant. His Democratic-greenback opponent was John R. Baldwin, a lifelong resident of Lynn. Four years younger than Cabot, he had received a common-school education, and then had attended Harvard College in the class of 1877. He had never held public office, except on the school board of Lynn, where he was a practising lawyer.

Cabot Lodge always insisted that he was defeated in 1881 by what he called "slanders promulgated at the eleventh hour." Election day was November 8. On November 7 the *Lynn Item* carried a full-column advertisement from Mr. Baldwin. It said: —

It was not intended by the founders of our State that these districts should in any way resemble the English rotten borough system, which enabled a man wherever he resided, by purchase to represent any district that he might desire. . . . Our system was to remedy this very evil. Our representative was to be a citizen, a portion of that very community he represented. He should not be a citizen for a single purpose, a citizen merely by a strict legal construction, but he should be a citizen in intent, in interest, in aspirations, in affections and tastes.

It was a telling blow. Even more cruel was this: "Why should the citizens of Lynn and the first district lend their aid to, why should they be interested in, the personal aspirations and ambitions of Mr. Lodge? His followers openly announce their modest intentions. The position of State Senator is to be but a mere stepping stone, a friendly boost by the grateful people of the district, so that next Fall by a little more aid he will be able to be a Congressman." The advertisement then went on to tell of his Boston home and say that "wherever he may choose to call his domicile for financial and taxable reasons, he belongs to Boston . . . the thousand and one slight affections of [his] life are all Bostonian and encompassed in the circle of Beacon Hill society." Adams called him "Boston incarnate" — the Lynn Democrats called him "interloper" and "carpetbagger." Both were right.

Mr. Baldwin having made these same charges in a speech in Saugus on the Friday before the election, the Republicans were able, in the same issue, to print their side of the case. His youthful attainments were set forth, including the fact that he was a contributor to the *Encyclopaedia Britannica*. He was a "gentleman," above "personal controversy," who always placed "the interest of country above party." Of course, he was rich — but in brains as well as in money, and anyway his wealth was the result of the "honest industry and good New England economy" of his ancestors. With utter disregard of the genealogical facts the advertisement blandly asserted that "the Lodges have been an old Essex family for two hundred years and in this district. . . . How long has Mr. Baldwin's family been in the country?" the writer wanted to know. As to his living in the district: "His residence has been at Nahant since he was two weeks old and his mother's house in Boston is his headquarters when he has business to attend to. Is there anything very wrong with that?" Not much, except that the facts were slightly strained.

As the defender of Lodge, who signed himself "Fair Play," admitted, the controversy was "silly," but it was effective. Baldwin, the native son, carried the district by a vote of 2252 to 2080, and Lynn itself by the larger margin of 2117 to 1790. In Swampscott, Saugus, and Nahant, where ancestry and literary ability might be expected to carry more weight than in the city of Lynn, Lodge's margin was better than half.

Henry Adams, learning of the disaster, felt that perhaps now he might wean his protégé back to literature. After all,

73

literature was, as John Morse once coyly said, his lawfully wedded wife, and politics only his mistress. The woeful Adams warned him of "the remarkable way in which politics deteriorate the moral tone of everyone who mixes in them." But Cabot's mistress gave him something that he needed, something that literature, however much he loved her, could not supply. He was not to be successful at the polls again for six years, but politics was to be his passion to the end of his life.

VII

The Remarkable Way

IN 1882 Lodge decided again to seek the Republican nomination for Congress. In his own behalf he had made what his friend Charles G. Washburn described as "a most vigorous and unprecedented canvass," aided by his friends, but all their pleas were unavailing. The convention lasted two days and two nights, and 130 separate ballots were taken, but in the end he went down before Elisha S. Converse. It was, perhaps, just as well. Mr. Converse found he could not dam the Democratic tide that year and he, too, was frustrated in his ambitions to get to Washington by a one-legged Civil War veteran from the Lynn shoe shops.

Henry Adams was on hand to console Cabot. "You have lost nothing," he wrote, "and saved your chances for 1884."

This second defeat within the party was not fatal. A few months later Cabot was elected chairman of the Republican State Committee. The *Boston Herald,* in announcing that "young men are on the quarterdeck," declared that Cabot Lodge "has completely outgrown his political adolescence." He was to have a chance to prove his maturity very soon in a battle with a master politician.

Out of the Civil War had emerged one of the strangest figures of American political history. From the mill town of Lowell, Massachusetts,[1] to the city of New Orleans, he had

[1] When Cabot was one year old a Lowell mill posted this notice: "Whoever, employed by this corporation, votes the Ben Butler Ten Hour ticket on Monday next will be discharged." Since that year, 1851, Butler had been considered a dangerous radical and demagogue by all "right-thinking" people.

fought the good fight, stopping long enough in New York on the way to suppress the draft riots. Like many another Civil War general with ambition and gumption, this magnificent extrovert had found politics to his liking after the surrender of Lee (and even while fighting the war, his enemies said). In Washington, in the House of Representatives, he had won a reputation as one of the most dreadful spoilsmen of the dreadful decades. His enemies said he was unprincipled. His temperament was fundamentally Jacksonian, but Jackson's integrity was lacking from his make-up if his crudeness was not. He owned a yacht built with Navy Department funds, and he was the father of the infamous "Grab Bill" of 1873 which he blandly repudiated in the very next session of Congress. He had been Republican and Greenbacker; now he was a Democrat and Governor of Massachusetts.

To oust General Ben Butler from the State House became Cabot Lodge's immediate concern. It was an assignment to his liking. Besides, he knew that, were he successful, he could demand recognition and reward from the organization to which he had already given so much of his time and money. The major problem facing the Republicans was to find a candidate widely known and respected, for Butler not only held the advantage of possessing the office, but over the years, mainly through patronage in the post offices and navy yards, he had built up a formidable organization.

When the State Convention assembled, the choice was between George D. Robinson, a member of Congress from Chicopee, and Charles Francis Adams, Jr., Henry Adams's older brother. An informal poll showed that the delegates favored Robinson four to one over the gentleman from Quincy. Adams thereupon walked to the platform and moved that the convention draft and nominate Robinson by acclamation.

In his capacity as chairman of the State Committee, young Lodge sought out the gentleman from Chicopee, who, just by chance, was in a near-by hotel. Lodge escorted him to the platform amid enthusiasm and the gentleman from Chicopee then and there became the Republican candidate. Robinson was an able man whose chief disadvantage was the fact that, coming from the western part of the state, he was not well known in the urban eastern sections where Ben Butler had his strongholds.

Immediately after the convention Lodge, who had plenty of money to spend, began to gather together what one of them later described as "the greatest group of volunteer campaign workers ever known in the political history of the state." According to another observer, "in some manner the partisans of reform, and Lodge, their leader, begot for themselves a certain ill-repute during their struggle with the dreadful spoilsman. In fact, rumors of Lodge's Jekyll-and-Hyde character, circulating even at this time, had it that Butler's own shady methods had been turned against him; a hired 'rowdy' element seemed to have become uppermost in the respectable faction itself." The rumors, indeed, became so prevalent that Lodge had to deny them as "miserable calumnies" and once more he set forth the record of his ancestry, his past life, his position, his education, and his character, to show that such charges could not possibly be true.

However he accomplished his triumph, two things are certain: the campaign, known as the "Waterloo of Butlerism," succeeded in driving Butler from the presence of the Sacred Cod, and Henry Cabot Lodge's education in practical politics had been advanced another grade. It was not long after this campaign that Edward Henry Clement, editor of the *Evening Transcript*, was to devote part of his weekly letter to the *New York Tribune* to young Lodge of Boston, saying, "The gentleman and scholar in politics is without the guilelessness and squeamishness of said gentleman and scholar."

Important as it was, the crushing of Butler was only a prelude to the great campaign of 1884 — the campaign which marked the turning point in the career of Henry Cabot Lodge and showed how easily and quickly one might go down that "remarkable way" which Henry Adams had warned him to avoid.

In the spring of 1884 it was no longer fair to refer to Lodge as "young Lodge of Boston." Not only was he thirty-four years old (in May of that year) but, as they would say around Republican headquarters, he had already "been through the mill." He was seasoned and tough. He knew all the local leaders, those who controlled the silk-stocking districts and those who brought in the votes in the Irish slums. A friend of his described him at this period as "repellently cold, with no mellowness or warmth of speech." Similar characterizations dogged him all his life, and not without reason. One day, after Theodore Roosevelt had become President, the couple were walking in Rock Creek Park and Cabot expressed impatience with a magazine article which called him "cold, reserved, a Boston Brahmin." He asked Theodore why he was always charged with being frigid and aristocratic. "I can tell you why," said Roosevelt, with a chuckle, "because you are." He was born superior, and he took pride in his superiority; although with his intimates, and with his family, he was genial, witty, generous, human. His Boston crustiness became as much his political trademark as a dearth of socks was Congressman Jerry Simpson's, or black clothes and a string tie were the trademark of his fellow irreconcilable, Senator Borah. He fostered it, for he reveled in his title "the scholar in politics," but it was not an act — it was a fundamental part of his nature. It worked with the

Boston Irish and it won the heart of that old renegade, Pitchfork Ben Tillman. Because his crustiness was not "put on," after one recovered from the first chill one accepted it, and many who were the quickest to ridicule it were its secret admirers.

As might have been expected, it was Carl Schurz who sounded the battle cry of 1884. Early in May this Independent, although without standing in orthodox Republican circles, warned that if James Gillespie Blaine were nominated, the Republican Party would be split in two. Blaine, and Blaine alone, was to be the party issue of 1884. His character and his record were to raise questions which, asked on every hand in 1884, are still unanswered. Perhaps they can only be approached now, as they were then, by an application of one's own standards, one's own interpretation of morality and honesty, one's own conscience. Was he an innocent man or a culpable man? Did his "moral delinquency" overshadow his admitted ability? Certainly Blaine never disproved the charge that he had perverted the high office of Speaker of the House of Representatives for financial gain. Certainly he never mitigated his reprehensible conduct by an explanation satisfactory to the impartial reader of history. And yet he was an able man, if impetuous, and like Arthur he might also have proved, in the dignity of the White House, that he was capable of personal development and national leadership. But that is speculation. By the record, in spite of his magnetic personality and his command of oratory, he earned the appellation of Charles Edward Russell: "No other man in our annals filled so large a space and left it so empty."

Henry Cabot Lodge was as aware of Blaine's "decidedly mottled record" as was Theodore Roosevelt, who wrote to him from New York nearly a month before the convention, urging him to "avoid the Blaine devil." There is no question that, at least until the time he left Boston as a delegate to the Republican National Convention in Chicago, Cabot Lodge considered Blaine utterly unscrupulous and quite untrustworthy of political leadership. So did all those members of the Brahmin caste whom he respected and admired and with whom he had worked for the advancement of political morality — George Cabot Lee, Moorfield Storey, Charles William Eliot, Henry and Brooks Adams, Josiah Quincy, George William Curtis, Roger Wolcott, and many, many more.

The independent Massachusetts Republicans, unwilling to support Arthur for a second term, were expected to concentrate their strength on Senator George Franklin Edmunds, the chilly Vermonter who had received their support four years before. When Cabot Lodge was elected delegate at large from Massachusetts in May it was generally conceded that he was an Edmunds man. He made a speech at that time supporting Edmunds and Robert T. Lincoln. In New York Theodore Roosevelt, who had just been elected a delegate at the Utica convention, was swinging his friends to the Vermonter's support. The two men had been in correspondence for some time. On May 5 Theodore invited Lodge to a meeting of independents at Delmonico's, then New York's most famous restaurant. Lodge went, had his dinner and much talk, and then he and Roosevelt moved on to Washington to look the situation over. They did not find much sentiment there for Edmunds in their talks with the "many interesting people, leaders in politics — many Senators" whom they saw, and they were worried over the evidence of "plenty of support visible for Blaine and for Arthur." Lodge admitted he "made little effective headway" trumpeting for Edmunds, but the trip had one significant result: Lodge and Roosevelt became the closest of friends during it. Previously Roosevelt had addressed his letters "Dear Mr. Lodge"; after they had returned to their respective homes he was writing to "Dear Lodge"; by the time the campaign was over it was "Theodore" and "Cabot." And so it was to remain between them until Theodore's death.

In later years Lodge insisted that both he and Roosevelt had agreed "as a matter of simple honesty and good faith" to enter the convention "expecting others to support our candidate if fairly nominated," and that they in turn would support the convention's choice — whoever it might be. He claimed to have said to Godkin of the *Nation:* "Of course, if we go to the convention and Blaine is nominated, we shall have to support him." [2]

The Republican National Convention opened to noisy confusion and the usual prayer in Exposition Hall on Tuesday, June 3. The delegates had been arriving since Sunday. By Monday afternoon they had sized up the situation. The strategy of the independents was to stop Blaine at all costs, hopeful of bringing about another deadlock which would only be broken by the nomination of Edmunds or some dark horse acceptable to them. Throughout Monday night the little group — George William Curtis of New York, Senator Hoar, Governor Long, Roosevelt, and Lodge — scurried about the Chicago hotels, working late and earnestly, conferring with the leading Arthur men and canvassing the other delegations. The Blaine supporters, they had learned, were under orders to name Powell Clayton of Arkansas as temporary chairman. Clayton was a notorious carpetbagger

[2] Lodge's own version of his stand regarding Blaine, and his version of Theodore Roosevelt's course at the same time, may be found in *Selections from the Correspondence of Theodore Roosevelt and Henry Cabot Lodge, 1884–1918,* Vol. I, pp. 11–12. It is by no means a satisfactory explanation and the only witness called upon by name, E. L. Godkin, editor of the *Nation,* was dead at the time of publication, 1925.

who made it a point never to contradict the assertion that he had lost a leg in the Civil War — although it was well known to his intimates that it had been cut off in a quite non-military accident. If the independents could stop Clayton's nomination they would be a long way towards upsetting Blaine's plans. When they retired in the early hours of Tuesday morning they were, for once, sanguine of success.

Almost as soon as the convention was called to order Powell Clayton's name was offered. Immediately Lodge, whom the *New York Sun* described as "a pretty clever young fellow . . . the real head of the Massachusetts delegation," climbed upon a chair with as much dignity as he could muster under the circumstances, and in his thin voice offered an opposing motion. Recognized, he thereupon nominated John R. Lynch of Mississippi, a neatly dressed, dignified Negro who, like Lodge, wore a mustache and goatee. Immediately a New York delegate seconded and George William Curtis arose to say that "we ought to have a representative of these great people who, in great part, constitute the Republican Party of the South." As he sat down Theodore Roosevelt threw off his straw hat and scrambled to his perch on a chair with what, in a memorable phrase, a *Times* reporter the next morning called "juvenile activity." But when he spoke, this same reporter added, it was "not with the voice of a youth, but that of a man." His telling speech clinched the nomination for Lynch. The vote was 424 to 384.

The next day the evanescent limelight played upon Lodge and Roosevelt as the Eastern newspapers praised them for their temporary victory over Blaine. But although the two young men worked as well as they could to further the cause of Edmunds, that colorless individual stood no chance. The only other victory won by the independents was the defeat of a Blaine resolution which would have held every delegate in honor bound to support the nominee, whoever he might be. Another able and eloquent speech by Curtis forced the resolution to be withdrawn. Thereafter about all the independents could do was to sit back and watch Blaine win. Their own candidate had only ninety-three votes when the balloting began. On each successive vote this number was reduced. On the fourth ballot Blaine was nominated and the most violent and colorful election campaign since the Civil War was under way.

At the convention Lodge commanded more attention than he ever had before. He impressed the reporters with his earnestness and his capacity for work. The *Sun,* an irreverent Democratic organ, claimed that he "works while Mr. John Milton Forbes orders dinners and Mr. George Frisbie Hoar contemplates his own perfection. He seems to know what he wants. Many of his associates in the delegation really don't know what they want and some don't want anything except to look distinguished. Mr. Lodge is bigger than Mr. Hoar. The young man will never be unduly conceited if he never receives higher praise than this."

Cabot Lodge did know what he wanted. His aim was to be elected to the Congress in the fall. He had already announced his intention of seeking the nomination. The choice of Blaine, however, left him in a most troublesome position. If he were to believe his friend Schurz's observation — "this is the hour and the minute which will go down in history as marking the death of the Republican Party" — would it not be best for him to bolt? He knew, even then, that many of his closest friends were considering taking such action. He knew, too, that the eyes of the rank and file of Republicans were on him, for he had openly expressed his contempt for Blaine and his record.

It was, indeed, a most unhappy Henry Cabot Lodge who pushed aside Schurz's view of the situation as a "question of political ethics" and said to a representative of the *Boston*

Advertiser, while packing his Gladstone bag: "Blaine is obnoxious to our people, but I shall give him my support."

Overnight he had made his resolve. He had chosen the path he was to follow. From June 5, 1884, until his death, Henry Cabot Lodge never again wavered in his loyalty to the party to which he bowed that day. He had irrevocably offered himself to the man whom he had once described to his own wife as a "rascal" and an "utterly worthless scamp."

That personal ambition led him to take this step, while all around him members of his own class — his closest friends and fellow reformers — were preparing to bolt, seems certain. In Nahant the rumor spread that he was contemplating a similar rebellion. An alarmed Judge Wilson, who had a fine contempt for all irregularity, rushed to Worcester where he boarded the train carrying the returning delegates. The judge was greatly relieved to find that Lodge had made up his mind the night before.

Perhaps on the long train ride back from Chicago the scholar in politics had thought of some words he had written two years before concerning Alexander Hamilton's decision to vote for adoption of the Constitution, despite his own dislike for many of its provisions: —

Had he been an agitator or a sentimentalist of muddy morals and high purposes, a visionary and an idealist, he would have stood up and howled against this constitution. . . . As he was none of these things, but a patriotic man of clear and practical mind, he knew that the first rule of successful and beneficial statesmanship was not to sulk because one cannot have just what one wants, but to take the best obtainable, and sustain it to the uttermost.

One of the first things Lodge did after his return was to write his friend Roosevelt, who, still grieving over the death of his young wife, had hastened off to the Bad Lands of

84

Dakota to wrestle with his conscience in the wilderness. Roosevelt's answer lends weight to the belief that there was no early agreement between them to support Blaine and Logan. Certainly the young New Yorker was disgusted with the results of the convention and his mind was all but made up, if not to bolt with the other Mugwumps, as the reformers were now known, at least to take no part in the campaign. He understood Lodge's unhappy position clearly, and he urged him to be cautious in what he did and said, and above all to keep on good terms with "the machine." The exile added, a little patronizingly, "I am very anxious you should take no steps hastily, for I do not know a man in the country whose future I regard as so promising as yours."

Having formally announced his regularity Lodge could not very well have joined the general exodus of liberal spirits from the Republican Party. The desertion reached its height on July 10, when the Democrats nominated Grover Cleveland, the first really dangerous contender that party had offered since 1856. When Carl Schurz heard of Lodge's choice he wrote sorrowfully to his faithless protégé. The election of Blaine, he declared, would be a virtual endorsement of corrupt practices by the American people.

"You are a young man," he reminded Lodge. "You have the advantages of affluent circumstances. You have the promise of an honorable and useful career before you. That promise certainly will not be damaged if you follow a noble impulse at the risk of temporarily compromising your party standing and of obscuring the prospect of immediate preferment.

"Do not," he begged, "run for Congress on the Republican ticket." To do so, he warned, would be to raise the suspicion of having suppressed upon "an important occasion [your] best impulses for the purpose of getting quickly into place."

In one last appeal he wrote that there was a "moral limit" to the concessions one must make to the organization.

Lodge's reply, although courteous, was cool and specious. The course he had chosen was "the only honorable one to take. . . . If I had announced to the Massachusetts Convention that if Mr. Blaine were nominated, I should bolt him, they never would have sent me to Chicago," he pleaded. It was his intention now to proclaim his formal adherence to the Republican ticket, to resign as State Chairman of the Republican Committee,[3] and to accept the nomination to Congress if it were proffered.

"On the mere grounds of expediency," the young man lectured his mentor, "it seems to me that no party was ever founded on opposition to a single man or ever will be. Whatever the result of the election, the parties will remain. By staying in the party I can be of some use. By going out I destroy all the influence for power and good I may possess. . . . I want you to realize that, however mistaken I may be, I act from a sense of duty and from a conviction that I have a debt of honor which I must pay, no matter how disagreeable and distasteful it is."

To this Schurz replied with the last letter he was ever to write Henry Cabot Lodge: —

Our duty to the country which we discharge at the ballot box is in all respects paramount to any duty we may owe the party.

For Henry Cabot Lodge this was the first of many deep friendships that ended forever in the summer of 1884. Moorfield Storey, who had dined so often at his home and who had shared with him the high hopes of their political adolescence, maintained for forty years the independence forged in this bitter campaign and did not speak to him again. There were others, of his own class, who likewise

[3] He offered his resignation but it was not accepted.

turned their backs. There were some, on the other hand, who understood. The late Louis A. Coolidge, Lodge's one-time secretary, once wrote: —

The bitterness against him grew and flourished among his former social and professional associates about Boston, who, unversed in the necessities of politics and unfamiliar with the exigencies of party organization and loyalty, could not comprehend that one might still remain true to his own, high, political ideals while remaining true to the only organization which could give effect to those ideals through men and agencies perhaps not altogether satisfactory.

Two days after Carl Schurz had written his penultimate letter of warning the campaign was formally opened in Massachusetts by a Republican ratification meeting that filled Boston's Tremont Temple to overflowing. Huge portraits of Blaine and Logan were hung on either side of the organ and a brass band played stirring music as the more or less prominent Republicans invited by the State Committee filed to the tier of seats on the platform. Conspicuous at the meeting was the slim figure of Henry Cabot Lodge. He cannot have been a completely happy man. Perhaps in the inner pocket of his neat and expensive dinner jacket lay the letter from Carl Schurz. Beside him on the platform sat such worthies as Governor Robinson, who presided, Senator Hoar and Senator Dawes, former Representative Crapo, and former Governors Long and Rice. They had decided in advance upon the "party line": that this was to be a contest not of men, but of parties. And this was the line that Lodge, the first speaker, presented. Quickly passing over the question of candidacy he turned to his own predicament: —

"I was one of those delegates who were opposed to these nominations. My fellow delegates decided against me, and by that decision in honor and good faith as a delegate, I propose to abide."

Having thus confessed, he announced his entire loyalty to that great party which had "honored and trusted him in this state." Then, after asserting that a choice must be made between the two parties, he reviewed in sarcastic terms the Democratic platform and the recent work of the Democratic Congress, contrasting it unfavorably with previous Republican achievements. After a sneer at the Democrats' attitude towards civil service reform (which he and Roosevelt were to hang to for years as their own private brand of liberalism) he tore from its context an old and scathing criticism of the Democratic Party, once uttered by George William Curtis, and sat down to polite applause.

It was old Senator Hoar who waxed most satirical about the bolters and who uttered words that ought to have made Lodge squirm in his seat: "President Eliot expresses the sentiment of a little body of men about Cambridge. I am happy to believe he does not represent Harvard, whose influence . . . has tended to infinitely degrade the public life of the Commonwealth. These men have taught our educated youth to be ashamed of their own history. Their eyes are microscopes which can see a blemish on the skin, but cannot take in a fair landscape or a hearty human figure. There is hardly a man who has taken any of the responsibilities of public life who has not been compelled to undergo the contemptuous criticism of these gentle hermits of Cambridge. . . ."

Senator Hoar's seemingly gratuitous assault upon his and Lodge's college was not without significance. At Commencement this very year Lodge had been elected to the Board of Overseers. But President Eliot was now in the forefront of those who had gone over to Cleveland, a group whose rolls contained the name of many a prominent son of Harvard. Indeed, Harvard was a hotbed of Republican secession.

The *Boston Herald* had bolted Blaine, as had the *Advertiser*, the *New York Times*, and several leading independent Republican papers – the *New York Evening Post*, the *Springfield Republican*, and the *Boston Evening Transcript*. The *Herald* now mockingly referred to the meeting as "a crow banquet," and for Lodge, who once had professed "no faith in reform within the church," it must have been just that.

Two days later Theodore Roosevelt, who had made no definite admission of his plans, came quietly on from Dakota. He went immediately to Nahant and there, on a warm Thursday night, the two men sat on the broad veranda overlooking the restless sea, talking into the late hours. They must have thrashed out the whole matter, then and during the next day. On Saturday afternoon Roosevelt went to Boston, where he made his presence known to a *Boston Herald* reporter. He prefaced his remarks with a disavowal of any previous "interviews" credited to him, and said: "I intend to vote the Republican Presidential ticket. While at Chicago, I told Mr. Lodge that such was my intention; but before announcing it, I wished to have time to think the whole matter over. A man cannot act both without and within the party; he can do either, but he cannot possibly do both." It was the voice of Theodore Roosevelt speaking, but the words were those of Henry Cabot Lodge.

To Roosevelt, such men as E. L. Godkin, Carl Schurz, Charles Francis Adams, Jr., or Cabot's old friends Leverett Saltonstall, William Everett, James Freeman Clarke, Josiah Quincy, Winslow Warren, or Richard H. Dana, proved themselves by their desertion of Blaine and Logan to be suffering from "a species of moral myopia, complicated with intellectual strabismus." He found that his friends in New York were surprised that he had "not developed hoofs and horns." In putting up a good front in his letters to his friend,

he professed amusement because the Boston independents
"circulated . . . the idea that I was a misguided weakling,
who would have liked to be honest, but who was held in
moral thralldom by the unscrupulous machine-manipulator
of Nahant."

On the other hand old white-haired Senator Hoar, his
younger colleague Dawes, Andrew D. White, and even
George F. Edmunds, the reformer's own candidate (all men
whose basic integrity was unquestioned), accepted Lodge's
position, and saw nothing opprobrious about it, and supported Blaine. Bishop William Lawrence, Lodge's friend and
biographer, confessed many years later that, although he
was opposed to Lodge at the time, he had come to believe
that his schoolmate was right in 1884. As Mr. Fuess once
pointed out, the Mugwumps had no monopoly of virtue,
and Lodge, deep in his soul, "was a strong partisan, just as
he was a strong nationalist. Loyalty to institutions and to
country was ineradicable in his personality."

The first reward of this Massachusetts Abdiel was the
unanimous nomination for Congress when the Republicans
of the Lynn-Nahant district held their convention in the
shoe city on September 10. After the enthusiastic Republicans had named him, he arose to remark: —

"I shall not utter any vain formulas about the nomination
being unsought and unexpected. I have sought it in the past.
I expected it today, and I am none the less grateful and
appreciate your action none the less on this account."

That evening, after he had driven to his estate in his
phaeton, a crowd of enthusiastic supporters in festive spirit
boarded barges and went from Lynn to Nahant, where they
celebrated the candidate. Later an anonymous bard composed a song in his honor, and if its poetic qualities may
have grated upon an ear trained in childhood to the cadences
of Pope and Shakespeare the scholar in politics no doubt

appreciated its intent. One verse, in which prophecy outran poesy, claimed: —

> Then vote for Lodge, you men who toil
> You'll find that he will dare if
> The Democrats attempt free trade
> To fight hard for the tariff.

Lodge spoke in practically every town and village in his district. His campaign was well covered by the *Herald* and the *Advertiser* for, although these newspapers could not stomach Blaine, their blessing, strangely enough, was bestowed upon Cabot Lodge. In October, at the insistence of Lodge, Theodore Roosevelt (who had abandoned his intention of taking no part in the campaign although he was reported to have said, when further "Mulligan letters" were made public in the heat of the campaign: "I hope to God he will be defeated") came on to make several speeches in Lodge's behalf. At the Melrose Town Hall, Lodge was greeted with "uproarious enthusiasm" according to the *Advertiser*, and Roosevelt, received with "tumultuous applause," praised him as "one of the most conspicuous examples of independent republicanism." In Lyceum Hall in Winchester, Roosevelt sandwiched in a tribute to Lodge in a speech mainly devoted to the national campaign but which he concluded by expressing his delight in remaining "where by inheritance and education I feel I belong — the Republican Party." The phrase fitted Cabot Lodge better than himself.

But neither the poetry of the unknown party-singer nor the witticisms of Theodore Roosevelt availed. Like Blaine and Logan, Henry Cabot Lodge was defeated in the election of November 6, 1884. In the Democratic landslide, made possible in good measure by the defection of the Mugwumps, Lodge's old opponent, Mr. Lovering of Lynn, won out again. Lodge was defeated by 265 in a total of 30,000 votes.

When Theodore Roosevelt heard the bad news he hastened to console his "dear Old Fellow," blaming the Republican disaster on "the cursed pharisaical fools and knaves who have betrayed us."

"You have," he wrote, "a hold on the party . . . and beyond question you will take the stand you deserve in public life."

VIII

Washington at Last

HENRY CABOT LODGE had to wait two years before he was able to take the stand he deserved in public life. They were not idly spent. When he was an old man he wrote rather pompously about the virtues of work, which was, he said, the best of friends. "Without it one can never enjoy either leisure or a vacation, and work, free from anxiety, is always a tonic, and in some of the darkest hours an anodyne. I do not believe that it ever did anyone anything but good, provided that a man takes plenty of exercise, which I have always done, hunting in the autumn, and in summer living in and on the water, and always varying my amusements out-of-doors by much walking and the simple labor of chopping and sawing wood."

The months following the Blaine disaster were dark. Lodge was unhappy, even despondent. He threw himself into a self-appointed task. If it brought him neither wide fame nor great fortune it at least took up his time and salved his New England conscience. He was still at heart a scholar as well as a politician and now he lost himself in editing the complete works of his great hero, Alexander Hamilton. The first of the nine resultant volumes appeared in 1885 and the last came from the press in 1887. It was a tremendous task and one of which he was proud. No other editor of Hamilton's writings had accomplished as much as he in gathering together the speeches and writings of the Federalist.

In 1882 he had, of course, written his short biography of Hamilton, the first of his many books in which prejudice supplanted scholarship and his strong anti-democratic leanings found full expression. This was followed by a short biography of Daniel Webster. Henry Adams found that there was a "visible effort" in Lodge's "elaborate excuses and apologies" for Webster, while another scholarly critic sighed because the author appeared ready to accept almost any story about the statesman-lawyer. For years to come the American attitude towards Webster was slanted by Lodge's book, which found wide popularity. It was short and well-written. Perhaps the harshest criticism that could be made against it was that it contained, as Allan Nevins once pointed out, many flagrant errors of perspective; his attribution to Webster of the entire constitutional argument against secession, for one thing, was patently preposterous. Reading the book several years later Theodore Roosevelt exclaimed: "Lodge is not as big a man intellectually as Webster, but he is a far better man morally."

These two biographies fed his ambition. One day, between his election to Congress and the convening of the House, he walked into the library where John T. Morse, Jr., was seated at his desk before an open fire. Lodge was in a gloomy mood and sat there for several minutes before speaking. Suddenly he turned and said, "John, I should like to write the Washington for your series; will you give it to me?" The biography of the first President was destined to be, of course, the most important volume in the American Statesman Series, and Morse, understandably, had reserved it for himself. Indeed, he had already started upon it and several of the first chapters lay in manuscript on the desk that separated the two men. Startled, Morse did some rapid thinking and replied, with a generosity probably unparalleled in editorial history: "All right, Cabot, it is yours." A few minutes later when Lodge had left the room Morse reached for his manuscript and threw it into the flames.

To this day there is a difference of opinion over the two-volume *Life of George Washington* which Lodge wrote between 1887 and 1889. When the *Life* first appeared William Dean Howells sang its praises, saying that, for the first time, Washington had been rescued from "fable land" and that Lodge had at last succeeded in presenting a "purely human as well as thoroughly American Washington." Although Lodge did show a Washington far different from that incredible creature imagined by Parson Weems, his portrait helped establish another fable that was almost as far from the truth. To Henry Cabot Lodge the father of the country was a sort of war lord who "sniffed the air of battle from afar and was glad," rather than the peace-loving and worried Washington whose one sustaining dream during the Revolution was to get the business done so that he might return to the peace of Mount Vernon. Lodge's Washington was essentially an early American militarist and not the Washington who wrote: "How much more delightful to an undebauched mind is the task of making improvements on earth than all the vain glory which can be acquired from ravaging it by the most uninterrupted career of conquest."

Aside from misunderstanding and misinterpreting Washington's character, he went astray, according to competent critics, in giving an account of Washington's military career. This, perhaps, was not surprising, for Lodge had no knowledge of military history, knew nothing about tactics. In discussing Washington as a politician, he saw him primarily as one who proved for all time the virtue of loyalty to a party. Indeed, his chapter on "Washington as a party man" may be read as an expression of Lodge's own credo, post-1884.

During the years preceding his election to Congress

Lodge had written, for the *Atlantic Monthly* and other magazines, a number of essays on historical subjects. Published in 1885 as *Studies in History,* they revealed the intense partisanship of the man. In some instances brilliantly written, they invariably imposed upon the reader his own political and economic predilections. They showed him as a most capable interpreter of the ideas and achievements of Hamilton, Marshall, Adams, and others of the anti-Republican party; and as one incapable of doing justice to those on the other side. American historical writing contains few less just portraits of Jefferson, Madison, Monroe, or Gallatin than those penned by Henry Cabot Lodge. He could never understand, much less appreciate, Jefferson, whom he saw through the eyes of his own great-grandfather as one who represented all the evils of democracy.

His literary activities, while exacting, had not been so overwhelming as to shut him out from politics, nor had his literary ambitions overshadowed his yen for public office. He remained as chairman of the State Committee through 1885. In that year he took charge of fashioning the Republican platform. His plank on civil service reform attracted attention far beyond Massachusetts. The New York newspapers, with the exception of the *Post,* praised it, mentioning him by name. Teddy Roosevelt congratulated Lodge for his "reappearance in politics" in such a decisive manner. Writing from Oyster Bay, where he, too, was momentarily following a "literary career," Roosevelt predicted that Lodge would soon be in the United States Senate and urged him not to run "in that damned Congressional district" again.

The Republicans of the "damned Congressional district," however, were not adverse to having Lodge try his luck there once more and he was duly nominated by his party in 1886. The Democrats again nominated Mr. Lovering. The campaign was rough. M. E. Hennessy, the *Boston Globe's* seasoned veteran of Massachusetts political reporting, recalled it, at the time of Lodge's death, in these words: —

Lodge's district included Democratic Charlestown. He was not without Democratic support. The Navy Yard played an important part in the spirited fight for Congressional honors. There was no Corrupt Practices Act in those days and money was spent lavishly for influence and votes. The leaders of both parties generally selected a candidate with a barrel and proceeded to tap it for the benefit of the "boys." For years the financial echoes of that campaign plagued the successful candidate and his friends.

Perhaps it was because Lodge had more money at his command than Lovering; perhaps it was because the electorate, Republican and Democratic alike, saw in Lodge the better man; but whatever the reason, after the speech-making, parading, and red fire had died down, and the ballots had been counted, Lodge was the victor by 728 votes.

When Lodge entered the House he looked upon his new office as little more than a steppingstone to a seat in the Senate. There he could be a statesman, free in great measure from the petty annoyances that dogged a Congressman. But he was content to bide his time, work hard at his new job, and make a name for himself. He was not above seeing to it that his constituents were "taken care of," that deserving Civil War veterans were given pensions or increases, that certain G.A.R. posts got the cannon they wanted to decorate their headquarters.

From the very beginning Henry Cabot Lodge of Massachusetts was looked upon with mingled awe and suspicion by the Representatives from the South and West. The Southerners were soon to have good reason to hate him; the Westerners regarded him as an effete and even effeminate dude. He was thirty-seven years old when he took his seat in the House but he looked younger, in spite of his beard. His figure was then as always slight and trim (he was more at home in a saddle than many of the Westerners who derided him) and the close-fitting clothes he wore accentuated the slightness and trimness. He had a way of standing with his hands in his pockets, which were cut on a vertical slant at a time when the style was horizontal; Congressmen from the hinterland detected an insolence in his manner of which he chose to be completely unaware. But they disliked most his cutting New England accent. They delighted to imitate it, with exaggerated twang and broader "a," in the privacy of the cloakroom.

Although Lodge was aware of the limited prerogatives of a freshman in Congress he had no intention of remaining a nonentity for long. He was placed on the Elections Committee during his first session, a post which ordinarily would have afforded him but little opportunity to attract attention. Fortunately for him this committee was called upon to decide an issue potentially of wide political significance.

In the fall elections of 1886, Speaker John G. Carlisle of Kentucky had come dangerously near defeat. He and his Democratic backers, with singular indifference to the temper of the times, had apparently taken it for granted that his re-election was assured. The Republicans had offered no opposing candidate and the only obstacle to Carlisle's victory was the nominee of the Knights of Labor, a little-known mechanic named George H. Thobe. When the first votes were counted on November 3 the Democratic machine was astounded to find that Thobe had corralled a majority in the city of Covington and throughout Kenton County. Hundreds of workers from the shops and factories of Cincinnati, just over the state line, had taken the day off to vote for the Knight of Labor, with the result that it looked momentarily as if an unknown candidate of an unrecognized party had defeated a national statesman. The back-county vote, however, showed a bare majority for Carlisle.

Charges of fraud immediately were raised, and through the state rumors spread that Democratic politicians had sped at midnight in closed carriages to stuff forged ballots into the boxes in the outlying district in order to save the day for Carlisle. As a result of the suspicions, Thobe filed with the House what the cynical Washington correspondent of the *New York Times* called a "frivolous and diaphanous suit" in a desperate effort to unseat Carlisle. Carlisle, whose personal integrity was unquestioned, left the appointment of the Elections Committee to Crisp of Georgia, whom he called to the chair for that purpose. When the House refused to appoint a special committee to take up the matter, it came before this committee. On January 17, 1888, the committee unanimously agreed that the allegations of Thobe had been disproved. Nevertheless, a minority wanted the case reopened, if for no other purpose than to give Thobe a chance publicly to be heard.

The outstanding defender of workingman Thobe's right to a hearing was the Boston aristocrat, the dude of Nahant — Henry Cabot Lodge. His motives were not entirely altruistic. Carlisle was one of the strongest antagonists to the Republican tariff theory in Congress and, as Speaker, he was in a powerful position. If it was impossible to remove him, it was at least of good purpose to embarrass him. Depending as he did upon the votes of Lynn shoe workers, it could do Lodge no harm to defend a Kentucky mechanic. And so he arose in the House to argue that, although there was no definite evidence warranting such action, the case should be sifted again because of the "enormous disparity of political position between the contestant and the contestee." Such a course was justified, Lodge pleaded, if only it would do something toward removing the feeling among workingmen that the "power of corporations, the power of trusts, the power of rings, the power of men in high authority, backed by money and influence, has enormous weight in all legislative bodies in this country."

While Lodge did not deny that the "workingmen" may well have had good reason for their belief he added, cautiously, "It is an unwholesome and dangerous belief. It is the kind of vague theory to which agitators opposed to every form of order and society appeal."

As a consequence of Lodge's speech Thobe was given his day before the House. Three days later the Democrats secured a quorum and declared Carlisle elected. In Oyster Bay Theodore Roosevelt read about the case in the newspapers and congratulated "Dear Cabot." "You have made your mark," he said. George Thobe went back to Kentucky to take up his trade of mechanic and to disappear from the public gaze.

Lodge's constituents were given no reason to believe that the scholar in politics was ignoring issues in which they might be presumed to be interested. When it was proposed to appropriate $100,000 for a drydock in the Brooklyn Navy Yard he protested on the ground that the Navy Yard at Charlestown had adequate facilities which were not being used. He was "sound" on the tariff, from a Massachusetts point of view, whether the goods involved were curled hair, codfish, or rattan. He supported the bill for an eight-hour day in government yards, and when certain citizens of the fishing port of Gloucester protested against the ratification of the fisheries treaty with Great Britain he duly presented their petition to Congress.

It was the fisheries question that allowed him to play with international affairs for a brief moment. The rights of American fishing vessels in Canadian waters had been in almost constant dispute since the creation of the Republic. An attempt to define these rights had been made in 1818; now through the expiration of subsequent treaties the matter was back almost where it had started. Lodge approved the belligerent "retaliation bill" which passed both Houses and which empowered President Cleveland to employ measures against Canada for the seizure of two American ships. In the course of his defense of the bill he took occasion to criticize the President for making the foreign policy a party measure. "A feeble foreign policy is bad," he said, "but it is not necessarily disgraceful. To use the honor and dignity of the country as a stake in our foreign relations for political ends or to bluster to foreign nations for political effect would be disgraceful in the President of the United States." This was the basis of Cleveland's intense and lasting dislike of Cabot Lodge. The treaty was rejected by the Senate by a strict party vote of 28 Democrats for and 30 Republicans against.

Although Harrison failed of a popular majority in 1888, he won over Cleveland by 65 votes in the Electoral College and the Republicans carried both Houses of Congress. At the same time Cabot Lodge was re-elected to Congress by the largest majority he had yet won: 5294 votes.

Cabot Lodge knew what was likely to be popular at home. His secretary, Louis A. Coolidge, who had come to him from the *Springfield Republican* and who later was to become treasurer of the United Shoe Machinery Corporation, once said that Lodge understood the value of never neglecting a personal or political promise and of attending to such things himself. A few days after the inauguration of President Harrison Lodge was writing to Theodore Roosevelt: "I am harassed to death and if this accursed patronage does not kill me politically and destroy my health and temper, nothing will." At that very moment he was taking care of a bit of patronage for Theodore himself — arranging with Tom Reed, Secretary Blaine's son Walker, and other influential members of the administration to induce President

Harrison to appoint Roosevelt to the Civil Service Commission.

It was not long after his re-election before the matter of "accursed patronage" arose to plague this outspoken advocate of civil service reform. His local enemies had kept alive the intimations of irregularities in Charlestown in 1886 and now, in October 1889, his former friend and fellow Mugwump, George William Curtis, was to give them national circulation. In the course of a speech in Philadelphia attacking the Harrison administration's stand on civil service, Curtis had suggested that Lodge had been guilty of playing politics with Navy Yard employees. Lodge was forced to make a public denial. He said he had confined his action at Charlestown to the dismissal of a few relatively poor subordinates who had been appointed during the Cleveland administration and to the "reinstatement in their places of good men, who were also war veterans."

The so-called "Navy Yard charges," although embarrassing, came to nothing and did little ultimately to mar Lodge's reputation; but they did reveal to a certain extent how Lodge kept his hold over the electorate. They marked the beginning of what for many years was known as the "Lodge machine" in Massachusetts.

At this time, however, Lodge was best known to the general public as an advocate of civil service reform. He made many speeches on the subject, both within and without Congress, and in March 1889 made a dramatic gesture to show how, even in the Post Office Department, his favored principles might work towards eliminating the "spoils system."

"Under the existing system," he said, "postmasters are selected . . . from the party in power and the office of postmaster in every town and city has been made a party office. I believe strongly in taking all the routine offices of the government out of politics and this is a reform I hope to see accepted ultimately."

He chose the town of Winchester, Massachusetts, as the scene of his experiment and there he induced the Republicans to hold a caucus for the choice of postmaster. (The Democrats, of course, were not invited: that obviously would be taking things a little too far out of politics.) As a result William F. Fitch was "elected" by the townspeople, and Lodge duly presented his name for confirmation to John Wanamaker, the Postmaster General. Although Lodge's "Winchester system" attracted its mild share of editorial attention, and was tried out in an upstate New York village, it never caught the public fancy.

Not since the revolt against Grant in 1875 had the Republicans controlled both the administration and the two Houses of Congress. The party was greedy and expectant and quite determined that no such nonsense as Cleveland's radical and unbusinesslike attempt to revise the tariff downward should be repeated. In order to facilitate matters the high-tariff Republicans were determined to have their own man in the Speaker's chair. As it turned out, both contenders for the Republican choice could be depended upon to do their party's bidding, but the Eastern members were convinced of the superiority of Tom Reed over "Uncle Joe" Cannon.

Cabot Lodge had sat next to Thomas Brackett Reed since his first day in the House and had acquired deep admiration for the "fat man from Maine," as Lodge playfully called him, whose service on the Judiciary, Ways and Means, and particularly on the Rules committees had taught him nearly all there was to know about Congress. Lodge had with keen appreciation watched Tom Reed slump, silent and sleepy, on his spine while many a verbose Representative raged and ranted upon some subject dearest to him, and then rise and, with caustic tongue, puncture the offender — while the House and the galleries roared at his sallies of ready, and sometimes cruel, wit.

The friendship of the two men soon extended beyond the halls of Congress. Reed became a steady frequenter of the literary-political salon in Lodge's charming, book-lined home, which was fast becoming a Washington fixture. Besides their friendship there was another good reason why Lodge preferred Tom Reed to "Uncle Joe" — the latter was an unlettered rustic whose manners to a Bostonian were as deplorable as his lack of schooling. Lodge, therefore, threw himself into the fight that raged within Republican circles and, although the nature of his persuasive efforts does not appear upon the record, we have the late Governor Samuel W. McCall's word for it that it was mainly through "Lodge's efforts in the caucus" that Reed triumphed over Cannon and went on to defeat Carlisle for the Speakership by a majority of twelve votes. Passage of the tariff bill in the House was assured.

When President Harrison had stood in the rain on March 4 to deliver his long inaugural address he made a passing reference to the possible need for Congressional action to eliminate ballot abuses in the various states through federal control of elections. Although he did not specify, everyone knew that he was speaking against the disqualification of Negroes in the South. This was a subject which had long rankled in Republican breasts. Since the abandonment of Reconstruction the vote of every white Southerner had possessed far greater weight in national affairs than the vote of a Northerner. In the South, where the Negro was denied the ballot, he still was counted in the population as a basis for Congressional representation. Inasmuch as the South was Democratic, this was a situation that cried for a remedy — by the Republican Party. In Massachusetts, Henry Cabot

104

Lodge's heart was torn by the plight of the Negro voter and, as potential heir to the seat of Charles Sumner, he pledged himself to remedy the intolerable situation.

Strength was lent to his reconstructive ambition by a Republican caucus which endorsed the principles embodied in President Harrison's speech and which designated a committee to prepare a bill. Besides Lodge this committee was made up of a battle-scarred Union soldier from Illinois, Jonathan H. Rowell, who would "have seated every Negro who made a contest, and Thomas H. Carter of Montana. Rowell wrote the first draft of the bill, crudely phrased but biting in form. Lodge took it to his library where he rewrote it in milder form and in better English. He then introduced it in the House, which promptly referred it to the Elections Committee, of which Lodge was the chairman. Lodge promptly reported it out of committee for consideration by the House.

Although many of Lodge's friends insisted in later years that he was not in "entire accord with the provisions of the bill" which he then so carefully shepherded, when he arose in the House on June 26, 1890, it was to deliver a speech that could only have been prepared after weeks of careful consideration and deep study.

"We have clothed the Negroes with attributes of American citizenship. We have put in their hands the emblems of American sovereignty. Whether wisely or unwisely done is of no consequence now; it has been done, and it is irrevocable . . . The Government, which made the black man a citizen of the United States, is bound to protect him in his rights as a citizen, and it is a cowardly government if it does not do it."

There were other telling passages: "The great safeguard to the public welfare is publicity. The business of the people must not be transacted in dim corners or locked room." And, in order to show that the law was needed elsewhere than in the South, he produced elaborate tables of figures to prove that the election of 1870 in New York had been rife with fraud and corruption, the blame for which he neatly tossed on the doorstep of Tammany Hall.

Not since he had been in Congress had Lodge uttered so dramatic a speech as this. It spread anger and consternation through the South and the Northern Democrats sprang to their feet to condemn it. One prominent Massachusetts Democrat wrote W. C. P. Breckinridge in Washington that Lodge's course disgusted "the best people here."

The Force Bill,[1] as it was generally known except among those who supported it, was passed by the House under the helpful "Reed rules" by the slim margin of six votes. Most impartial observers were predicting its speedy passage in the Senate when it suddenly became involved in one of the most dramatic political struggles the country had witnessed in years. The powerful Republican majority of the Senate was expected to stand behind it, if not for any altruistic reason at least to rectify the situation pointed out by Lodge: "The people of the North will not continue to permit two votes in the South to count as much as five votes in the North."

Such Republican leaders as Senator Matt Quay and Don Cameron, the Pennsylvania bosses, however, had but one idea — the safe and quick passage of the McKinley tariff. The plight of the Negro was a matter for indifference compared with bigger profits for Northern manufacturers.

---

[1] The Federal Elections Bill of 1890 provided that federal officials should be appointed on election boards in any part of the country upon the petition of 500 voters in any district. These officials not only could inspect and verify returns but also had power to pass upon the qualifications of voters and receive ballots refused by local officials. Senator Hoar claimed that its important provisions were borrowed from the English election law of 1868.

Cameron, who was to become one of Cabot Lodge's closest friends, expressed the hard viewpoint when he said: —

"Northern capital has been flowing into the South in great quantities, manufacturing establishments have been created and are now in full operation, and a community of commercial interest is fast obliterating sectional lines. . . . The Election Law would disturb this desirable condition and produce ill feeling between the North and South."

Leading the opposition to the Force Bill was Senator Arthur P. Gorman of Maryland, who realized the strength of the Republican insurrectionists and made a deal with them. He would not oppose the tariff if they would force abandonment of the election law. By virtue of this bargain the Force Bill was squelched until passage of the tariff measure. Senators Hoar of Massachusetts and Aldrich of Rhode Island were apparently not included in the bargain. The incorruptible Senator Hoar boldly asked for consideration of the bill. The vote on his motion, 41 to 30, plainly indicated that it was far from dead. Alarmed, the Democrats met in caucus the next day and decided they would start a filibuster.

After thirty-three calendar days of verbose obstruction the Force Bill was effectively shunted into oblivion. The Democrats breathed easy again — and the Negroes of the South still are kept away from the polls.

Cabot Lodge's association with the Force Bill of 1890 did not leave him either unscathed or unpraised. While the Senators were wrangling over it "Gumshoe Bill" Stone,[2] a virulent Missouri Congressman, made a long speech that bristled with personal abuse and that had little to say effectively in opposition to the measure. In the course of his

[2] William J. Stone, 1848–1919. He was chairman of the Senate Foreign Relations Committee at the time of his death. He had been Governor of Missouri and became Senator from that state in 1903.

107

harangue he called Cabot Lodge "the Oscar Wilde of statesmanship." Lodge was not in the House at the time but the following day he answered the attack in a short and effective speech. When the good gray poet, John Greenleaf Whittier, read it in snow-bound Amesbury he sent this note to Lodge: —

DEAR FRIEND — Let me thank thee for thy manly speech. It has the ring and is worthy of the best days of Massachusetts — of Webster and Sumner and John Quincy Adams. I am truly thy friend.

Although it is obvious that Lodge was motivated by partisanship as well as by philanthropy in introducing the Force Bill he must have been aware of the political dangers inherent in it. If nothing else, it fastened upon him the charge of being an intensely partisan Republican, and it alienated much of the Democratic support which he had been able to count upon in recent years. Nevertheless he felt he was strong enough again to run for Congress. Opposing him was Dr. William Everett, son of Edward Everett, the former President of Harvard, ex-Senator and one-time Secretary of State. Dr. Everett, whose real home was in Quincy, was in truth a "carpetbagger" imported into the district by the Mugwump clique among the Democrats as the one man able to cut short Lodge's Congressional career. This former Unitarian divine, who was known as "Piggy" to his Harvard friends, had campaigned as a boy orator for Abraham Lincoln, and had unsuccessfully been seeking public office since 1884. He had left the Republican Party that year — now, once again, he was trying his luck.

A great deal of money was spent during the campaign. The Republicans contended that the Sixth District was flooded with funds sent down from New York by Tammany

Hall, which hated Lodge's Force Bill as deeply as did the most unreconstructed Rebel. Throughout the country the newspapers kept their eye on the Lodge-Everett fight, realizing that it was one of the most spirited of any on the whole Congressional front. Lodge had to pitch in vigorously to maintain his advantage. All around him in Massachusetts the Democrats were getting support in the reaction to the conservative Harrison administration. It was, indeed, a Democratic year almost everywhere in the country. In the Bay State the popular William Eustis ("Billy") Russell was elected governor, the third Democrat and one of the youngest men in the history of the Commonwealth to hold that office.

Henry Cabot Lodge, however, ran ahead of his ticket that year, showing how well he had built up his personal machine and the imposing position which he held in Massachusetts Republicanism. He defeated the elderly and somewhat eccentric Dr. Everett by 1040 votes.

IX

On the Threshold

ANCESTRALLY, connubially, and economically Henry Cabot Lodge was destined to be an Imperialist. His home overlooked the Atlantic and the money earned for him by his forebears had come in good measure from the sea lanes once traveled by the *Storm King* and the *Kremlin* of his father's fleet. When Alfred Thayer Mahan came along to put a theory into words, who was better prepared to understand them than the Boston historian turned legislator, now avid for a program that might lead him to statesmanlike heights?

In his second term in Congress, Lodge had been placed on the Naval Affairs Committee, where his rank was next to that of the chairman, Charles A. Boutelle of Maine. At the same time he was also a member of the Immigration Committee. From the eminence of both positions his thin, Yankee voice was to be raised in argument, and apt quotations were to roll in cultured accent to help decide the destiny of a nation that had been too long asleep.

Lodge had been acquainted with Captain Mahan for some time prior to 1890 and undoubtedly had listened understandingly to the naval theorist's exposition of ideas that were to be given wide circulation with the publication in May 1890 of the first volume of *The Influence of Sea Power upon History*. Nor must Mrs. Lodge be forgotten in this connection. Raised in an atmosphere of Navy talk, and the daughter of an admiral of considerable intellectual and scientific attainments, she had never allowed her interest in the service to wane. It was said of her that she knew the names and technical details of almost every ship in the Navy and that she could discuss the controversies of staff and line vividly and accurately with any sea dog or trim executive who might drop over from the Navy Department for afternoon tea. Since Lodge never prepared a speech or essay without submitting it to her for verification of sources and quotations her influence upon him in such matters was hardly negligible. And Lodge's closest friend, Theodore Roosevelt, fancied himself as a student of naval history. In the months following his graduation from Harvard had he not delved deeply and studiously into the subject while writing his first book, *The Naval War of 1812?* And had he not sounded the keynote in 1888 when he told the Union League Club that our lack of battleships was a disgrace, leaving us at the mercy of a "tenth-rate power, like Chile"?

There had been a restlessness in the Navy Department for many years. In 1884 this had led to one notable advancement, the establishment of the War College at Newport, with which Captain Mahan had been associated for some time.[1] Throughout the 1880's naval construction had gained momentum, if hardly in the deep-sea direction desired by Captain Mahan. The development of heavy industries in the country had spurred on the program — here was a market for machinery, ordnance, and armor plate that the manufacturers were hardly likely to ignore. President Harrison, although one of the most reactionary of Presidents, was outspoken in his advocacy of a larger fleet. His Secretary of State, Mr. Blaine, had long since foreseen America's entrance into the world picture, a vision from which armed ships were not absent. His Secretary of the Navy, Benjamin F. Tracy, was "a man of ability and initiative," which meant that he,

---

[1] He first went there to lecture on naval tactics and history in 1886; was its president 1886–1889 and again 1892–1893.

too, saw the Stars and Stripes flying proudly over many ships on the two oceans that guarded the United States. When the hurricane of 1889 sent three American war vessels to the bottom of the harbor at Samoa, thus denuding the Pacific Fleet, these men, and Lodge, and many others, knew that the time to push forward had arrived.

Those who agreed with Captain Mahan, and Lodge was first among them, anticipated the day in the not too distant future when the United States would spread its influence and its territories overseas. In order to do this the country must have a new navy, not just a larger navy. In 1890 the United States owned no battleships; few people, even those living along the seaboard, expected that we ever would. Monitors, to defend our harbors, and cruisers to harry any enemy that might attack, were deemed sufficient. But those who looked beyond the horizon realized that nothing less than a fleet of capital ships could keep open our ports.

There was, in 1890, no widespread public demand for this program. In January, nevertheless, the Navy's Policy Board offered a report that outlined a program "in terms, not of present requirements, but of the imperialistic program envisaged in Mahan's larger conception of sea power." From all quarters a storm of protest was raised. Even the Republican *New York Tribune*, for many years the Navy's stanchest advocate and later imperialism's bellicose mouthpiece, called such belligerent and grandiose ideas "naval fanaticism."

In the face of this outburst shrewd political maneuvering was called for; in the House the Messrs. Lodge and Chairman Boutelle issued a report endorsing the most important section of the Policy Board's recommendations: that which called for fleets for the Western Atlantic, the Caribbean, and the Eastern Pacific.

The name "battleship," however, was anathema to peace-loving ears and if, in framing the appropriations bill to forward their expansionist aims, the embryo war hawks had used the term without qualification they would have been unmercifully beaten. Astutely, therefore, they softened the implication contained in their request for funds by providing for "three sea-going, coastline battleships designed to carry the heaviest armor and most powerful ordnance." The insertion of the innocent word "coastline" cloaked their ambitions. Lodge could be counted upon further to disarm the critics. With his reputation as the scholar in politics and the great historian he was able with impunity to tell the House that the battleship proposal introduced nothing new but was "merely the continuance" of a policy "settled" by the War of 1812 and followed consistently thereafter. That this was a "palpable inaccuracy" there was no one then to point out.[2] That Lodge knew its falsity, also, there is no doubt.

Although the so-called "battleship clause" provoked opposition, the House passed the appropriations bill by a vote of 131 to 105. Later, by a vote of 33 to 18, the Senate made it into law. Before the year ended hammers were ringing in yards on both the East and the West Coasts of a nation whose fleet had engaged no foreign enemy since 1812, and the battleships *Indiana, Massachusetts,* and *Oregon* were building on their ways.

The Congressional debate over the battleships in the winter of 1890 marked the turning point in America's relationship with the rest of the world. It was not long before the gospel of imperialism found its advocates in high places and was widely and vigorously preached by many of the leading thinkers, teachers, and publicists of the day. "But it was Mahan, and his politically influential friends and satellites, Henry Cabot Lodge and Theodore Roosevelt, who sounded the call to action, marshalling the ideas of national

[2] See Harold and Margaret Sprout, *The Rise of American Naval Power, 1776–1918,* 1939; pp. 212–213.

security, commercial expansion, cosmopolitan philanthropy, national honor and national prestige, in support of a breathtaking program of imperialism and naval aggrandizement." [3]

At the same time that Henry Cabot Lodge was seeking to expand the national power on this front he was also attempting to contract it on another. Again acting in accord with his social and economic background, he sought to shut the gates of America against the hordes of the Old World and of the Orient. His theories on immigration were in keeping with his theories on imperialism; both, he rationalized, were calculated to further the strength of the United States.

"Let every man honor and love the land of his birth and the race from which he springs," he had told the New England Society of Brooklyn in 1888. "But let us have done with British-Americans and Irish-Americans and German-Americans, and so on, and all be Americans. . . . If a man is going to be an American at all let him be so without any qualifying adjectives; and if he is going to be something else, let him drop the word 'American' from his personal description."

These were the words of the patriot — and later the sentiments of the jingo. In Lodge's mind one of the first great signs of America's awakening had come in 1882 when an alarmed Congress had passed the first Chinese Exclusion Act. When he thought of the hordes of Chinese laborers [4] sweeping through the Golden Gate and taking the bread from the mouths of honest American workingmen he trembled with rage. When he saw the hordes of Italians, Czechs, Slovaks, Russians, streaming through the ports of Boston and New York, bringing their smells and bad manners and

[3] *Ibid.*, p. 226.
[4] There were 132,000 Chinese in the United States in 1882. In 1940 there were 77,504, of which 40,262 were American citizens born of Chinese parents.

poverty to the mills and mines, he was equally disturbed. With the poet Aldrich he asked: —

> O Liberty, white Goddess, is it well
> To leave the gates unguarded? . . .

and with the poet he answered: —

> Have a care
> Lest from thy brow the clustered stars be torn
> And trampled in the dust. For so of old
> The thronging Goth and Vandal trampled Rome,
> And where the temples of the Caesars stood
> The lean wolf unmolested made her lair.

As a historian, of course, he realized that there had been a time when it had been necessary rapidly "to fill up the country," but he deeply resented that to this "practical advantage" America had joined "the sentimental and generous reason that this free country was to be a haven of refuge for the unfortunate of every land."

The time had come to put a stop to such nonsense. "The question of regulating and restricting immigration," he told the House in February 1891, "is one of the gravest which now confront the country. . . . It has been said . . . that we are in no danger of being overcrowded in the United States. We are certainly in no present danger of being overcrowded by desirable immigrants, but we are at this moment overcrowded with undesirable immigrants."

It was easy enough for the aristocratic Lodge to differentiate between the two classes. Those who came from the United Kingdom, from Germany and the Scandinavian countries, he was willing to accept; but he shuddered at the influx of immigrants from Italy and the Slav countries, from Russia, Poland, Hungary, and Bohemia.

As his first move toward shutting out the undesirables Lodge, in 1891, introduced a bill which required that all

115

who sought entrance to America should know how to read or write in their own language.[5] Few citizens of the ghetto had ever had an opportunity to learn to read or write, although thousands of them turned to America, the land of opportunity, so that their children at least might grow up with these forbidden advantages.

"I do not want to see the quality of American citizenship decline," Lodge said, "beneath the effects of an unrestricted immigration, and I am utterly opposed to a system which is continually dragging down the wages of American labor by the introduction or the importation of the cheapest, lowest, and most ignorant labor of other countries."

Lodge was not so cynical or conscienceless as to accuse the ignorant immigrant of always coming to America of his own volition. He knew that thousands were imported under contract by vicious entrepreneurs who gathered them together in their European slums and sent them here to work "at wages far below the American standard." And so Lodge supported amendments to the Immigration Law which would have barred the importation of aliens under contract or an agreement to perform labor. This was not only humanitarian, but vote-getting.

It was not until he had become Senator, however, that Lodge revealed his doctrines of race purity. His speech of March 16, 1896, which was widely read and quoted, summed up the thoughts that were forming in his mind during his last years in the House.

"More precious even than the forms of government," he said on that occasion, "are the mental and moral qualities which make what we call our race. While those stand unim-

---

[5] After a lively contest this bill passed both House and Senate but was vetoed by President Cleveland three days before his term ended. The House passed the bill over the veto but the Senate did not get around to it in time for action.

116

paired all is safe. When those decline all is imperilled. They are exposed to but a single danger, and that is by changing the quality of our race and citizenship through the wholesale infusion of races whose traditions and inheritances, whose thoughts and whose beliefs are wholly alien to ours and with whom we have never assimilated or even been associated with in the past."

When Lodge voted for the expansion of the United States Navy and for the restriction of immigration he acted strictly in consonance with the political philosophy that was to find its national expression in the words and deeds of many leaders before the decade was done. Not the least among these was Henry Cabot Lodge himself.

X

The Statesman

IT WAS a Massachusetts tradition that one waited for the
Senatorship to be thrust upon one, but in 1892 Cabot Lodge
was taking no chances. He had learned "the hard way" that
when one wanted office he asked for it. It may have been
true, as Henry Adams wrote John Hay, that "dear Cabot
seems to be the only man who has the people with him. True
heart! Pure people's patriot! He and Cleveland. Two stuffed
prophets" . . . but "the people," as Lodge well knew, didn't
elect Senators. That was a job for the party managers and the
legislature. And one didn't persuade either body of men
purely by popularity. It had to be arranged within the
inner circles of the party and without undue publicity.

Fully aware of the situation, Lodge began his under-
cover campaign immediately after the second state-wide
defeat of his party in 1891. In that year he was among the
most outspoken critics of the State Committee. With several willing henchmen he turned his guns fully upon Chairman Burdett. As the leader of a powerful junto he let it be
known that he felt the disaster at the polls had been the
result of inefficiency and want of political tact on the part of
certain committeemen. In due time, the chairman's decapita-
tion followed. In the ensuing struggle for the chairmanship
Lodge threw his support to that eminent manufacturer of
webbings and gorings and leading spirit of the Home Market and Arkwright Clubs (both organizations of high protectionists), Eben S. Draper of Hopedale. At that time Mr.

Draper was not even a member of the committee, but this little disadvantage was quickly remedied through the resignation of a Lodge adherent. Mr. Draper was given his place and the chairmanship, thus making Lodge's hold upon the State Committee stronger than ever.

Lodge was now able to go before the State Convention to force through a resolution favoring the settlement of the Senatorial question by a caucus of the Republican legislators in November, three months before the election of Senator would take place. The purpose of this unprecedented move was to prevent a coalition of Democrats and minority Republicans who might be hostile to his interests. Six years before Senator Dawes had gone back to the Senate only after the Democratic supporters of Patrick A. Collins had swung to his aid at the last moment. Otherwise he would have been unable to gain enough votes against the other Republican contenders, former Governors Long and Robinson, who between them controlled 107 votes to Dawes's 79.

The bosses of Tammany Hall could have taken lessons from Lodge as he ran the Republican machine with an iron hand in the autumn of 1892. With plenty of money at his disposal — Draper was one of the state's wealthiest manufacturers — he campaigned for the election of members of the legislature favorable to himself. He canvassed the entire state, holding conferences here, making suggestions there, pressing his cause from Cape Cod to the Berkshires. Nor did he neglect his own Congressional campaign. His resolution for the holding of the caucus brought him a great deal of criticism, but the legislators met as he had planned; and, as he had hoped, proffered him the nomination.

So cleverly had Lodge paved his way that on the first, and only, ballot, when the Senate voted, Lodge had 29 and his opponent only 10 votes. In the House the count was 160 to 69.

Having achieved at last the great ambition of his life, Lodge resigned from the House and on March 4, 1893, he was assigned the desk that for twenty-three years had been occupied by Charles Sumner.

In Washington an excited and happy Theodore Roosevelt rushed to congratulate Mrs. Lodge as soon as he received dear old Cabot's wire telling him of the result. Still excited, he dashed off a gushing note to Nahant: "I am glad of your triumph, first, for your own sake, next for the sake of honest government, and because of the premium thus put upon integrity, ability, industry, and a high standard of public morality. . . . Hail, friend!"

In New York George William Curtis sat down at his editor's desk at *Harper's Weekly* and wrote: —

Had Lodge remained true to his standards . . . he would have struggled hard to preserve the political traditions of his state; he would have fought to the bitter end to keep his party in Massachusetts free from machine rule . . . but, instead, it was he who introduced and developed machine methods in government; he pressed upon the legislature a "gerrymandering" scheme from the shamelessness of which even his followers recoiled; he devoted himself to the running of caucuses and conventions like an old machine hand. Had he given the ability and time and labor he squandered in the miserable business of machine building . . . to the earnest study and treatment of public questions . . . he would then have sat in the Senate with a consciousness of dignity and independence, owing his position to his own worth, unhampered by any obligation to greedy henchmen, and free to do his best for the welfare of the people.

In the face of this, Lodge (who, as Henry Adams put it, had "the misfortune of becoming not only a Senator but a Senator from Massachusetts") was not unduly discouraged. Washington, even in a depression, was a pleasant place and his home on Massachusetts Avenue, with its rose gardens and its library, was the center of its most delightful aspects. There were rides and walks to be enjoyed along beautiful Rock Creek with his cronies, all men of culture like himself, and many of them politically aware.

It was better than being a professor at Harvard, better even than being a lion in Boston. Here one could be a national figure, with his hand deep in stirring events. "What funnily varied lives we do lead, Cabot!" Theodore wrote at about this time. "We touch two or three different worlds, each profoundly ignorant of the others. Our literary friends have but a vague knowledge of our actual political work; and a goodly number of our sporting and social acquaintances know us only as men of good family, one of whom rides hard to hounds, while the other hunts big game in the Rockies." There was going to be more political and less literary work from now on for both, and less riding to hounds and hunting in the Rockies, as these scholars in politics reached out for the power and the glory they thirsted for.

The Washington that Cabot Lodge knew and loved in the 1890's was as nearly a little world unto itself as the Boston of his childhood. He and his friends set up a fence against the crass and vulgar manifestations of democracy and drank their tea, sipped their Scotch, collected their books, and had their dinner parties and musicales without interference from that other world of Western Senators, of Populists, of Knights of Labor, of silver-voiced orators that was also Washington as the nineteenth century drew to its close. What a superior crowd they were! The dulcet Henry Adams, the chipper Cecil Spring-Rice, the bearded John Hay, the volatile Theodore Roosevelt, towering Tom Reed, the exacting Elihu Root, and striving Albert Beveridge of Indiana.

Gathered together in their fastidious homes they professed scorn for the alliance of big business and corrupt politicians that they saw all around them and convinced themselves that they were above this. Whenever Lodge looked in the mirror he saw a statesman. Marcus Aurelius Hanna was not his friend; neither was E. H. Harriman, the railroad tycoon. He had little patience with money-getting and equally little understanding of the economic issues of the day. At heart both he and his closest friend, Roosevelt, were conservatives. Never once did they think that they need go very deeply beneath the surface to make this a better world; nothing fundamental had to be changed. Their only rebellion was against the older leadership of their party, not against the party itself or against anything for which it stood.

No longer was Lodge interested in history for scholarship's sake, but as a means to buttress his own arguments as he went about the business of making history on Capitol Hill. He had a reputation to maintain and he had already chosen the field for his new endeavors. The silver question, the tariff question, and other purely domestic problems afforded the drudgery of his work; the joy lay in foreign affairs.

At the outset of his Senatorial career, however, he could not escape involvement in the one burning domestic issue of the day. The financial panic which had gripped the country almost simultaneously with Cleveland's second occupancy of the White House cried for immediate political action. Not only politicians anxious for a whipping boy but the leading economists of the day seized upon the Silver Purchase Act of 1890 as major cause of the disaster which had been marked by the closing of banks, the driving of railroads and other industries into receivership, widespread unemployment, and the shaking of public confidence in business and in government. From the banking centers of the East arose a great cry for the repeal of this iniquitous act and the immediate return to the single gold standard. These circles set up a cry for "dear money" which, in their opinion, was the only "sound money," and they asserted that legislative tinkering with exchange was an "immoral" act. Gold alone, they screamed, was the true money.

With the Eastern bankers Senator Lodge begged to differ. Not then, nor for several years, was he a gold bug. He believed in the use of silver for currency along with gold, although he tempered this theory with the further belief that bimetallism was most workable if established on an international scale. His hope was for a convention of the leading gold countries which would resolve the issue and place them jointly on a dual monetary standard.

The Silver Purchase Act had been enacted only with the connivance of an Eastern cabal which had accepted it in order to enact the McKinley tariff and of a Southern clique which had gone in on the deal in order to sound the death knell of the Force Bill which Lodge had maneuvered through the House. The statute of limitations on political deals is elastic: in 1893, as far as the Silver Act was concerned, it had run out. President Cleveland was willing enough to have the depression blamed on a law passed by another than his own administration. At heart deeply conservative, he honestly believed that repeal would have a salutary effect, and soon after he took office he determined to call a special session of Congress for this purpose.

Late that spring, however, the President's physicians informed him that an ulcer in the roof of his mouth presented symptoms of malignancy that made necessary an immediate operation. This dictum presented Cleveland with a personal problem to be added to the political crisis which he faced. Vice President Adlai E. Stevenson was a stanch silverite. If news of the impending operation leaked out, fears of new economic uncertainty would at once assail the country. After all, who knew if Cleveland would survive the surgeon's knife? President Cleveland called Congress into session for August 7 and then, accompanied by a small party of friends, boarded a yacht ostensibly for a cruise. While the vessel steamed slowly in the calm waters of New York Harbor he submitted to the operation. By the time Congress met he had fully recovered and was able to send his message recommending repeal.

Lodge's first action as a Senator was to introduce a resolution calling for immediate action in regard to the law. There were other resolutions of a similar nature. At once the various interests began jockeying for position. Sectionalism rather than partisanship was to determine the drawing of the lines. The East, bulwark of the great financial interests, stood pitted against the West, where the silver mines were, and against the agrarian South, where the sentiment for free and unlimited coinage of silver was strong. But partisanship as well as sectionalism played its full part once the lines were drawn. Three weeks after Congress convened the great fight started when the leader for the administration reported a House measure in the Senate. At once the silver Republicans and the "farmer" Democrats threw their allied troops into the field. Talk was to be their weapon as a hitherto unprecedented filibuster got under way.

Although Senator Lodge was soon to write a learned article for the *North American Review* on the dangers of "Obstruction in the Senate" he was not, at the start, averse to the tactics employed by the opponents of repeal. He well understood the political benefits arising from the cleavage within the Democratic ranks — a split that was to contribute as much as anything toward keeping the Democratic Party out of power from 1896 to 1912. He even expressed himself as wishing fervently that the dissension might continue unabated, at least until after the fall election back home in Massachusetts. He had his wish. The filibuster lasted until the last week in October, during which time one Senator filled 100 double-columned pages of the *Congressional Record* with a speech it took him seven days to deliver and Senator Stewart of Nevada crowded nearly 250 pages with his various verbal contributions.

By September 21 Senator Lodge apparently felt that everything was safe in Massachusetts for the Republicans even if neither party had yet held its State Nominating Convention, for he joined with Senators Hoar, Platt of Connecticut, Hill of New York, and Gallinger of New Hampshire in a desperate effort to shut off the flow of words. Every proposal to close debate through majority action evoked another torrent of debate until finally, in exasperation, Lodge arose to tell the Senate that in his opinion "there is another right more sacred in a legislative body than the right of debate, and that is the right to vote." This declaration caused Senator Teller of Colorado, one of the vocal advocates of silver, to reply that "there is nothing in the world more wicked and cruel than the majority; and governments are instituted and preserved to protect minorities against majorities. Majorities protect themselves." To this Lodge made no reply.

It was not until October 24 that the Senate decided the time had come to exercise the sacred right to vote. It was said that when this decision was reached Senator Voorhees, the administration leader, suddenly looked ten years younger. During forty-nine of the past fifty-seven calendar days the Senate had been in session; it might have gone on indefinitely had not the administration used pressure to force into line enough silver Democrats to assure a vote. When this was finally accomplished, on October 30, the Repeal Bill was passed, 43 to 32 votes, and the Democratic Party, then controlling administration, House, and Senate for the first time in thirty-two years, was on the way out.

Even as he was not completely convinced that only gold

was pure, so was Lodge not wholly in favor of a high tariff in the year 1894. But the tendency of his thinking was more and more in the direction of both. Coming as he did from the industrial state of Massachusetts and owing his election to the Senate in no small measure to the machinations of high-tariff organizations, it is little wonder that he should espouse their cause. By April, he had rationalized his thoughts on the subject sufficiently to incorporate them in a speech, which he had widely distributed in Massachusetts.

The tariff, Senator Lodge said after aptly quoting Carlyle, was not merely a matter of dollars and cents but "in its largest sense" a part of a general theory and system of government which "in its farthest results may affect a nation socially, morally, and politically." Indeed it may "so modify the distribution of wealth as to give it a wider and better scope and by defending wages and standards of living may influence the whole arrangement and growth of society." On the other hand, he warned, "a tariff policy in the usual and narrow sense, and especially from the standpoint of a free-trader" — whose attitude of mind, he added, has "all the imperishable charm of springtime" — "is purely an economic matter, a question of the pocket, of dollars and cents, and of the national method of doing business. In this latter aspect there is nothing sacred or moral about a tariff system." Having thus raised the issue to a level where it might be discussed by a "scholar in politics" Senator Lodge prated at length, and with due recognition of Adam Smith, about the "pathway to be pursued by enlightened selfishness in its search for national prosperity." And then he asked: —

Are we to sit down with our great civilization and bring about free trade in order to be gradually overwhelmed by the labor of the tropics after a desperate struggle with the overcrowded people of our own race in Europe? Are we to be told that the laws of supply and demand, of buying in the cheapest and selling in the dearest markets, are eternal truth and that everything would be right if we only adhered to them? Are we to accept these shattered dogmas and yield without a struggle to the ruin of our labor and the degradation of our standards of living?

How well his argument fitted the imperialist pattern he was tracing! But there was more to it now than there had been before, when he had first raised his voice against immigration. There was now England, England which "took up free trade, not because she was suddenly convinced of its scientific truth and believed that it ought therefore to prevail, even if the heavens fell . . . but because she was satisfied that it would pay!"

Many of his friends were astounded at the bellicosity of his voice when he mentioned England. Some attributed his anti-British expressions to his desire to appease the great Irish vote in Boston, and undoubtedly this had much to do with it. To others it seemed only right that a true Yankee should scorn perfidious Albion.

Within a week of his scornful attack upon Britain he was starting another agitation directed against that country. The revenue bill was up for discussion and to this measure he added a seemingly innocuous amendment. In effect his measure would have compelled England to go on a silver currency basis under threat of stopping trade with her if she did not. His amendment would have placed discriminatory duties on English goods, a tax upon American consumers of them. It was a bold, if futile, bid for the extreme protectionists, the silverites, and the Anglophobes. The *New York Times* felt that nothing more "shifty, frivolous, unstatesmanlike or unscrupulous" had ever been suggested by a Congressman, and that eminent newspaper was shocked that Speaker Tom Reed should lend it his encouragement. Fortunately for the peace of nations, the amendment never came to a vote.

These attacks on England were, in a way, manifestations of national growing pains. Senator Lodge, reading the future, was laying his plans for the return to power of the Republican Party in 1896 (an event of which he felt reasonably sure) when nothing could stop his America from exercising its mature strength.

XI

Prophet and Imperialist

In the year 1895, one of the most decisive in his life, Senator Henry Cabot Lodge was already a familiar figure on the Washington scene. He might be observed almost any day darting briskly from one committee room to another in the Capitol as he attended to his many affairs. He was a member of the committees on Civil Service and Retrenchment, Education and Labor, Immigration, and the Organization, Conduct and Expenditure of the Executive Departments. Not for another year would he be given his coveted post on the Foreign Relations Committee but that did not deter him from expressing himself at the slightest provocation on all matters dealing with foreign affairs. Indeed, on no other subject was he more vocal. Not even the tariff or silver absorbed his time and attention as continuously. Playing at Statesman, he let his imagination roam across the Atlantic and the Pacific and rest possessively upon Cuba, Samoa, the Hawaiian Islands, and defensively upon Venezuela, which he would save from enslavement at foul British hands.

For diversion there was scholarship. Between 1891 and 1895 Cabot Lodge published four books. Of these only one was original in character, a brief history of the City of Boston. Two were collections of his speeches and essays. The fourth was done in collaboration with Theodore Roosevelt. Entitled *Hero Tales of American History*, it was designed for youthful readers and it became, at least financially, one of his most successful efforts. But there was really very little

129

time for the study, except as a place in which to prepare speeches. These always were done with care. When he read them in the Senate even those who never could agree with a thing he said were on hand to listen, for his literary skill was obvious and the way he brought in an apt allusion, a pat verse or two, and the manner in which he cited the classics as if they were personal friends, tickled the fancy of even the opposition roughnecks.

If Mrs. Lodge was not quite the leader of Washington Society, she came very close to it, sharing that honor only with Mrs. Don Cameron, Henry Adams's confidante. To be recognized by either lady set one apart. Nannie Lodge had more time now to devote to society and to checking the sources of her husband's speeches. Their daughter Constance had become engaged to Augustus Peabody Gardner in the autumn of 1891 and had married the wealthy cattle breeder and polo enthusiast from Essex County the following June. In 1894 she was to give the Lodges their first grandchild. Her brothers, too, were growing up. John was being tutored for Harvard and George Cabot Lodge, who was known to the family and all his friends as "Bay," was already showing signs of becoming a poet, although he was not to be graduated from Harvard until that June.

On Capitol Hill, Senator Lodge was still considered cold and austere by his fellow politicians. Most of them felt towards him as did Pettigrew of South Dakota. One day that pungent Senator, annoyed at being checked up on some points of logic by the gentleman from Nahant, paid his respects to the latter by interjecting: "Mr. President, I pause to remark that the Senator from Massachusetts is in some respects like the soil of his native state — highly cultivated but very thin." Such friends as Adams, Reed, Roosevelt, and a very few others addressed him as Cabot. To everyone else in Washington he was invariably "Mr. Lodge." In public his self-assurance, heightened by his bright blue eyes and his cocky Vandyke beard, irritated many of his colleagues, but in his own home, or among close friends, he was kind and gracious. When young Cushing Stetson, John's tutor, arrived home between eleven and eleven-thirty at night he invariably found his employer reading in the book-lined library. After discussing the news of the day Lodge would start talking to the young man, and often his discourses on literature, history, poetry, or the English novel would go on until a score or more of books had been dragged down to buttress his didacticisms and the clock had struck two. Sometimes Stetson would surprise him in the midst of preparing a speech. With his hands behind his back, Lodge would be pacing up and down the library floor, forming his phrases out loud in his precise voice. His really important speeches he wrote out in longhand and then the library floor and tables would be littered with books from which he had filched the quotations that studded them as thickly as though they were essays by Hazlitt. When he delivered them he seldom had to refer to the prepared script, he knew them so thoroughly.

During his first two years in the Senate those few people who expected great things of the scholar in politics had but little chance to make up their minds about him. On the credit side they could point to his advocacy of an International Copyright Law, to his apparently honest efforts for the civil service, and now, in January 1895, to his and Senator John T. Morgan's bill which was designed to take the consular service "out of politics." This last-named was an idea imposed upon him by Henry White through the intercession of Theodore Roosevelt. On the debit side was his uncertainty as to his own stand on silver. Many a Boston banker would have felt happier if he would only stop flirting with the international bimetallists. And many a New England manufacturer wondered if he really were as sound on the tariff as he pretended to be.

In the meantime Captain Mahan was advocating the annexation of Hawaii, not only as a naval necessity but also as the "first fruit and a token that the nation in its evolution has aroused itself to the necessity of carrying its life . . . beyond the borders that heretofore have sufficed for its activities." Lodge read and noted the article with satisfaction, and sniffed when his one-time friend, Carl Schurz, pointed out that the United States was only inviting attack by acquiring vulnerable outposts.

Senator Lodge spent the following summer at Nahant refreshing himself on the history of Hawaii and pondering the problems of American imperialism. He was startled to read in the newspapers that the United States warships, long stationed at Hawaii, had been withdrawn. He smelled real trouble and laid his plans accordingly. He does not appear to have expressed himself publicly on the matter at this time, but he kept in close touch with the situation and apparently learned of secret goings-on among the Queen's men. He was ready to let go a blast when Congress met again. For one thing he had rediscovered the Monroe Doctrine, that summer, and had appropriated it for his own use.

On December 22 Lodge arose in the Senate and opened fire. His career as imperialist began that afternoon. Did not the interests of the United States and its citizens require the presence of at least one war vessel at all times in the harbor of Honolulu? Let the Secretary of the Navy answer that question. He then picked from his desk a copy of a letter which Rear Admiral J. G. Walker had written while bringing the *U.S.S. Philadelphia* back to the United States. As Admiral Walker had left Honolulu Harbor he had noted that a British warship remained behind. What was the purpose of this, if it were not part of a surreptitious plot on the part of

England to seize the "ripe pear," or at least to restore the fallen monarchy, while American backs were turned? Let America beware. The Queen and the British were plotting and very soon a royalist uprising would rend the islands again. Having sowed the seeds of suspicion, Mr. Lodge sat down.

Whether Lodge actually knew, or only suspected, the existence of a "royalist plot" is a matter of conjecture, but on January 7, heartened by Cleveland's previous assertion that "we have no right to meddle in the domestic affairs" of Hawaii, a small group of rebels attempted to seize the government. After a skirmish on the beach they were arrested by the Honolulu police. Because of lack of modern communications word of this did not immediately reach Washington.

On January 9, President Cleveland, who, Lodge felt, was despicably susceptible to British influences, sent a special message to Congress suggesting that the Hawaiians be allowed to lease uninhabited Necker Island to England as a way station for the proposed telegraph cable between Canada and Australia. He could have done nothing better calculated to stir the ire of the Senator from Massachusetts.

For the past six years Lodge and others had advocated the laying of an American cable to Hawaii and here was the President of the United States ignoring that patriotic necessity and making it easy for England to get there first. The implications of treachery were enormous. Six years before, even the British Minister had admitted the islands were "thoroughly American." Why should the British control the only means of fast communication to them? Add to this Cleveland's expressed desire to withdraw from the tripartite Samoan alliance and you had in the White House a very dangerous man.

While Lodge was stewing in his study over what his friend Theodore called "Cleveland's base betrayal of our interests abroad" word came of the abortive royalist rebellion. Not only did this set Lodge up as a prophet of sorts but it confirmed his worst suspicions of a British plot. The quick despatch of the *Philadelphia* to the scene was not enough. Nor was he alone in his anxiety. An aroused Senate was flooded with resolutions calling for immediate annexation. Presenting his own demand (in which he inserted a plea for prompt action towards constructing an American cable to the islands' capital) he warned against "any other government" being allowed, at any cost, to obtain "a foothold upon any part of the Hawaiian Islands." The Senate, however, refused to be stampeded and on January 25 reaffirmed its previous policy of nonintervention and in general upheld President Cleveland's stand.

Senator Lodge was not to win his fight for annexation while Cleveland remained as President. But he did not surrender. On February 9 the Senate took up consideration of the Diplomatic and Consular Appropriations Bill to which had been attached an amendment providing half a million dollars to help defray the cost of constructing the much-debated cable. This was adopted by the Senate without appreciable debate but it ran into difficulties in the House. President Cleveland let word get abroad that he would veto the bill if it passed with the cable amendment, since he, like Secretary Foster, felt it was contrary to American traditions for the government to intervene in private enterprise. Nor would he lend his support to "boom the annexation craze."

Definitely determined not to let the President lie down before the British Empire, Senator Lodge prepared a fiery speech which, in angry tones, he delivered in the Senate on March 2. Even if it meant an extra session — or "ten extra sessions" — the gentleman from Massachusetts was determined that the bill must be passed.

"I would never vote to strike out that cable as the first

step toward the development of American commerce," he declared, "toward the taking of what belongs as of right to the American people in their onward march."

He then delivered an exposition on sea power as one of the controlling forces in history and, applying it to the United States, said: "Sea power consists in the first place of a proper navy and a proper fleet; but in order to sustain a navy we must have suitable ports for naval stations, strong places where a navy can be protected and refurnished." At this point he unfurled a huge map of the world on which in brilliant red Maltese crosses were marked the far-flung naval stations of England on both sides of the North American continent. Pointing to the British stations at Vancouver and in the Falkland and Fiji Islands, he cried out: —

"In that great triangle marked by these three points Great Britain does not hold a naval station. There in the center of that triangle, heart of the Pacific, where I am now pointing, lie the Sandwich Islands. They are the key of the Pacific."

Senator Lodge then deprecated any thought that Great Britain desired war with the United States, but since we were her "natural commercial rival," and since she had always "opposed and thwarted" the United States, we must be on our guard and take advantage of the opportunity to strengthen our position against her in the Pacific.

Senator Lodge had not begun his Senate speech without due preparation. For several weeks he had been busy working out his thesis for an article entitled "Our Blundering Foreign Policy" for the *North American Review*, which was even then in the hands of its subscribers. He justified his own imperialism. "We have a record of conquest, colonization, and territorial expansion (Westward — as Washington taught!) unequalled by any people in the 19th Century." After taking a pot shot at Canada, which, he said, had never

135

lost any opportunity of injuring us, he reached his climax, which, as far as he could shape it, was to become the foreign policy of the United States within three years.

Not to the south should we move, but "from the Rio Grande to the Arctic Ocean there should be but one flag and one country. Neither race nor climate forbids this extension and every consideration of national growth and national welfare demands it. In the interests of our commerce and of our fullest development we should build the Nicaraguan Canal and for the protection of that canal and for the sake of our commercial supremacy in the Pacific we should control the Hawaiian Islands and maintain our interest in Samoa. England has studded the West Indies with strong places which are a standing menace to our Atlantic seaboard. We should have in those islands at least one strong naval station and when the Nicaraguan Canal is built, the island of Cuba, still sparsely settled and of almost unbounded fertility, will become to us a necessity. Commerce follows the flag, and we should build up a Navy strong enough to give protection to Americans in every quarter of the globe and sufficiently powerful to put our coasts beyond the possibility of attack."

In spite of his impassioned plea Hawaii ceased temporarily to be a political issue and the Senate went on to other matters.

The adjournment of Congress found Senator Lodge back in Nahant girding himself for the great battle which he well knew would get under way when Congress met again in December. This was to be over the long-contested issue of the Venezuela-British Guiana boundary. Briefly, the dispute was this: Several years previous, Venezuela had suspended diplomatic relations with Great Britain as a result of the larger nation's arbitrary drawing of the boundary line. The United States had offered to arbitrate, but each time had

136

met with rebuffs. Since 1884 Great Britain had stiffly refused to do anything.

In May, Secretary Gresham died and a few weeks later President Cleveland induced his Attorney General, Richard Olney, to become Secretary of State. When Senator Lodge heard of this he wrote: "As long as Cleveland is obliged to take a man in sympathy with his foreign policy, he could not do better. Olney is a gentleman, a man of training and education, and a very able lawyer." Olney was all that; he was also a lonely, puritanical, despotic New Englander, and a corporation lawyer who had always been a Democrat, like his father before him, less because of any deep-rooted love for the principles of Thomas Jefferson than because of an inherent Yankee contrary-mindedness. He was a man of action, who had won wide approval among the comfortable classes for his ruthless advice to Cleveland to break the railroad strike on the ground that United States mail must go through. He knew nothing about foreign affairs when he became Secretary of State but he was not at all averse to learning quickly and dangerously.

In the opinion of Senator Lodge, whose attitude towards Hawaii perhaps made him an expert in such matters, it would be hard to find "a worse case of land-grabbing from an inoffensive state" than England's encroachment upon Venezuela. He spent the early part of June studying the matter and preparing another article for the *North American Review*. He had two purposes in mind. As he wrote his friend Henry White: "I wanted first to call attention to the facts but little known here, and second to pave the way for *a stiff declaration of the Monroe Doctrine by the next Congress*. You know that has never been done. The next Congress will do it and we shall serve notice on the world that we shall regard infringement of the Monroe Doctrine as an act of hostility." Since these belligerent words were written in a private letter to a close friend they may be taken as proof that in the summer of 1895 Henry Cabot Lodge was spoiling for a fight with England. No other nation then was in a position to threaten the integrity of the Monroe Doctrine, whether strictly or loosely construed.

At the same time President Cleveland and Mr. Olney were studying the Monroe Doctrine on their own account and the blunt and vigorous President had come to the conclusion, as a logical isolationist, that the time was at hand to check sharply any imperialistic designs on the Western Hemisphere of Great Britain or any other European power. On July 20 Mr. Olney sent his famous message to Lord Salisbury — which Cleveland called his "twenty-inch gun" — in which he asserted that any attempt at a forcible ratification of the Venezuela boundary would be a violation of the Monroe Doctrine. His words had the unmistakable ring of authority when he declared that "today the United States is practically sovereign on this continent, and its fiat is law upon the subjects to which it confines its interposition." Lord Salisbury was somewhat taken aback.

In the meantime the ladies of the Lodge and Adams ménages had been putting their heads together, preparing for a trip abroad. "The Lord only knows what has induced the Senator from Massachusetts to go over with wife and sons, to Europe, where he has not been these five and twenty years, and which he detests almost as much as I do," sighed Henry Adams, "but go he will, and probably he will revisit the dreary old capitals as though he were still twenty, and as though Napoleon III were still reigning."

The "little family party," Senator and Mrs. Lodge, their two sons, Henry Adams, and Mrs. Brooks Adams, who was Mrs. Lodge's sister, arrived in London before the middle of July. Never one to waste time, the Senator at once plunged into a round of activities which left him little opportunity for sight-seeing. He dined with the Curzons, met the Asquiths, lunched with Balfour. With journalists and politicians of every stripe he talked about bimetallism and grew more confused than ever on the subject when Joseph Chamberlain on one day told him that silver was on the agenda of that great man's party and on the next the Duke of Devonshire said he suspected very little would be heard of the subject after the general election. He chatted with the Duke of Sutherland, with Sir Edward Grey and Lord Lansdowne — and with Mrs. Humphry Ward, whom he found "pleasanter a good deal than her books." Everywhere he listened to conversations as various as the breeze and before he left England, as Adams remarked, he had seen and known the great and virtuous British statesmen, both Radicals and Tories, and had had a wonderful time. "He that kicks the Britisher gets his reward," Adams chuckled. "Cabot is treated with the utmost civility." As Cabot himself wrote to Theodore (who was having a delightful time being Police Commissioner of New York that summer), "I have seen pretty much all the interesting men."

For a month Lodge "dawdled about in country houses" and went to "bimetallic symposia" and kept in touch with affairs back home through the columns of *The Times* of London and letters from Theodore. The thing that most impressed him was the growth of the United States. "You feel it here better than at home — and oh, how glad I am to be an American!" His mind was constantly on politics. When he heard rumors to the effect that Cleveland had beaten him to the draw on the Monroe Doctrine he wrote, "We should beat him to death on the third-term issue." He worried about Roosevelt's political situation and he kept constantly in mind his scheme for making Tom Reed President in 1896. He grew angry when he read in *The Times* "that there is no general interest in the United States in the

Monroe Doctrine, that only a few jingoes talk about Venezuela, that there really is no objection among our people to England's going there, that the Irish brogue can be read in every line about Trinidad," and rushed off orders for Theodore to have a good talk with George W. Smalley, the American correspondent of the Thunderer, and put him right.

Even in Paris, whence the group went after a month in England, he could not refrain from indulging in politics and wrote happily that he had met two Americans who wanted "a strong foreign policy." But once Adams got him away from the city he doffed his Senatorial toga and became the charming travel companion that he had been a quarter of a century before when he and Nannie had been on their honeymoon. Henry Adams has given a delightful picture of him at this time. "The Abbey is marvelous," he wrote his friend Elizabeth Cameron, "we passed our time wholly in enjoying it from all sorts of points and passed hours studying the details of the church, and the perfection of its taste. The boys dragged me up and down walls and moats, cliffs and beaches, and Cabot beamed with satisfaction in history. He ought to have been professor at Harvard College, as I meant him to be when I educated him. He showed it at Mont St. Michel where the church is not so religious as military. . . .

"Bay Lodge is a very good fellow, with illusions and ambitions and an exaggerated idea of Parisian standards. John is less sympathetic and more commonplace, and much too old for his years. Their father is a sort of elder brother to them, and all three are so young that the weary world stops in its orbit to wonder at them. John alone approaches nineteen. They are pleasant companions, fresh, intelligent and good natured."

It was while in Paris in mid-September that he wrote

Theodore a most prophetic letter. "I am a fair judge of political forces," he boasted; "I am no dreamer either about you or myself. . . . There are to be two Republican Senators from New York soon — one very soon. There is a good chance for you to get the first one . . . I do not say you are to be President tomorrow. I do not say it will be — I am sure that it may and can be."

After France the Lodges went to Spain to look the situation over. The people and the landscape — "desolate dreary plains and here and there a dying town" — depressed and repelled him. He found the Spanish were "beaten, broken and out of the race, and are proud and know it." In Madrid he talked cautiously with the Spanish Premier about the situation in Cuba. He found the Spanish in a "state of mind" and "dreadfully afraid that we shall intervene" and recognize Cuban belligerency. Of course, Lodge was in favor of such action. Spain made him want to get back to the United States. "I love that great land of mine across the sea so much better than anything else!" he said, from the heart.

Back again in Paris Lodge heard the news that Great Britain had no intention of allowing the Venezuela matter to be arbitrated. This put him on pins and needles, as he said, to get home. "If we allow England to invade Venezuela nominally for reparation . . . really for territory our supremacy in the Americas is over. I am worried and angry beyond words at what I see. England is simply playing America for what she can get."

Early in November he recrossed the Channel and prepared to return home. But before he embarked he gave a long interview to the *London Chronicle* in which he redefined the Monroe Doctrine for the edification of the British public. Once more he predicted that Congress would formally declare by resolutions of both Houses that the Doctrine was an integral part of the policy of the United States, to be maintained at all hazards. The following day the correspondent of the *New York Times* cabled: "Senator Lodge's exposition of the Monroe Doctrine has not profoundly interested the British public." A day later the Senator sailed for home.

XII

The War Hawks

THE country was startled and excited after reading President Cleveland's special message to Congress on December 17, 1895. In this he asked for the immediate creation of a special commission which would study all the facts in the case and decide exactly where the Venezuelan boundary lay. His words were stern and stubborn. "When such a report is made and accepted it will, in my opinion, be the duty of the United States to resist by every means in its power, as a wilful aggression upon its rights and interests, the appropriation by Great Britain of any land or the exercise of governmental jurisdiction over any territory which after investigation we have determined of right belongs to Venezuela."

Those were words to please the most bellicose jingo. They gratified Senator Lodge. Those were brave (or boastful) words coming from a commander in chief who had at his disposal an army of 27,160 men and officers compared to Great Britain's 155,455, and two battleships (second class) to Britain's forty-four! But Mr. Cleveland, of course, had left himself a way out: he threatened nothing until after a report had been made and accepted. Nevertheless, he had spoken up to England in a way that thrilled the American soul. When the message was read to the Senate that august body cast aside its traditional reserve and the chamber rang with applause. The Republicans were even more hearty than the members of Mr. Cleveland's own party. In the House the message evoked loud cheers.

143

The message was hardly on the telegraph wires before stocks began tumbling on all the exchanges and America was in for its worst war scare in many years. While the first headlines screamed, Representative Robert P. Hitt of Illinois, chairman of the Foreign Affairs Committee, was introducing his resolution calling for the commission and appropriating $100,000 to its use. The debate was brief, fervent, and ringingly patriotic. Within two days, having been approved by the House, the bill was placed before the Senate.

In the excitement of the moment, Senator Lodge remembered his adage that when it came to foreign affairs he always placed his country's weal above party consideration. He did so now, eloquently. Not in the entire Senate was there a more ardent supporter of the Democratic President than this Republican. Cleveland was a humorless man; otherwise, even at so tense a moment, he must have been amused to find Lodge, whom he despised, rushing to his defense. But Cleveland was saying now, in statesmanlike terms, what Lodge had said so waspishly the previous spring. It called for little charity on the Senator's part to say that he "cordially agreed" with the President's message. After all it was only "the right, the sound, the American position for the United States to take." That being the case, what was now "of the utmost importance is that we should show to the world that we are united, without distinction of party or section, in support of the policy which the message outlines. We should be able to say, as Webster said in the House of Representatives, that our politics stop at the water's edge, and that when we come to deal with a foreign question we deal with it simply as Americans!"

Senator Lodge sneered at the charge made in the British newspapers — and in that "small part of the British press which is published in New York City" — that the Venezuela affair was "a matter of politics." "That is the most mistaken view ever uttered," he declared, without true regard for the facts of the national temper. "The American people, without distinction, believe in the maintenance of the Monroe Doctrine and are prepared to uphold it at any cost." The commission was not to act as a board of arbitration, he warned, but to inform the United States "on what line they ought to stand when they prepare to resist further aggressions on American soil." He did not say, however, when such aggression would take place, nor by whom.

There should be no delay in getting this report, the Senator said. He himself had examined every map and document in the case, and it should not take the commission more than five months to do likewise. "We want nothing indefinite about the commission. We want them to report as soon as possible, and then we will sustain the Monroe Doctrine with all the strength of the Republic!"

In his haste Senator Lodge ignored an important political implication. But Senator Sherman, who was not deceived into thinking that politics had nothing to do with the case, did not. It was never out of his mind that, should the affair lead to a glorious war with England, the credit for this desirable state would go to a Democrat! That this might be forestalled he urged that the bill be sent to the Foreign Relations Committee for further study, and when it promptly came back, Senator Lodge's time limit had been dropped. By that time Lodge, reminded of the election that was less than a year away, had seen his error and no longer pressed the point. If war was inevitable it was better to have it prosecuted with the right party in power. The bill creating the commission was signed by President Cleveland just five days after he had asked that it be set up.

On the whole the country rallied around Cleveland — and inferentially around Senator Lodge. Cleveland's stand was, after all, as Theodore Roosevelt quickly pointed out, a "remarkable vindication" of Lodge's point of view. "Let the fight come if it must," the Police Commissioner wrote the Senator. "I don't care whether our sea coast cities are bombarded or not; we would take Canada." This was a private expression of what was a popular belief among those whom Mr. Godkin called the "mostly ignorant and completely secluded" democracy, whose great contempt for history and experience was urging the country at this moment to use its great strength against "anyone who comes along" — and "without knowing how to do it."

The bankers howled in anguish and deluged Senator Lodge's office with telegrams and letters of reproach written in terms, as Henry Adams said, that no Copperhead in 1861 surpassed. State Street was frantic, the anger of "the Harvard crowd" was great, and Boston's year-old Twentieth Century Club violated its own constitution for the first and only time in history to register its unanimous protest. Henry Higginson "raged and whined and threatened" — but Senator Lodge was not perturbed. He knew that if it were not Venezuela now it would be Cuba in the spring or Canada at some other time.

Bubbling with excitement, the Senator would not let the matter rest. On December 30 he was ready once more to lecture the Senate on his favorite theme. For one hour that afternoon he held the attention of his colleagues of both political faiths, and the crowded galleries. The only interruptions were from certain spellbound Democrats, who, obviously impressed with his words, asked pointed questions designed to strengthen his stand. His speech is important in that it set forth the dual belief in isolationism and imperialism on which was founded the philosophy of the expansionists. As usual Senator Lodge called up the spirits of George Washington (who would "form no entangling alliances and take no part in the affairs of Europe") and of

146

Thomas Jefferson (who urged "America, North and South" to have "a system of her own, separate and apart from that of Europe") to buttress his own arguments. "The words of Jefferson," he said, "may be commended to those who think the operations of a foreign power in South America of less importance than the temporary price of stocks."

England, of course, was the villain of his piece. He compared her action in claiming territory in Venezuela, to which, he said, she had no just claim, to "seizing and holding new territory in the Americas by right of conquest." This was an absolute violation of the Monroe Doctrine and its only purpose was to give Great Britain "control of the Spanish Main and make the Caribbean Sea little more than a British lake."

"For thirty years," he said, "the American people have been absorbed in healing the ravages of civil war and in completing the conquest of the great continent which was our heritage. That work is done. The American people have begun to turn their eyes to those interests of the United States which lie beyond our borders and yet so near our doors."

As a sort of afterthought he deprecated hostility with Great Britain, whom he termed the "aggressor" in this case. On the whole he was far more cautious than usual in his references to England, but still it was, in effect, an inflammatory speech. Possibly, in spite of his bombast, he really expected no war and hoped that after a certain amount of necessary bluster England would submit the question to arbitration. Anyone as close as he was to the state of the American Navy must have been a little frightened at the possibility of a fight, but there is no question that Senator Lodge believed that only through the fire of conflict at some time could the United States reach the state of greatness he desired. All his previous twistings of the Lion's tail had been acts for the amusement of the home folks. Now he was speaking to the world. Too cynical to have the trust in Providence that Cleveland professed, he knew he was playing a dangerous game. Nor was he alone. Professor Woodrow Wilson emerged from his study of history to praise the President's stand. Theodore Roosevelt, Elihu Root, Henry Adams, and many others believed with Cleveland and Lodge that the national honor and the national future demanded of the government strong words backed by conviction.

Even as Senator Lodge was pouring forth his hour-long peroration in the Senate, events were transpiring in distant parts of the world — in the old European world of which we were, and should be, no part — which lent some credence to the widely held belief that we were being led to our manifest destiny by the hand of God. Had they not occurred we might very well have been forced, by the passion of our patriotism and the fiery words of our statesmen like Senator Lodge, into a position where we, who were so unprepared for battle, would have had to fight. Luckily, there was South Africa — and the German Kaiser.

Just three days after Senator Lodge's address a small group of Englishmen raided Jamestown in the Transvaal in the hopes of fomenting an uprising against the Boer State. On January 3 the Kaiser publicly congratulated President Kruger for repelling with his own forces and without appeal "to the help of friendly powers" the armed forces which had "broken into your country." In the shock of surprise that followed Wilhelm's bold if undiplomatic utterance England's minor quarrel with the United States over an obscure jungle boundary suddenly seemed of puny significance — to the English. The danger of a cisatlantic war disappeared overnight. British foreign policy changed with the snap of the Kaiser's finger. Joseph Chamberlain urged upon the

Prime Minister the necessity of "coming to terms" with America.

It was Chamberlain who expressed the new British stand: "We do not covet one single inch of American territory. War between the two nations would be an absurdity and a crime. The two nations are . . . more closely allied in sentiment and in interest than any other nations on the face of the earth. While I should look with horror upon anything in the nature of a fratricidal strife, I should look forward with pleasure to the possibility of the Stars and Stripes and the Union Jack floating together in the defense of a common cause sanctioned by humanity and justice."

To the very end of the argument Lord Salisbury insisted that the United States should never have raised the controversial issue of the Monroe Doctrine. But he was convinced of the dangers inherent in the dispute and, within a few weeks of Mr. Chamberlain's telling speech, his government and that of Venezuela agreed, in principle, to arbitrate.

Senator Lodge read one morning in the newspapers that the Danish government was willing to sell its possessions in the West Indies, as well as that ill-defined and mysterious island lying in the sea of ice between Baffin Bay and the Arctic Archipelago — Greenland. Although nobody else seemed to care, Senator Lodge at once pounced upon the item like the wire-haired terrier of which he reminded so many people. His excited yelps became even shriller when he read further, in the unconfirmed newspaper story, that Denmark might very well consider a bid from Germany if the United States showed no interest. In short order he prepared and introduced in the Senate a resolution demanding an immediate investigation.

As Senator Lodge very well understood, American interest in the West Indies islands was nothing new. Secretary Seward, impressed during the Civil War with the need for an

American naval coaling station there, had "literally teased" Denmark in 1867 into agreeing to sell the islands of St. Thomas and St. John for $7,500,000. A plebiscite in the islands had shown that a majority of voting natives favored annexation with the United States and the King of Denmark accordingly had released them from his sovereignty. For a variety of reasons, including a rather widespread belief that Mr. Seward had made a bad bargain in buying a useless "iceberg" called Alaska, the Senate not only declined to sanction the treaty of sale but even refused to discuss it. Political partisanship, of course, was at the bottom of this insult to friendly Denmark. When Grant became President that eminent statesman would not take up the matter, rudely washing his hands of it on the ground that it was an "affair of Seward's" with which he would have nothing to do. At that time proponents of the treaty made the same argument Senator Lodge was now to repeat: the United States would be in a most awkward position should Denmark decide to sell to another power. We either would have had to repudiate the Monroe Doctrine or to invoke it on behalf of the very islands which the Senate would not let us buy.

Burning as he was with expansionist fever, Senator Lodge told the Senate that "we need more than ever today" the same coaling station that Mr. Seward had failed to obtain. After his usual lecture on American history he said, "It is in the interest of the United States that no opportunity should be offered for any of the great powers of Europe to secure additional territory in the Americas." Of course, the safe and sensible way to resist such a transfer, obviously a violation of the Monroe Doctrine, would be to take the islands now by "peaceable cession." And while we were about it, we should also take Greenland. In some future day that island would benefit us as much as Alaska. Not only would it afford us another base but we would find it "profitable in minerals" too.

Few Senators and fewer journalists took Senator Lodge seriously. Particularly did his plea for the acquisition of Greenland fall upon deaf ears. He tried in vain to interest Secretary Olney in the project, but, as he later put it in an indignant note to President Roosevelt, "the idea was looked upon as a joke." Nevertheless, being blessed with true Yankee tenacity, the Senator did everything in his power to keep the subject alive. If he filed it away in 1896 he did not forget it. He reintroduced his resolution, still to no effect, in March 1897. But in 1902, he almost saw the sale completed. It received the approval of two thirds of the Senate — only this time the Danish upper house, with poetic justice, rejected the treaty by a vote of one!

While Senator Lodge was unsuccessfully seeking support for a realistic application of Captain Mahan's theory of how to make a great nation, the matter of Cuba, which had been momentarily forgotten in the excitement over Venezuela, again was brought to the attention of Congress. All at once a flood of resolutions descended upon both Houses demanding recognition of Cuban belligerency, Cuban independence, and even calling for a war. At the same time many other bills were before the legislators requesting armaments, battleships, torpedo boats, the reorganization of the Army, coastal defenses, and other items of "national defense."

In Senator Lodge's name was an amendment to the general fortifications bill proposing a $100,000,000 issue of coin bonds to be sold at popular subscription, the proceeds to be kept in the Treasury as a separate fund for coast defenses. As the Senator from a state that might expect any day to be bombarded, by whatever enemy it was we were preparing against, he could be expected to do no less.

Early in February the Foreign Relations Committee put

its seal of approval upon according belligerent rights to the Cuban insurgents and on February 20 the debate began. It was not long before the Senators had recklessly plunged into a discussion of the policies of the friendly kingdom of Spain in language "so inaccurate and so insulting" as to bring the debate, in the words of Walter Millis, "to the verge of simple blackguardism."

Senator Lodge, who was once described as "that cautious firebrand," did not join in the general billingsgate. He was, as usual, too much of a gentleman for that. Ever the scholar, even in the midst of the alarms of war, he would preface his remarks by quotation. To Lodge, who knew his Milton, "among all the Spanish-American colonies Cuba was the Abdiel; 'among the faithless faithful only he . . .' Her reward was the title 'Faithful Cuba' and that was the only reward she ever received." Having paid his aptly allusive tribute to the island he became realistic again: "Our immediate pecuniary interests in the island are very great. They are being destroyed. Free Cuba would mean a great market for the United States; it would mean an opportunity for American capital invited there by signal exemptions; it would mean an opportunity for the development of that splendid island." That was not all. There was a broader political interest in her fate: "She lies athwart the line which leads to the Nicaraguan canal!"

In this speech, at least, it appeared as if Senator Lodge favored freeing the Cubans. He did — in public utterances. In private conversations, he expressed doubt that Cuba, if granted independence, would ever be able to set up a "stable government." For that reason he felt that annexation was the necessary answer. In the confused and often ignorant debate which led, in April, to the Congressional recognition of a "condition of public war" in Cuba, he was frequently vocal. But even he succumbed to the Senatorial habit of loose speaking when he quoted as an actual proclamation by General Weyler a newspaper guess as to what the General would probably say. Such proceedings disgusted his colleague, the venerable Senator Hoar, who had been in Washington too long to be taken in. He knew that most of the commotion caused by his junior colleague and the other war hawks was "no proof of any disturbance in our foreign relations but that there is a presidential election at hand."

Senator Hoar, of course, was speaking the truth. Senator Lodge, younger and far more cynical than the old man from Massachusetts, knew it too. He never for more than a moment forgot the political implications of anything. Particularly did he not forget them in 1896.

Since they had first sat together in Congress in 1887 Senator Lodge's admiration for Tom Reed had steadily grown. Upon more than one occasion, particularly after Lodge had gone to the Senate, they had teamed up in behalf of legislation. The Democratic papers often spoke disparagingly of the firm of Reed and Lodge, and the *New York Times,* whose editors still remembered the campaign of 1884, seldom referred to the latter without implying something evil in the relationship. They felt that Lodge exerted a corrupting influence upon his older friend. But even if Reed did consort with the renegade from Massachusetts there was no question that the powerful Speaker of the House deserved well of the party he had wholeheartedly served so many years. He had been faithful, he had a forceful character, his intellect was on a par with, if not above, his colleagues', and his wit was brilliant. Although it may not have been a political attribute, his friends, both young and old, delighted in his keen Yankee sense of humor. Furthermore, he was not notoriously a war hawk. His attitude towards England and Cuba was conservatively safe. His mental processes were closer to those of the Eastern businessman than were those of his fervent admirer. As a potential candidate, though, he had one fault: he was not a friend of Mark Hanna.

When it came to the Republican nomination Reed was a Barkis. He had — or thought he had — more friends than enemies. By March the political writers were taking his candidacy seriously. In the Senate, however, Lodge made little headway in finding active supporters for his cause. In New York young Roosevelt, already becoming bored with the Police Department and yearning for Washington again, was still at odds with "Boss" Platt and the Republican machine and he found it difficult to advance the cause of Reed. And there were moments, during the winter, when both became impatient with their friend. They suspected he could work a little harder to push the coastal defense bills through the House. They detected an inertia which they could not understand.

"Upon my word," Theodore burst out in March, "I do think that Reed ought to pay some heed to the wishes of you and myself. You have been his most effective supporter; and while my support does not amount to much, it has yet been given at a very serious cost to myself."

But Reed was, as Henry Adams pointed out, a stubborn man, "too clever, too strong-willed and too cynical, for a bankers' party." By that he meant the Republican Party as now controlled by Mark Hanna. And Mr. Hanna, his hand deep in his pocket, had his own man in McKinley.

Roosevelt wavered. Lodge remained firm. His support was not entirely sentimental. Nor was it unselfish. As the junior partner of the firm of Reed and Lodge, were luck to be with them, he could name his reward. Everyone in Washington knew that if Reed went to Washington Mr. Lodge would go to the State Department. No other post would interest the rediscoverer of the Monroe Doctrine who had just been appointed to the Foreign Relations Committee. But the Reed boom did not gain momentum. Mr. Hanna kept taking his hand out of his pocket and in the South, and even in New England, people who had been talking Reed began talking McKinley. Mr. Hanna was a businessman and knew how to get results. He had more money than Senator Lodge. By early spring it was even doubtful if Reed could command the delegation from his own state.

Although Lodge could not drum up much enthusiasm for his fat friend in the Senate cloakroom, he held Massachusetts in the hollow of his hand. When Lodge left Washington in late March to preside over the convention which was to name the delegates to the Republican National Convention, he knew no opposition worth mentioning awaited him.

In a brief and orderly meeting, which was charged with a spirit of confidence, Senator Lodge was quickly chosen delegate at large and chairman of the delegation. Two of the other delegates at large were Curtis Guild, Jr., and Lodge's old friend, Eben S. Draper. A third was a silent, thin, whispering man, the head of a large paper factory at Dalton, Massachusetts, and reputedly very rich. This was to be his second National Convention. In the fall he was to be elected Lieutenant Governor of Massachusetts. His name was Winthrop Murray Crane. All four were in favor of Tom Reed, as, indeed, were all but one of the twenty-six other delegates chosen that day.

The Massachusetts delegates were among the first to arrive at St. Louis but even so they did not get there before Mark Hanna had appeared on the scene to take things in hand. This was to be Mr. Hanna's convention all the way through. He was to run it with an iron hand and make his candidate the party's choice. Senator Lodge – who might have been the convention's chairman had not Speaker Reed's boom collapsed so miserably – was to have a brief moment

155

or two in the spotlight, but his first essay at President-making was an abject failure.

Even before the arrival of the early birds on Saturday it had been decided — by Mr. Hanna — that the one dangerous issue confronting the party should be side-stepped as neatly as possible. This was the currency question. He and his junto were determined not to allow a rancorous debate over silver, the bête noire of the Easterners, to wreck the party's harmony. Having arranged everything with the peaceful nomination of Major William McKinley in mind, to be followed by a quiet campaign in which the tariff would be the outstanding topic of discussion, it was not the Ohioan's purpose to allow anything to happen which might perforce lead to a bolt of the silverites. And so the fateful word "gold" was not to be mentioned openly at all. Hanna and his protégé felt that in good season both wings could be reconciled on an innocuous plank supporting bimetallism.

When Senator Lodge unpacked his bags in his rooms at the Southern Hotel on Sunday afternoon he was of an entirely different mind than Boss Hanna. He had made it pretty clear before leaving Boston that he would do everything in his power to have a "gold plank" written into the platform. Therefore, he hustled off for a conference with Boss Platt, the Senator from New York, whom he soon left, convinced that this estimable gentleman would back up Massachusetts in its insistence that the word "gold" be used. He then went to pay his respects to his friend Police Commissioner William Henry Osborne of Boston, who, by virtue of being McKinley's cousin, was in charge of the Ohio delegation. Cousin William showed Lodge two tentative drafts of the currency platform. Neither mentioned gold.

In a determined mood Lodge hastened to the Hanna headquarters. Unceremoniously he burst into the room

156

where Mr. Hanna, his nerves on edge from lack of sleep, sat in a dense cloud of cigar smoke perusing the speech which the temporary chairman, Charles W. Fairbanks, was to deliver at the opening session. Without further ado the impetuous gentleman from Massachusetts burst out: —

"Mr. Hanna, I insist upon a positive declaration for a gold-standard plank in the platform."

The startled Hanna looked up and barked, "Who in hell are you?"

"Senator Henry Cabot Lodge of Massachusetts."

"Well, Senator Henry Cabot Lodge of Massachusetts, you can go plumb to hell. You have nothing to say about it."[1]

Senator Lodge, who was not used to being talked to in this manner, must have been somewhat taken aback, but he retained presence of mind enough to threaten to take his fight for the gold standard to the floor of the convention. And this, of course, was exactly what Hanna wished to avoid. Hanna, however, was confident of his own ability to crush any opposition. He told Lodge to make his fight where he pleased, for he knew damned well that Massachusetts alone could not secure a vote.

"No," the Senator said, "but Massachusetts will not be alone."

"I am informed otherwise," snapped Hanna, and the painful interview was over.

H. H. Kohlsaat, the Chicago editor and newspaper publisher, who was present, was worried. He wanted to mollify

[1] Quite a controversy raged for several years over the colloquy. H. H. Kohlsaat, who claims to have been present, is author of the above bit of pungent dialogue. (See *Saturday Evening Post*, May 28, 1922; *New York Times*, May 28, 1922.) Senator Lodge denied it ever took place. Contemporary newspaper evidence seems to show that Hanna and Lodge met, before the convention opened, and had a verbal row over the plan. (See *New York Times*, June 15, 1896; also Dunn, *From Harrison to Harding*, and James B. Morrow in *Washington Sunday Star*, December 15, 1918.)

the Senator by showing him the plank which Hanna had accepted, but the Ohio boss growled. "You cannot trust the blankety-blank man," he said. "He will give the plank to the press." The trusting editor, however, insisted, and chasing after Senator Lodge let him not only see but make a copy of the plank. In some manner it did leak out, being printed in a St. Louis newspaper under a Boston date line. Hanna was furious, but apparently only he and one or two others saw the item. Undoubtedly Hanna thought that Lodge had deliberately let the story out, hoping to bring about a break in the McKinley ranks and thus further the candidacy of Tom Reed, whose animosity to the silverites had never been aggressive.

The misunderstanding was patched up. Hanna and Lodge met again and the latter stubbornly insisted that his demand for a gold plank was the better tactic for the party to pursue. He was adamant, in spite of the fact that he carried in his pocket a cablegram from Senator Hoar urging him to stand out for a declaration in favor of "the restoration of silver as legal tender in company with gold," and in concert with other nations, which the patriarchal senior Senator had sent him from Paris. "You are the most stubborn man I ever met," Hanna told Senator Lodge. In the end the plank was written as Lodge wanted it, with a specific endorsement of "the existing gold standard." Lodge had seen correctly; but just how correctly none knew until after William Jennings Bryan made his famous "Cross of Gold" speech two weeks later and set the temper for the violent and bitter campaign of the summer and fall of 1896.

Throughout the East there was rejoicing over Lodge's victory. Even Senator Hoar, who often looked with amazement upon his younger colleague, was to admit that by his insistence he had "saved the Presidential election" for the Republican Party. Lodge, who sometimes modestly disclaimed having actually written the famous gold plank, never was known to blush when he was given credit.

Lodge may have saved the Presidential election but not for Reed. But neither did he desert his candidate as some others did under pressure from Boss Hanna. When the roll was called on the nomination of candidates, he was quickly on his feet. In a brief speech he offered the name of Tom Reed to the convention. Any hope of a stampede for Reed quickly died. Hanna's convention could not be stampeded. When it came time to vote, Reed ran a bad second to McKinley on the only ballot, corralling 84½ votes to the Ohioan's 661½.

The defeat of Reed does not appear to have deeply affected Senator Lodge, but Reed, who said bitterly that he was used to "waiting for others to pass," felt that he had been betrayed. "Hanna's coarse ways are pretty hard to stand," he wrote Roosevelt, "especially when you appreciate that a great office can be retained by purchase as well as obtained by purchase." Soon, thereafter, the brilliant Speaker decided to retire from politics, and Lodge made his peace with Hanna and his satellite. Roosevelt did, too.

The abortive effort on Reed's behalf and the successful fight for the magic word "gold" did not occupy all of Senator Lodge's time in the hot and smoky rooms of the Southern Hotel or in the noisy environs of Convention Hall. His practised hand helped hew the party's plank on Foreign Policy. His words are seen: —

Our foreign policy should at all times be firm, vigorous, and dignified and all our interests in the Western Hemisphere should be carefully watched and guarded. . . . The Hawaiian Islands should be controlled by the United States and no foreign power should be permitted to interfere with them. The Nicaraguan Canal should be built, owned and operated by the United States. . . . In Turkey . . . and everywhere American citizens and American property must be absolutely protected at all hazards and at any cost . . . the Government of the United States should actively use its influences and the good offices to restore peace and give independence to . . . Cuba. . . .

Having contributed his full share to the week's good work, Senator Lodge hastened homeward. In New York, where he paused overnight, he and Theodore gloated together over Lodge's golden victory. The Senator was, indeed, "on top of the wave." Had he not gauged the situation better than Hanna and McKinley? A few days later, when he was introduced at the Harvard Commencement and applauded as the author of the gold plank, he experienced a momentary glow. As Theodore wrote his sister Corinne, Lodge was "able to emphasize his triumph most in the presence of the men who hate him most." No doubt, as he took his bow, he was thinking of what President Eliot had called him that spring — "a degenerated son of Harvard." Indeed!

Senator Lodge threw himself with a will into the campaign for the election of McKinley. In many speeches he invariably warned that a victory for Bryan and the silver Democrats — who were "masquerading under the livery of the old Democratic Party" — would bring a "period of panic, a diaster of misfortune unequalled in the country's history." The dreadful Bryan, he charged, as the huge crowd in Carnegie Hall cheered, was an enemy of mankind because it was the Commoner alone who had raised the issue of "the classes against the masses" and thereby threatened the very existence of "American institutions and American prosperity." Later Lodge and Roosevelt stumped New York State, speaking to large crowds in such Republican strongholds as Utica and Buffalo.

The national campaign of 1896 was, as everyone now realizes, more than any other up to that time exactly what

Lodge said Bryan had made it — a struggle of mass against class. It was also a life-and-death battle between Western agrarianism and Eastern capitalism. Class and capital, being the better organized and having access to greater funds, could not lose. Bryan's great eloquence, reaching magnificent heights though it did, and often touching upon the fundamental truth about America, was no match for the wealth that poured without urging into Hanna's war chest. The shipowner and coal magnate, now turned politician, no longer had to use the old, crude methods of buying votes. Frightened capital, facing dread inflation and repudiation of debts, gave of its own free will, and press and pulpit rose without prompting to the defense of the *status quo*.

Never for a moment did Senator Lodge have any qualms about the rectitude of Massachusetts. No other state in the Union, perhaps, had to the square mile as many "idle holders of idle wealth" as did the Bay State. Massachusetts did not have to be told by Senator Lodge, or anyone else, to vote for McKinley and gold and safety. As M. E. Hennessy once remarked, every Democrat who owned a checkbook left the party that year and voted for McKinley.

The first thing that Senator Lodge had to do after the election was to establish himself firmly with Major McKinley. After all, he was not an "original McKinley man." Although he had worked as hard as any party man for his victory it was necessary for him to get himself "in" as solidly as possible with the President-elect. Even a scholar in politics has to look after the "accursed patronage." He had already taken steps in the right direction. Immediately after his New York speaking tour during the campaign, he and Roosevelt had gone on to Akron, whence, after a bad night in a garret room in what Lodge remembered for twenty-five years as "an alleged hotel," they had visited the Major on his front porch at Canton. When John Hay heard of this he chuckled and said they had gone there to "offer their heads to the axe and their tummies to the hari-kari knife" for the good of the cause. It was at least certain that Major McKinley would not have to ask, "Who in hell are you?" when Lodge should see him again.

After the election the impelling subject of conjecture was the Cabinet. When word leaked out that McKinley had offered the post of Secretary of the Navy to his old friend and fellow Representative, John D. Long of Massachusetts, Senator Lodge was furious. For years Mr. Long had been prominent in the Peace Society, a strange place, the Senator thought, in which to recruit an adviser on naval affairs. He at once entrained for Ohio, hoping to persuade McKinley to withdraw his offer to Long. His choice was T. Jefferson Coolidge, a wealthy Boston manufacturer and former Ambassador to France. He arrived on Monday, November 30, just in time for luncheon in the plain frame house where Major McKinley lived.

The two men got along well. Across the luncheon table they talked of Hawaii (at Lodge's behest) and of Cuba (which was greatly on McKinley's mind). The Senator was impressed at the President-elect's attitude on the latter subject, for it seems that McKinley hoped the crisis would be reached before he took office. If war there must be, let Cleveland have it and leave the peacemaking to him. Such a program would hardly interfere with his one "great ambition . . . to restore business and bring back good times." Over the coffee Lodge was at last able to broach the subject of the Navy Department. He quickly perceived that McKinley was determined to have Long but his disappointment over the rejection of Coolidge did not prevent him from bringing up another subject he had well in mind when he came to Canton. Two days later he wrote from Washington to "My dear Theodore": —

162

Later . . . I said to him: "I have no right to ask a personal favor of you, but I do ask for Roosevelt as the one personal favor." He said very warmly: "You must not say that. I have no feeling about what went before the nomination. You have a perfect right to ask a personal favor and I understand what you want." When I was leaving after lunch I said, just as we were starting, that I was very much obliged to him and had enjoyed our talk and that he knew the one thing which was near my heart and that I should say no more about it. He said very cordially that he did. In a word he gave me every encouragement. But after all I am not one of his old supporters. . . .

Senator Lodge had started the ball rolling. Although neither could have realized it at that moment, Theodore Roosevelt was on his way to the White House at last.

XIII

That Splendid Little War

THE War Hawks, in the spring of 1897, were in the minority. William Randolph Hearst, however, was on their side, with oceans of red ink and bastions of huge type and conscience-less reporters like Karl Decker and reluctant artists like Remington at his imperious command. And in the long run it was Hearst's voice which was heard. A few years later both Lodge and Roosevelt were to say unkind things about the publisher, to rank him among the anarchists with Governor Altgeld; but in 1897 he was doing their work with remarkable if sometimes ungentlemanly efficiency. One atrocity story in the *Journal* was worth far more than any number of speeches in the Senate.

Indeed, it was not as much by any of his speeches as by a quiet bit of political conspiracy that Senator Lodge furthered the cause of expansion and helped change the history of the Western World.

Ever since Lodge and Roosevelt had become close friends the latter had made no important decision, at least in his political life, without having first courted Lodge's advice. There was, of course, more than friendship involved in Lodge's moves at this time. He wanted an active and dependable ally in the Navy Department.

Having asked McKinley "for Roosevelt as the one personal favor," Lodge set to work within a week of his return from Canton. The first person he approached was Tom Platt of New York, no friend of Roosevelt, but one whose consent would be necessary to put his man across. Lodge was on friendly terms with the "Easy Boss" at the time, having joined forces with him at the convention during the fight to get the word "gold" into the platform. Realizing that the major argument against Roosevelt, as far as Platt was concerned, was that he could not be trusted to "play ball" with the machine, Lodge pointed out that he would not have his hands on any important patronage, but would be concerned only with "the big questions of naval policy." In the recent past it was only through Lodge's counsel that Roosevelt had not had an open break with Platt and now, again at Lodge's insistence, he swallowed his pride and visited the Boss to tell him he would be a good boy if Platt would not stand in his way. Next Lodge lined up Senator Wolcott, an old and intimate friend of themselves and of Mark Hanna, who promised to plead Roosevelt's cause in the right places. Another ally was the labor-hating Senator from Minnesota, Cushman K. Davis, soon to head the Foreign Relations Committee. Lodge's argument was that the Navy Department needed a vigorous man like the New York Police Commissioner and that the party owed him the job.

By Inauguration Day Lodge was certain that he had "enough friends earnest for you to make a Secretary of State." Platt was convinced by now that Roosevelt would do less harm to the machine in Washington than in New York and, since the appointment would not be credited to him anyway, he decided to stand aside. Both President McKinley and Secretary Long felt a little the way Boss Platt did, that Roosevelt was not to be trusted; and it was not without a sense of prophecy that the Secretary wondered if the ebullient New Yorker would make a tractable subordinate. By April, however, McKinley had weakened to the supplications of Lodge and his co-conspirators. Roosevelt was given the post of Assistant Secretary of the Navy.

"It was Lodge who engineered it," Roosevelt wrote his sister, "at the end as well as at the beginning, working with his usual untiring loyalty and energy," thus proving he was Theodore's "dearest friend" and "the most faithful and loyal man" Roosevelt had ever known.

Untiring energy was, indeed, a characteristic of Senator Lodge and none knew it better than his colleagues on the Committee on Foreign Relations. They all were glad enough to have the energetic Lodge as their associate, for he was quite willing to do most of the hard work of the committee. Chafed by ambition, Lodge was not to rest content until he became chairman. He grew bitter in the long wait: it was not until he was an Elder Statesman that the post came to him in 1919. He was, of course, the victim of the old Senate rule of seniority. While this irked him, there was nothing he could do about it, especially during the years when the Democrats were in power. Upon one occasion he even delivered a stinging lecture in defense of the rule to Theodore Roosevelt when the latter suggested, in 1899, that Albert J. Beveridge, a comparative newcomer to the Senate, should be made chairman of the Committee on the Philippines. Able though Beveridge was, Lodge said in effect, let him keep his place and wait his turn! [1]

If foreign affairs were uppermost in Senator Lodge's mind they were something that President McKinley would dearly have liked to keep in the background. He had, however, inherited the Olney-Pauncefote Treaty, and something had to be done about it very soon. Mr. McKinley anticipated no difficulty. He had not then learned, as John Hay was to learn a few years later, that any treaty entering the Senate "is like a bull going into the arena: no one can say just how or when

---

[1] Lodge was appointed to the Foreign Relations Committee on December 30, 1895; he became the ranking Republican member in 1913 and chairman on May 28, 1919.

the final blow will fall, but one thing is certain — it will never leave the arena alive."

The so-called Olney-Pauncefote Treaty was a straightforward and simply worded document calling for the reference to arbitration tribunals of all disputes (except those involving title to territory) which might arise between the United States and Great Britain. Although negotiated by a Democratic Secretary of State, the idea of a general arbitration treaty of this nature had originated in the Fifty-first Congress when the Republicans had entire control of the government. In 1890 a joint resolution calling for such a treaty . had passed; three years later it had received the approval of the British Parliament. Mr. Olney and Lord Pauncefote had signed the treaty, which endeavored to carry out the expressed wishes of the two legislatures, early in 1897. President Cleveland had duly sent it to the Senate. There it lay untouched.

In his inaugural President McKinley, recognizing the universal approval the treaty had received when it was made public, gave it his enthusiastic endorsement. Even Mr. Gladstone, who didn't care too much for arbitration as a general rule, gave it his open support. Republicans found no fault. But when Lodge and his committee confreres reported the treaty, on St. Patrick's Day, they had already stabbed it in the back.

When the treaty emerged from the committee, it carried with it a proviso that every agreement to submit a question to arbitration must be individually submitted to the Senate and be approved by two thirds of that body. This, in effect, meant that the Senate had no intention of arbitrating, but would merely consent to submit questions to arbitration after any chance of settlement by diplomacy had failed. Other hamstringing amendments also were added, and the treaty came to a vote on May 5. A majority of the Senate favored it, in the weakened form, but the vote of 43 to 26 failed by three votes of the necessary two thirds. The treaty was rejected.

To Richard Olney, and many others, the rejection was a calamity of "world-wide proportions." He angrily blamed the disaster upon the cheap politicians, among whom he included Senator Lodge. The jingoes, the intense partisans who hated anything emanating from the Cleveland administration, and the big-navy advocates, came in for their share of his and others' castigation. These undoubtedly had much to do with the rejection. All were categories into which Lodge fitted neatly. Senator Frye, oldest member of the Foreign Relations Committee, blamed Great Britain, pointing out that as a gold-standard country she had never shown any willingness to enter into any international agreement regarding free silver. Whatever the real reason, Senator Lodge, in his wily way, had been as much to blame as anyone. Too cautious to come out flat-footedly against the treaty, he and his Republican colleagues had wrecked it by insisting upon the amendments — and then had sought to ratify the wreck!

In Senator Lodge's old age a treaty far more important to the peace and welfare of the world was about to come before the Senate. One day Senator Watson of Indiana turned to his colleague and said despairingly, "It appears to me that 80 per cent of the people are for it [the Versailles treaty] . . . and I don't see how it is to be defeated." Senator Lodge must have thought back, at that moment, to a long-forgotten spring of 1897 as he made his now famous answer: "Ah, my dear James, I do not propose to beat it by direct frontal attack, but by the indirect method of reservations."

It is possible that Lodge did not set out to beat the arbitration treaty by this method. But there can be no doubt that he learned the method then, and that he found it one of the most valuable lessons of his life. Upon more than one occasion, leading up to the great and tragic climax of 1919, he made effective and damaging use of the tricks he was taught as the treaty of 1897 was driven to its doom.

The arbitration treaty did not occupy all of Lodge's time and attention that winter or spring. Among other matters, such as patronage, there was the Navy and there was Cuba. Although he was not a member of the Naval Affairs Committee [2] Senator Lodge actively supported every measure designed to increase the size and strength of the fleet.

As Lodge had anticipated Theodore Roosevelt was taking his duties in the Navy Department seriously. Much to their joint surprise he seemed to be getting along quite well with Secretary Long. Only once did Lodge have to warn his "dear Theodore" to take things a little easy, and consult with his superior officer before going off half-cocked. Even President McKinley got over whatever fears he may have entertained for his Assistant Secretary and had the young man at the White House for an evening's talk. Theodore took advantage of the opportunity to propagandize for "the upbuilding of the Navy," and Mark Hanna, who was present, seemed impressed. He had not been in office more than four months before Secretary Long was confiding to Senator Lodge how pleased he was with his assistant, whose spirit of work and service, so he said, was a real inspiration to the department. True, both the Senator and the Secretary were a little apprehensive about Roosevelt's passion for floating drydocks, but the former, at least, was reassured when Theodore told him that what the Navy really needed was concrete docks — "and especially one concrete dock at Boston." Close as the two men were, when Lodge sought Roosevelt's help in securing increases in pay for certain shipkeepers in his district the latter adroitly "passed the buck" to Secretary

[2] His committees were: Foreign Relations, Immigration, Civil Service, Printing, and Railroads.

169

Long. But in spite of these minor differences one cannot read the correspondence that passed between "Dear Theodore" and "Dear Cabot" at this time without being aware of the conspiratorial atmosphere in which the pair were playing an exciting and dangerous game. They were, indeed, concerning themselves mostly with "big questions of naval policy," although none but themselves knew how far they were prepared to carry out their plans.

Congress had already resolved that Cuba should be independent, but even more important, in many respects, was its warning to the parties to the Treaty of Great Britain — Great Britain, Germany, Austria-Hungary, France, Italy, Russia — that they should live up to their obligations by protecting American Christians against Turkish atrocities. America, looking at the world, was on the verge of assuming its part in it.

Many Americans looked upon the outward trend with disfavor. They did their best to counteract the hysterical outbursts of Mr. Hearst's and Mr. Pulitzer's contending newspapers which, day in and day out, whipped up a new frenzy calculated only to draw us into a war with Spain.

One might have expected that the scholar in politics would have eschewed cheap tactics. Such was not the case. He indulged in them along with all the rest. In his zeal he was as nearly nonpartisan as he ever could become. The anti-imperialist newspapers frequently referred to the "jingoes of the Lodge-Morgan school," the Morgan referred to being that doughty ex-Confederate general, Senator John T. Morgan of Alabama, surely a strange bedfellow for the author of the Force Bill. But on the subject of expansion they saw eye to eye and behind the closed doors of the Foreign Relations Committee they worked hand in hand. They harried the State Department throughout February 1897 for a list of the American claims against Spain and a list of American citizens who had been arrested in Cuba by the Spanish authorities. From these latter they selected the name of one Julio Sanguilly and prepared a resolution demanding his immediate and unconditional surrender, which Senator Morgan, with appropriate solemnity, presented to the Senate.

Some pretty unbridled and irrelevant oratory followed and the documents pertaining to Mr. Sanguilly were put in the record. During the long and wordy harangues white-haired Senator Hoar listened intently, and then arose in his ancient majesty to point out that, on the strength of the record, Mr. Sanguilly was no more an American citizen than the Senator from Virginia, who had just been upholding America's honor, was a citizen of Cuba. This was quite a shock. Senator Lodge jumped up to save the day.

"Mr. President," he said in his precise and haughty way, "the committee on Foreign Relations did not think it necessary to go behind the record of a court of record of the City of New York."

When he had finished his defense Senator Hoar again rose to point out that, on the very date the court of record had accorded him his citizenship, Mr. Sanguilly, by his own documentary admission, was fighting in the Cuban insurrection! Flushing, Senator Lodge asked, "Does my colleague think his statement overthrows the record of the court?"

"I do," replied the rugged old gentleman. "There were 60,000 fraudulent naturalization papers issued from the same New York superior court within three days. . . . Those records are of the slightest possible importance." He then turned squarely on the junior Senator and said, "If we are going to plunge this country into war, let us have something to stand on! Let us have some facts!"

The next morning Mr. Olney announced that Mr. Sanguilly had been pardoned through the intercession of the State Department, that his citizenship was indeed doubtful, and that he had admitted he was guilty of the charges on which he had been arrested.

When the Senate met the following day the Foreign Relations Committee came in for considerable joshing. Senator Hale, his eyes twinkling, solemnly inquired if it were in order to move to substitute another island for Cuba. Amid titters Senator Lodge replied, in his most icy, Cabotian tones, that it was no matter for "sneers," and strode angrily from the floor.

Although McKinley had assured Carl Schurz that there would be "no jingo nonsense" in his administration, visitors who left the White House after discussing the Hawaiian situation reported a change coming over the President. They felt he was merely awaiting the "best opportunity" for presenting the matter.

Senator Lodge, of course, had paved the way. During his pre-inaugural visit to Canton he had arranged for H. E. Cooper, the Hawaiian Secretary of State, to have a talk with McKinley. Just before the inauguration a delegation arrived in Washington with full power to conclude a treaty of annexation. A few weeks later Japan, which in 1893 had favored American annexation, vigorously protested the Hawaiian Government's efforts to restrict Japanese immigration.[3] Overnight the peril of the yellow race became a far more effective weapon in the hands of the expansionists than Senator Lodge's often expressed fear of British designs. The Senator and his co-conspirator, Theodore Roosevelt, as might have been expected, made the most of the opportunity. The latter, who told Captain Mahan that he was "fully alive to the danger from Japan," which was then building two warships in England, wanted characteristically to take the islands

[3] In 1893 there were more than 20,000 Japanese in the islands. The number had materially increased by 1897. (*Expansionists of 1898*, by Julius W. Pratt, 1936; pp. 125, 217 ff.)

and settle the details later. Senator Lodge was more cautious, but he did nothing to discourage the Assistant Secretary of the Navy.

Roosevelt was keeping track of all the ships and had before him an outline of what to do "if things looked menacing about Spain" or if there was any likelihood of "the Japs chipping in." Hovering over his shoulders at all times was that "evil genius," Senator Lodge. Together they conceived a comprehensive plan of action to take effect just as soon as an excuse arose. Boldest of their conceptions was the seizure of the Philippine Islands, which they plotted in secret throughout the winter and spring, although they were to have no chance to do anything effective for several months.

As a matter of fact, the spring and summer of that year passed without any appreciable threat of war blackening the horizon. Senator Lodge divided his vacation between Nahant and the idyllic, ocean-washed retreat of his friend, William Sturgis Bigelow, on Tuckernuck Island off the southern Massachusetts coast. He was happy because his son John, who had been ill, had got through his Harvard year with no mark below a C and because Bay, returned from his studies in Paris and Berlin, was getting together a book of his poems. At Bigelow's place he bathed in the sun and lived in luxurious primitiveness, discussing all those esoteric subjects in which the shy and sensitive Bigelow — he who had sown Japanese seeds in the Arnold Arboretum and who at one time had almost became a Shingon priest — delighted. They shot pistols at targets and watched the plover which they would shoot in the fall.

It was not until after the first regular session of the Fifty-fifth Congress was well under way that events on the Cuban front began getting out of hand. President McKinley, still peaceful-minded, nevertheless devoted most of his annual message to this disturbing topic.

As early as October the *U.S.S. Maine* had been detached from the fleet and ordered to stand by for orders at Port Royal, South Carolina. In mid-December, at the suggestion of Consul General Fitzhugh Lee, the battleship had moved even closer to Cuban waters, this time at Key West. A month later pro-Spanish riots broke out in Havana and at 11 A.M. on January 25, the *Maine* passed Morro Castle and dropped anchor. Consul General Lee thought the move was ill-timed but since the ship had moved at Presidential order there was nothing he could do about it.

Senator Lodge and his more excitable fellow conspirator, Theodore Roosevelt, were convinced by now that there was going to be a war. Roosevelt looked around the Navy Department and, in the person of Commodore George Dewey, found an officer who could be entrusted with their larger plans of conquest. By astute maneuvering, with Lodge's *sub rosa* help, Roosevelt got for Dewey the sole command of the Asiatic Squadron and made it clear to the officer that at the first hint of strife he should proceed to seize the Philippine Islands, Spain's only outpost in the Pacific. This was done without consulting Secretary Long. When that peaceful gentleman learned what had happened he was a little put out, but he did not countermand the orders and Dewey left for the Far East.

In the meantime Hearst's unbridled journalism — with his fanciful tales of kidnapings, imprisonments, and the stripping of Cuban ladies suspected of being spies — continued to fan up excitement throughout the country. On February 9 Mr. Hearst's *Journal* printed a private letter of Spanish Minister Dupuy de Lôme, in which he spoke of McKinley as a weak bidder for the admiration of the crowd and in which he made other impious remarks. To Senator Lodge, as he later insisted, the letter "revealed the utter hollowness of all the Spanish professions" which in his opinion by no means were negated by the prompt resignation of Señor de Lôme.

On February 16 the *Maine* blew up in Havana Harbor, killing 260 of the 350 men and officers aboard. At first it was assumed to have been an accident. But Mr. Hearst's bright young men went to work. With diagrams and other "evidence" they proved the ship was the victim of a Spanish plot. Senator Lodge, who made no public pronouncement on the subject, agreed with them.

He was too cautious at this moment to scream for war. But he was not too prudent to prepare for it. He knew that "the slightest spark," as Secretary Long confided to his diary, was liable to result in war. Indeed, on January 31, more than a fortnight before the disaster, he had written an amazingly prophetic letter to Henry White in London, saying that "there may be an explosion any day in Cuba which would settle a great many things. We have got a battleship in the harbor of Havana, and our fleet, which overmatches anything the Spaniards have, is masked at the Dry Tortugas." We must assume that his reference to an "explosion" a fortnight before it actually occurred was merely a rhetorical indulgence on the Senator's part.

While the newspapers were speculating on the cause of the disaster and the board of inquiry was preparing to investigate, Senator Lodge cast his eyes to the Far East. On Friday, February 25, Secretary Long decided he needed a rest from the strain of office and left the Navy Department in the charge of Assistant Secretary Roosevelt. Senator Lodge chose this afternoon to pay the Assistant Secretary a call. The two spent one of the busiest afternoons of their careers. They were making history.

With Roosevelt's beloved maps spread before them showing the location of every ship in both the Atlantic and the Pacific Oceans, they laid their plans. Before the winter afternoon's darkness set in they started the wires humming with a series of orders for ammunition, the distribution of ships, the providing of guns for an auxiliary fleet not yet authorized, and the calling in of experts. They even sent a message to Congress asking immediate legislation authorizing the enlistment of an unlimited number of sailors. All this while Secretary Long dozed peacefully at home. No wonder when the Secretary learned, the next day, what had happened he felt that "the very devil seemed to possess" Roosevelt, and that he had come "very near causing more of an explosion than happened to the *Maine*."

But this was not all that the conspirators accomplished during their afternoon's adventure in international piracy, as Walter Millis once ironically described their scheming. The crowning achievement was a telegram they sent to their hand-picked Commodore. It read: —

Dewey — Hong Kong: Secret and confidential. Order the squadron, except *Monocacy*, to Hong Kong. Keep full of coal. In the event of declaration of war, Spain, your duty will be to see that the Spanish squadron does not leave the Asiatic coast, and then offensive operations in Philippine Islands. Keep *Olympia* until further orders. Roosevelt.

"I believe," Senator Lodge wrote, several years later, "he was never again permitted to be the acting Secretary. But the deed was done. The wise word of readiness had been spoken and was not recalled."

Once the war actually had begun the Senator became one of the busiest men in Washington. Each afternoon a group of correspondents would congregate in his committee room and discuss with him the progress and the conduct of the struggle. Senator Lodge referred to this select group as his "Board of Strategy." But in the press gallery they were referred to by a phrase that was to become famous in another respect thirty-four years later — the "brain trust." Throughout the war they met almost every day, and when the group later broke up Senator Lodge presented each of the "brain trusters" with a gold stickpin, bearing the golden eagle from the great American seal.

As usual, there were some members of the Senate who resented the Senator's stiff and snobbish attitude. One day, in the course of a speech, Lodge found occasion to use a Spanish quotation. He did not bother to translate it for the benefit of his less scholarly colleagues. Senator David Turpie of Indiana, no small scholar himself, replied: "The Senator from Massachusetts has seen fit to quote Spanish. I will take the liberty of quoting a Spanish proverb that applies to him: 'Pigmies stuffed and placed on Alps are pigmies still.'"

As soon as war was declared Roosevelt resigned from the Navy Department, ordered a uniform from Brooks Brothers, and went dashing off to form his troop of Rough Riders, exactly as he had told Senator Lodge he would do months before. Senator Lodge's son-in-law, Augustus P. Gardner, also received a commission and went to Cuba, and young Bay, who had spent the winter arranging his poems and acting as his father's secretary, joined the Navy.

Lodge was elated by the war. He was jubilant over the battle of Manila Bay, which he instantly recognized as an act of supreme importance. In that outburst America had suddenly emerged as an imperial power. Had he not helped plan for that day? Now the great thing was to keep the islands at all costs. He was determined that they must be ours under the treaty of peace. "The American flag is up," he said, "and it must stay."

"We hold the other side of the Pacific, and the value to this country is almost beyond imagination," Senator Lodge wrote Henry White in London.

Nervous lest pressure might be brought to bear upon the

administration to withdraw from the Philippines at the close of the war he made it his uppermost duty to fight for their retention. He had won a great victory in the annexation of Hawaii, which came about easily soon after the battle of Manila Bay. If he had his way we would soon own at least Manila and Luzon Island. And, of course, Porto Rico and Cuba would be ours in trust. He was sanguine of victory. As he wrote Theodore, then in Cuba, "the whole policy of annexation is growing rapidly under the irresistible pressure of events."

One salutary effect of the war was England's changed attitude towards the United States. The bellicosity of the German Kaiser, of course, had something to do with this; but our emergence in force upon the far Pacific had probably just as much. The lasting alliance of Great Britain and the United States was now being formed. Often as he had twisted the lion's tail in the past, Lodge realized now the value of such an alliance. Shortly after the destruction of Cervera's fleet and the capture of Santiago, when speaking of the fruits of the war, he said: —

"One of the most important is the friendly relations which have been established with England. Another is the expulsion of Spain from this hemisphere. Another is our entrance into the Pacific by the annexation of Hawaii and our securing a foothold at last in the East. . . . Lastly we have risen to be one of the great world powers, and I think we have made an impression on Europe that will be lasting. We are certainly going to have a very powerful Navy."

Congress had recessed the day after the Senate had accepted the annexation of Hawaii. Lodge spent the summer at Nahant and at Tuckernuck. Gus Gardner returned from his fighting in Porto Rico suffering from malaria; son Bay was discharged honorably from the Navy with the rank of ensign; Theodore was soon to be back in New York carrying

178

on his two campaigns — one for the governorship, which he won; and the other for a Medal of Honor from the War Department, which, in spite of all that Senator Lodge could do, he lost.

In the meantime the greatest problem facing the administration was the disposition of the Philippine Islands. It was generally agreed that the least the United States could be expected to ask was the retention of a harbor there to serve as a Far Eastern naval base. This was all that Secretary Day advised. The rest of McKinley's cabinet was divided on the question. When John Hay sent the word from London that Britain favored American ownership it was decided to leave the matter to the commissioners. The terms of the protocol signed August 12, however, ceded Porto Rico and other West Indian islands and another island in the Ladrones (Guam) to the United States, and allowed the United States to occupy Manila until the treaty of peace should determine the "control, disposition, and government of the Philippines."

On the whole the peace terms were acceptable to Senator Lodge, although as an alternative he had an ingenious scheme. He wanted the United States to take all the Philippine Islands at the start. Then the United States should retain Luzon, the most valuable, containing, as it did, Manila, which, as he told Roosevelt, was "the great prize, and the thing which will give us the Eastern trade." The other islands he would then trade to England in exchange for "the Bahamas and Jamaica and the Danish islands, which I think we should be entitled to ask her to buy and turn over to us." Secretary Day, to whom he broached this idea shortly before the signing of the protocol, was not in the least impressed by the ambitious plan.

Senator Lodge was fully prepared to see that the treaty passed the Senate. During the fall Congressional campaign, when President McKinley had openly urged election of Republicans so that the conclusion of the treaty might be made easier, Lodge had told the Republican State Convention in Massachusetts: —

"If we give a victory to his political opponents, we say not only to the United States but we say to the world . . . that the people of the United States have repudiated the results of the war and the man who has led it victoriously and is now leading us back to peace. . . ."

A few days later, in another campaign speech, he stressed the status of the President as the "constitutional representative" in the making of the peace. There is only one man, he said, who has to deal with "the extent to which we should go in the new policies involved in the war — that is the President of the United States. I have faith in him. I believe in his Americanism, and as the Constitution has charged him with this great duty, I, as one American citizen, am prepared to stand back and allow the constitutional representative to deal with it in the face of Europe and the world, and to settle it, and it is my desire, and I should think it should be the duty of every patriot, to stand behind him and to hold up his hands and not to cross him."

Although the treaty was not to be submitted to the Senate until January 4, 1899, Senator Lodge, a constitutional worrier, was already disturbed over its fate. Three days before it actually was signed he warned Theodore Roosevelt that trouble was brewing.

"How serious, I do not know," he wrote, "but I confess I cannot think calmly of the rejection of that Treaty by a little more than one-third of the Senate. It would be a repudiation of the President and humiliation of the whole country in the eyes of the world. . . ."

At that time he feared mostly the opposition of the Southern Democrats. He might well have feared his own senior

180

Senator from Massachusetts, George Frisbie Hoar, who behind his bland, his guileless, his cherubic countenance hid
an abiding passion for decency and human rights. Henry
Adams, who saw much of Lodge at this time (the day before Congress convened Lodge and Hay sat for an hour in
Adams's parlor "talking Senate and Treaty, and dreary Senatorial drivel"), said that at the start Lodge had "figured
out the defeat of the treaty." He at least was prepared for
a bitter fight.

From January 4 to February 6 the treaty proper was debated in executive, or secret, session, a procedure which
Senator Lodge found easy enough to justify. "The discussion . . ." he told the Senate, "is being conducted, and to
my mind properly conducted, behind closed doors, for there
is much that must be said affecting other nations and other
people which could not with propriety be said in public; but the treaty itself has been made public, and the
debate upon these resolutions, taking a wide range, has
covered, so far as could be fittingly done in open session,
the broad question of policy involved in the ratification of
the treaty."

At about this time Rudyard Kipling, who had been Lodge's
guest upon more than one occasion in Washington, published "The White Man's Burden." "Rather poor poetry, but
good sense from the expansion standpoint," thought Roosevelt when he sent Lodge an advance copy. Lodge thought
it better poetry, apart from "the sense of the verses," than
the Governor of New York did. It was gray-haired old Ben
Tillman who first read the poem to the Senate — as an argument against foisting upon the Filipinos a civilization
not suited to them and which they did not want. Not long
thereafter the phrase "the white man's burden" was taken
into our language. It inspired Mr. Dooley, while reading his
paper, to suggest as slogans for Senator Lodge: "Take up th'

white man's burden and hand it to the coons," and "Hands across th' sea and into somewan's pocket."

Senator Lodge was not so much worried by the verbal attacks as a less sensitive man might have been. He was honest in his stand. "The opponents of the treaty have placed their opposition on such high and altruistic grounds that I have preferred to meet them there." Therefore he would rather not discuss "the enormous material benefits to our trade, our industries, and our labor dependent upon a right settlement of this question, both directly and indirectly. For this reason I have not touched upon the commercial advantages to the country involved in the question of these islands, or the far greater question of the markets of China, of which we must have our share for the benefits of the working men."

Lodge and Senator Aldrich of Rhode Island guided the treaty over its rough waters. They had much to contend with, including a motion for public debate on the treaty itself. They managed to muster enough votes to defeat this suggestion, however. They also had the unsolicited support of William Jennings Bryan, who came on at the last minute to support ratification, whether for partisan reasons or for higher motives. Fifteen Democrats, Populists, and independents finally joined with the Republican majority, and, by a vote of 57 to 27, or one vote above the constitutional two-thirds requirement, the treaty was passed. The only two Republicans who voted against the treaty were Senators Hoar of Massachusetts and Hale of Maine.

Two days later Senator Lodge wrote to Theodore: —

Until the fight was over I did not realize what a strain it had been, but for half an hour after the vote was announced I felt exactly as if I had been struggling up the side of a mountain and as if there was not an ounce more of exertion left in any muscle of my body.

And well he might. It had been his fight. As he said of Aldrich and himself: "We were down in the engine room and do not get the flowers, but we did make the ship move." It was he, and not Chairman Davis of the Foreign Relations Committee, who kept the daily score on how the vote appeared to be going. Each day, too, he consulted with President McKinley. No wonder he wrote, "It was the closest, hardest fight I have ever known, and probably we shall not see another in our time when there was so much at stake."

XIV

The Wily One

"Cabot smiles because he has got his re-election, and all the world knows how great and good he is." So wrote Henry Adams in one of his chatty and catty letters to Elizabeth Cameron in the early winter of 1899. Cabot had good reason to smile. He had been re-elected almost as a matter of course by a strictly party vote of 190 to 72. He was a little annoyed because one Republican from the Springfield district had the temerity to vote against him, but this defection was offset by the support of two gold Democrats. When Theodore heard about the single anti-Lodge vote (it was cast by "a disciple of the *Springfield Republican,*" Lodge explained) he hoped that Dear Cabot would see that the renegade was made to understand "that the weak and silly variety of traitor is not particularly encouraged in the Bay State."

The friendship between the Governor of New York and the Senator from Massachusetts was at full flood. Nobody was ever more conscious of his own political potentialities than Theodore Roosevelt was at this time. In July 1899, he attended a reunion of the Rough Riders in New Mexico and, as he was quick to inform Lodge, then vacationing in Europe, at every station at which the train stopped he was "received by dense throngs exactly as if I had been a presidential candidate." Senator Lodge had already suggested that he utilize his unquestionable personal popularity and seek the nomination for the Vice Presidency. At first Theodore was inclined to follow this advice, even if Mrs. Roosevelt was opposed. It was not too easy a problem to solve. Should he remain as Governor, or try to become a Senator, or seek to get on the ticket with McKinley? He had never known a "hurrah to endure five years" and 1904 was definitely in his mind, as he confessed to Cabot. What should he do?

The letters that passed between the two men during the summer of 1899 were dominated by the subject. By the time Senator Lodge had returned to his duties in Washington in December, his opinion as to the wisdom of Theodore's taking the Vice Presidency had not changed. Even though he found that most people felt that Theodore would be foolish to follow that course, Lodge stuck to his guns. "I can put it most tersely," he wrote, "by saying that if I were a candidate for the Presidency I would take the Vice-Presidency in a minute at this juncture. Of course I may be all wrong, and I am not going in the least to push my opinion on you." But in the next sentence the "evil genius," as Roosevelt's friends so often called Lodge, became his wily self and recalled: "I did not hesitate to urge you to take the Assistant Secretaryship of the Navy, or the Police Commissionership of New York, but this is a very different matter."

Obviously disappointed in Roosevelt's hesitancy Lodge added: "When a man is candidate for the Presidency, no friend, however close, has the right to urge him to follow a course in the slightest degree against his own judgment. In such a very momentous matter a man himself must be sole judge." He thereupon promised to step out of the picture, resigned to the fact that Roosevelt had decided to remain as Governor. He would urge him no more. Let him make up his own mind. He could have the Vice Presidency for the asking. His re-election as Governor was assured. "I feel very sanguine about your future," Lodge said, "and I shall work along the line you prefer just as vigorously as if you were pursuing some other which I might think more favorable."

Theodore agreed the Vice Presidency was an "honorable place" but still it was one in which there was not much for a young man to do. And so he stalled along, never letting the matter get far from his mind. He next toyed with the idea of becoming the first Governor General of the Philippines or perhaps Secretary of War. Meanwhile Lodge was quietly playing with his latest toy; he conferred with Senator Platt, talked with others, and did not restrain himself from keeping after Roosevelt.

In mid-December he wrote: —

He [Platt] agreed with me that you had merely to say the word to have the V.P., so you see I am no dreamer on that point. Now think this well over. I am not going to urge you, but things are so shaping themselves that the V.P. is becoming stronger and more desirable for you than I had thought possible.

Theodore, however, did not trust Platt, even with Dear Cabot on hand to act as his protector. He surmised, and not without reason, that Platt was again plotting to get him out of Albany and to bury him in Washington. He also was inclined to take seriously his Western political friends, who were opposed to the idea. By January 1900, he had about made up his mind to run for Governor again and then resign to take the Philippine job, which Cabot assured him he could easily procure.

Late that month Senator Lodge talked the situation over with McKinley and hastened to tell Roosevelt that "the time has come when you should make up your mind whether to refuse to be the candidate for Vice President and run again for Governor of New York, or let your name be brought forward for the second place on the national ticket and remain quiescent in regard to it — which of course would be taken as a willingness to accept it." Again he said it was entirely up to Roosevelt, he would not urge him one way or the other, but still "the trend of events is steadily making your acceptance more desirable."

Roosevelt found one excuse after another. He could not afford it was his latest cry, but even as he wrote that he was weakening. "You are the only man whom, in all my life, I have met who has repeatedly and in every way done for me what I could not do for myself, and what nobody else could do, and done it in a way that merely makes me glad to be under obligation to you."

Senator Lodge on receipt of this letter hastened to assure Roosevelt that it wasn't the Vice Presidency for the Vice Presidency's sake that he was urging on his friend. He saw it merely as the steppingstone to the Presidency, or, if Theodore preferred, the Philippines. He even drew a seductive picture of the latter, as an obvious sop to Theodore's vanity, and he pooh-poohed Theodore's idea of not being able to live on the Vice President's salary of $8000 a year. The trend of events, he repeated, made it almost impossible for Roosevelt to decline. Lodge, at this juncture, undoubtedly thought he had won the reluctant Theodore over, and perhaps he had until Mrs. Roosevelt again intervened and convinced him that the inactivity of the post would be bad for him. He was too young, he would chafe at being a figurehead, he would be bored. With mutual expressions of love and fidelity Roosevelt and Lodge exchanged their views and Cabot reluctantly bowed to Theodore and Edith Roosevelt's views. Or so it seemed.

By April, however, Senator Lodge was back at the attack with all the wile at his command. He had not given up hope. He wrote Roosevelt several letters of advice, urging him not to go to the convention as a delegate because he just *might* be nominated and how then could he refuse? "If you stay away with your absolute declination," he said, "which you have already put out, I do not think you will be nominated." That drew the answer. ". . . I did *not* say that I would not under any circumstances accept the Vice Presidency!" Theodore snapped.

At this point Theodore recalled that Silas Wright had refused the nomination of Vice President on the ticket with Polk after he had been nominated, "came back and ran for Governor and was elected by a larger majority than that by which Polk carried the State." To this ingenious parallel Lodge, the historian, had a ready answer: —

I have forgotten the incident of Silas Wright but let me call your attention to the fact that he was never President, whereas Van Buren was!

Senator Lodge had done his work well. Almost alone, he had "softened up" Roosevelt, and won him around. Tom Platt and Boss Quay were to do the rest.

Occupied though he was with Roosevelt's affairs there were many other matters to claim his attention. For Cabot Lodge was, in the months between the closing of the Spanish War and the second election of William McKinley, "more important than ever," as Henry Adams expressed it with his usual irony. As a sideline he wrote a popular "history" of the Spanish War, receiving $4500 from *Scribner's Magazine* for six chapters. (Roosevelt thought it gave the best picture of the Rough Riders of any book of its kind.) He also finished his two-volume *Story of the Revolution,* which caused one astute reviewer to say: "When he began to write it was all the fashion to curse England, and he cursed her soundly. When he ended everyone was falling on England's neck, and he fell, blubbering with the rest."

Although Henry Adams, growing daily more querulous

was still friendly, he was becoming less and less satisfied with the conduct of his old friend. Adams and his crony, John Hay, hoped that McKinley would appoint William W. Rockhill, who once had explored Tibet in disguise and who now was wasting away in the State Department, as Librarian of Congress. In discussing the situation one day with Mrs. Cameron, Adams gave one of the most unforgettable pictures of the scholar in politics that he or anyone ever penned: —

. . . You know how hard I have been trying to get Rockhill into the Library. Hay strongly pressed him, and was supported by all the best interests in the cabinet, and by the President's own judgment. But Secretary Long[1] inspired a beaten Massachusetts Congressman named [Samuel June] Barrows to apply for the place, and Barrows invoked with more than usual violence the usual political machinery. . . . This alone should have excluded him, for Libraries ought not to be political jobs; but of course Long and Barrows invoked their Senators and, as usual, our noble statesman Cabot went every day to the White House to press on McKinley an appointment which he knew to be exceedingly unfit, and which he did not want to have made, and which he knew would disgust his own wife and children as well as Hay and me and the Senate. I never saw Cabot more apologetic; it was so bad that I retired into total silence; but you can imagine Hay's comments. Finally the President followed our wishes so far as to offer Barrows the Greek mission, with a view to shifting Rockhill to the Library. Barrows refused. Then the President yielded, and sent his name to the Senate, where Cabot now hopes it will be rejected!

As it turned out, Cabot had his wish. He and the other New England Senators suddenly discovered that Mr. Barrows, a former Unitarian divine, who had started his career

[1] John Davis Long, Secretary of the Navy and former Governor of Massachusetts, was also president of the Board of Overseers of Harvard. Adams called him "one of the cheapest of our cheap Yankee politicians."

189

as Secretary of State Seward's secretary and who for many years had been editing the *Christian Register,* was not qualified to be a librarian. Senator Lodge opposed confirmation on these grounds on the floor of the Senate. Herbert Putnam, reorganizer of the Boston Public Library, was given the post; Rockhill went to Greece; and Mr. Barrows devoted the rest of his life to prison reform in New York.

In spite of the row over Rockhill in March 1899, the Lodges and Adamses set off again for a European holiday. They visited Paris, Rome, Sicily. "Cabot rattles us through, on time, tourists such as Cook should love," Adams remarked. His Senate duties had tired Lodge and this year he spent the longest time he had ever spent away from the country. He did not return until late in September. When he arrived in Boston he found his mother, a woman of great vitality and constitution, showing at last the effects of her age. He spent several days with her at the old house on Beacon Street. The old lady adored her Senator son and followed his career with maternal admiration. Her keen Boston mind was still undimmed when she died the following March.

Senator Lodge returned to Washington for the first session of the Fifty-sixth Congress in December 1899. Two months later President McKinley sent to the Senate the newly signed Hay-Pauncefote Treaty and once more the Senator was in his element.

The treaty's terms allowed the United States to build and maintain a canal anywhere across the Isthmus, but it did not allow the United States to fortify or even to blockade it. It was always to be open, in peace or war, to vessels of both peace and war of all nations. At once there were loud and understandable objections to these terms. Theodore Roosevelt was quick to assail them. The clause forbidding us to close the canal in times of war would make us more vulnerable to attack than if we did not have a canal; the clause requiring adherence of other powers was contrary to the Monroe Doctrine. Senator Lodge at first approved and even openly applauded the treaty. He was ready to support it, even guide it through the Senate. Roosevelt's public attack came as quite a shock to him. He was torn between his friendship for Roosevelt and Secretary Hay. As Henry Adams maliciously put it, "Teddy appears disposed to paddle his own canoe and upset the machine. Cabot is in deadly terror."

The year 1900 was an election year and a Senator, even if he were not seeking re-election, had to be cautious. President McKinley, however, did not throw his weight behind Secretary Hay. This made it easier for Lodge. After taking one look at the Irish and another at the German vote, the Senator made his decision. He deserted Hay and declared against the treaty. Hay bore the brunt of the attacks and grew so angry over Lodge's defection, and the general assumption that he had allowed the British to put something over on him, that he twice verged on resigning his post. Only McKinley's personal plea restrained him. He called Lodge timid, accused him of shouting always "with what seems the voice of the crowd." Hay did not understand politicians. He was hurt when Lodge "was the first to flop."

The Senate adjourned in March without a final vote. In the interim Lodge issued a statement in which he reiterated his theory that a treaty is not a treaty when sent to the Senate, but merely a project for consideration by that august body. This greatly annoyed Hay, who despairingly said that, if adhered to, this attitude would make all negotiations with other nations impossible.

The amended treaty was ratified shortly after the opening of Congress. Senator Lodge thought that Great Britain should accept it in the new form. His attitude was that the original treaty had made a promise which the United States had no right to make. "We engage to keep the canal open in time of war as in time of peace, and thereby to allow an enemy's fleet, if we were at war, to pass unmolested through the canal if they could get within the three-mile limit," he said. "We either meant to keep that promise, or we meant, under stress of war, to break it. In either event I was against it."

As far as public opinion went, Senator Lodge declared, "the American people mean to have the canal and mean to control it." The only way England could prevent her would be by going to war. And "it would be ruinous [to England] if she did make war on us." Therefore, why not let us build the canal under the terms of the amended treaty? He warned that if Great Britain did not accept the amendments, Americans would suspect some sinister British motive and would hasten their demand for the canal. Lodge's opinions were placed before the proper British authorities by Henry White. But the British press and public attacked the amendments and the treaty was never accepted by England. Contemporary opinion was on Lodge's side and later events showed that he was right. At the time, however, his motives were suspect. It was said that he and other Senators had been influenced against the original treaty through pressure brought upon them by the great transcontinental railroads, which feared the competitive threat of a canal. This Lodge vigorously denied.

Secretary Hay, embittered and mistrustful of the Senate, went on to negotiate another treaty and Senator Lodge, convinced of the rectitude of his course, and not at all abashed at Adams's charge that he cut Hay's throat and "probably, within a twelve-month . . . will go back on Teddy," went to the Republican Convention in Philadelphia.

Governor Roosevelt, wearing his "acceptance hat" — the

sombrero of the Rough Riders of 1898 — was in attendance. He listened with enthusiasm as Chairman Lodge gave the keynote speech, which, in the absence of any great issue, was a bold challenge of the Democrats to battle, and, as usual, a lengthy recital of the accomplishments of the Republican Party. Mark Hanna was there, in telephone communication with the President, and after many consultations he agreed that Roosevelt, the "wild man," was acceptable. Boss Platt and Matt Quay, the Pennsylvania boss, worked together to get him the nomination. Those "in the know" said it was only because they wanted to shelve him, get him out of New York. Roosevelt felt this way too, in spite of the protestations of his friend Cabot Lodge. When all were agreed he was nominated. The demonstration that followed was a noisy, heartfelt tribute to his personal popularity. He beamed and waved his hat and his teeth flashed in the bright June sun.

Winthrop Chanler, of the Astor clan, whom both Lodge and Roosevelt knew intimately and called Winty, dropped Roosevelt a note: —

Long ago, when you first got the nomination for Governor, the astute Cabot told me that he wanted you to be Vice-President and enumerated all the advantages therein for you and the country. The Wily One has won the day, in spite of your titanic struggles to disappoint him. It is the first time you have been beat, old man. Let the thought that it took the delegates from every state of the Union to do so, console you.[2] I am glad because your being on the ticket makes a Republican victory almost a certainty. . . .

From Nahant, toward the end of June, the Wily One sent Roosevelt a long letter of advice. "We must not permit the President, or any of his friends, who are, of course, in con-

[2] The Massachusetts delegation, under Lodge's control, voted unanimously for Roosevelt.

trol of the campaign, to imagine that we want to absorb the leadership and the glory." Roosevelt must appear as McKinley's leading advocate and make this clear in everything he said. "Fortunately his policies on the great questions are our policies . . . and I am anxious that your advocacy of him should appear in everything you say. My purpose in this is to secure by every righteous means the confidence and support for you of the President and of all his large following . . ."

Writing in his Nahant library, his keen blue eyes looking out across the Atlantic, the Wily One went on: —

This is going to be of immense importance to us four years hence, and that is why I desire that you should appear, not only during the campaign but after the election, as the President's next friend, as Hobart[3] was. There is today no one who could stand against you for a moment for the nomination of the Presidency, but no one can tell what will happen in four years. I believe myself that by judicious conduct we can have it just as surely within our grasp four years hence as it would be today, but we should make no mistakes.

And then, lest Roosevelt become "too vain," he quoted from the *Springfield Republican*, which said that "the Republican party was now given over to the corrupt materialism of Hanna, the cynical political ethics of Lodge, and the swashbuckler fervor of Roosevelt. . . ."

When the votes were counted McKinley and Roosevelt carried Massachusetts over the striving Bryan by a majority of 80,000. Murray Crane was elected governor, again without making a speech, and ten of the thirteen Congressmen elected were of the Republican faith. There was, however, one ominous note that November: Boston turned in a plu-

[3] Garret Augustus Hobart, 1844–1899, Vice President from 1896 to 1899, whose death in office made it necessary to find a Vice Presidential candidate in 1900.

194

rality of 10,000 votes for Bryan, thus returning, for the first time in many years, to the Democratic column.

The winter, on the whole, was uneventful. The chairmanship of the Foreign Relations Committee fell vacant at the death of Cushman Kellogg Davis that year and Senator Lodge tried vainly to get the post he had coveted so long. Shelby Moore Cullom, who had been the law partner of John Hay's father, could not be "induced to get out of the way." Although Senator Lodge knew that "everybody wants me to have it on both sides of the Senate, in the Committee, and I think throughout the press," he had to bow to Mr. Cullom's seniority rights.[4] Secretary Hay soon came to depend upon Senator Cullom, for whom Lodge developed a deep dislike and at whom, according to the observant Adams, he would sneer "every ten minutes, in all companies."

As soon as his Senatorial duties were done Senator and Mrs. Lodge, and of course Henry Adams, fled to Europe once more. They went on to Warsaw and then on a wearisome trip in slow trains to St. Petersburg and Moscow. After Moscow the party broke up. Adams went to Sweden and the Lodges settled down in Paris. It was there that the Senator received the stunning news of the assassination of President McKinley.

He first read of it in the *Paris Herald*, but the news was meager. The American Embassy also lacked details. No definite word of what had really happened in Buffalo was forthcoming until Theodore Roosevelt thought of his absent friend and sent him a cable. Roosevelt's first word was reassuring, and Lodge wrote him a delightful letter, quoting some of the amusing things the Paris press said about

[4] By rights the chairmanship should have gone to Senator Frye of Maine, the oldest Republican on the committee, but he would not accept it.

Roosevelt, and urging him to guard himself well against all lurking anarchists.

Disappointed in not having received promotion to the chairmanship of the Foreign Relations Committee, Senator Lodge might well have coveted a place in President Roosevelt's cabinet. His son-in-law, Augustus P. Gardner, who had taken an increasing interest in politics since his return from the Spanish-American War, wrote to him at once, urging him to return home. At least two other friends also wanted him to hasten back. There was considerable newspaper speculation, during the week that followed McKinley's death, over who was to replace John Hay. Mr. Hay, the reporters intimated, was to be dropped because of his ideas on foreign policy which did not jibe with Roosevelt's. Anyone remembering Roosevelt's blast at the Hay-Pauncefote Treaty, and Senator Lodge's desertion of Hay at that time, could hardly be blamed for taking the report seriously, but Lodge's letter to Roosevelt, written from Paris on September 19, 1901, said: —

All sorts of reports as to the Cabinet are in the newspapers here, the one this morning being that Hay is going to stay. I am sure I hope so for then you will have both him and Root.[5]

Lodge made no apparent effort to get the post, refusing to hasten home. He appears to have had no further correspondence on the subject. Roosevelt kept Hay in the State Department.

Senator Lodge arrived in New York early in October and took the first train to Washington. He went at once to the White House. The two old friends talked over the entire situation late into the night. The Senator prescribed caution, as usual, and warned the President to stick closely to McKin-

[5] Elihu Root, Secretary of War in McKinley's second cabinet. He became Roosevelt's Secretary of State in 1905.

ley's policies. They argued over the first Presidential message that Roosevelt was preparing. Senator Lodge was afraid that his friend was perhaps a little too rhetorical in one or two places. He was most insistent that Roosevelt say or do nothing that would in any way jeopardize the second Hay-Pauncefote Treaty, which would be the Senate's first important business when Congress reconvened. He then returned to Nahant to prepare for the work that lay ahead.

XV

"Ever Yours"

"ROOSEVELTS are born and never can be taught," Adams wrote in his sixty-seventh year, "but Lodge was a creature of teaching — Boston incarnate — the child of his local parentage; and while his ambition led him to be more, the intent, though virtuous, was . . . restless. An excellent talker, a voracious reader, a ready wit, an accomplished orator, with a clear mind and a powerful memory, he could never feel perfectly at ease, whatever leg he stood on, but shifted, sometimes with painful strain of temper, from one sensitive muscle to another, uncertain whether to pose as uncompromising Yankee, or a pure American, or a patriot in the still purer atmosphere of Irish, Germans, and Jews; or a scholar and historian of Harvard College."

So was Henry Cabot Lodge painted, near the turn of the century, by a consummate artist who had studied his subject for fully thirty years. But there was more to the portrait, finer lines to be placed on with a sable brush to sharpen the general mass: —

English to the last fibre of his thought — saturated with English literature, English traditions, English taste — revolted by every vice and by most virtues of Frenchman and German, or any other continental standards, but at home and happy among the vices and extravagances of Shakespeare [1] — standing first on the social, then on the political foot; now worshipping, now ban-

---

[1] Senator Lodge never traveled without a thin volume of Shakespeare tucked in his coat pocket.

ning; shocked by the wanton display of immorality, but practising the license of political usage; sometimes bitter, often genial, always intelligent — Lodge had the singular merit of interesting. The usual statesmen flocked in swarms, like crows, black and monotonous. Lodge's plumage was varied, and, like his flight, harked back to race. He betrayed the consciousness that he and his people had a past, if they dared but avow it, and might have a future, if they could but divine it.

Even though he had now attained the dignity of two re-elections he was not immune to the scoffing that he had endured when his Harvard accent had been mocked in the cloakrooms of the House. One day, while he was acting as Roosevelt's spokesman in the Senate, old Ben Tillman, who admired him greatly deep in his heart and who requested, as he lay dying, that Lodge speak the eulogy at his funeral, could not restrain himself. He launched into such a gale of satire that the Senate was ordered into executive session. The galleries were cleared of an audience that was rocking with laughter and all of Tillman's remarks were expunged from the record. Among the remembered remarks that caused the pandemonium was this: —

"Like the Negro preacher and the telephone artist in the show, who on occasion gets into communication with the White House over the wire and acts as receiver and repeater, a veritable chameleon in his inaccuracy in reproducing White House colors, we have a Senator from Massachusetts, the home of the sacred cod, where the Adamses vote for Douglas and Lodge walks with the Almighty." [2]

[2] Thus, in 1907, did Ben Tillman paraphrase a toast given by "a western man" two years earlier at the 25th anniversary of the class of Harvard '80: —

> Here's to old Massachusetts,
> The home of the sacred cod,
> Where the Adamses vote for Douglas,
> And the Cabots walk with God.

Senator Tillman's description was apt. In all the Senate the President had no more faithful messenger than Senator Lodge. Hardly a day passed, at least during the earlier years of Roosevelt's administration, which did not see the two men in consultation. They rode horseback together in what, thanks to Roosevelt's interest in conservation, later became Rock Creek Park. (Unlike some of those invited by the President, Senator Lodge was an expert horseman. Roosevelt once chuckled: "Cabot didn't mind having the newspapers say he was head of the kitchen cabinet, but he was frantic with fury when they said he was learning to ride so as to go out with me!") The Senator had a door cut into his library and a stairway built from the courtyard of his Massachusetts Avenue home to give direct entrance from the outside, so that the President could call upon him without the formality of using the front door and going through the house. Even when the two did not ride together, Roosevelt as likely as not would pop in for a drink and talk in the late afternoon. Most of Roosevelt's messages were written only after consultation in the Lodge library. Often Mrs. Lodge was present at these discussions. There were few affairs of state to which Nannie Lodge and Edith Roosevelt were not privy.

The Roosevelt administration got under way with Roosevelt's first message to Congress, which was so eminently conservative and yet which appalled the businessmen of the

Three years later, in 1910, John Collins Bossidy at a Midwestern dinner of the Holy Cross College alumni gave the version that is best known: —

And this is good old Boston,
The home of the bean and the cod,
Where the Lowells talk only to Cabots,
And the Cabots talk only to God.

The Tillman episode is from an article by E. M. King, *New York Post*, July 5, 1919.

country who detected in it hints of the radicalism that Mark Hanna had feared. As far as the Senator was concerned its most important passages were those dealing with the second Hay-Pauncefote Treaty, which had been signed November 18, 1901, and was one of the first matters to come before the Senate. As it went to the Foreign Relations Committee it represented a compromise between the first treaty and the Senate amendments, the most vital difference being the omission of any article prohibiting fortification of the proposed Isthmian canal by the United States.

President Roosevelt was vigorously behind the new treaty. Senator Lodge, who took the credit for the defeat of the first treaty, was ready to see that it was quickly accepted. In the January 1902 issue of *Scribner's Magazine* he explained at length that the Senate had the constitutional right to advise the opening of a negotiation or advise against it, that it had the right to amend treaties, and that no treaty should be considered made until the Senate had approved it. He observed that Lord Lansdowne, the British Foreign Secretary, did not "seem to have realized that the Senate could properly continue the negotiations begun by Mr. Hay and Lord Pauncefote by offering new or modified propositions to His Majesty's government." Senator Lodge's belief was that the Senate had the full right to share in any or all diplomatic negotiations it wanted to. When the editor of the *Nation* read this amazing article, which in effect said the Secretary of State was the errand boy of the Senate, he wrote: "Diplomacy is at best a leisurely affair: this plan would make it a veritable dead march."

This time there was to be no dead march. England, as Lodge pointed out, had made all the concessions which the American critics of the first treaty had demanded. With Lodge as his able lieutenant, the Senators were rounded up by Roosevelt, lectured, and sent back to the Senate to carry out the administration's wish. On February 21, 1902, seventy-two Senators voted for the treaty; six, whom Roosevelt called "the irreclaimable cranks," voted against it. The way was cleared for a canal to be built by the United States, policed by it, and (at least by implication) fortified by it. John Hay, Cabot Lodge, Teddy Roosevelt, Elihu Root, were well pleased.

With the treaty out of the way Senator Lodge devoted most of the time to the Philippines. Grim stories had been coming back from the strife-torn islands. From disinterested men there came a demand for an investigation which could not be ignored, for the charges, seemingly well substantiated, concerned outrages perpetrated upon the natives by American troops during the suppression of the rebellion. It was alleged that whole villages had been needlessly burned, that native women had been raped by American soldiers, and that scores of natives had been forced to undergo the "water cure" — that same horrible form of torture inflicted by the Japanese upon American prisoners.

Under pressure, Senator Lodge introduced the bill calling for an investigation and forthwith the Senate appointed a committee. Since Senator Lodge, as chairman of the Philippine Committee of the Senate, was considered the Senate's leading expert on the Islands (which he had never seen), he was made chairman. Its next most important member was Senator Albert J. Beveridge, the cocky Indiana expansionist who had twice visited the Philippines.

The work of the Lodge committee does not constitute one of the brighter chapters of American history. The hearings began in January and continued until June. Among the witnesses called were Governor General William H. Taft, General Arthur MacArthur, Admiral Dewey, and a host of soldiers. Senator Beveridge set himself up as counsel for the defense. Senator Lodge, as presiding officer, left most of the questioning to Beveridge when witnesses were brought to the large and handsomely furnished room where the committee met. (For many years thereafter Senator Lodge made this room practically his private office.) There were no rules of evidence at the hearing. Senator Lodge had all the power of a judge and there was no question where his sympathies lay.

In spite of Senator Beveridge's skillful maneuvering in this frankly partisan investigation, the able Democratic Senators, who, in a sense, were the prosecutors, were able to prove that many of the alleged outrages had occurred, but not as often as had originally been charged. The Democrats had hoped to make a good campaign issue of the investigation, but the American people were tired of hearing about the Philippines, which, after all, were populated by the little brown men thousands of miles away, and so that effort failed. In fact, through Lodge's and Beveridge's obstructive tactics, it was made to look as though the Democrats had attacked the integrity of the American Army and the honor of the United States. That Lodge suppressed much of the most damaging evidence is admitted even by Claude G. Bowers, Beveridge's friendly biographer.

Almost as soon as Senator Lodge got back to Nahant early in June he heard that Associate Justice Horace Gray had resigned from the Supreme Court because of a serious illness. He at once sent word to Roosevelt that he had a candidate in mind as Gray's successor. As a matter of fact, Justice Gray had not then resigned, but he was on the verge of doing so. Senator Lodge's choice was the Chief Justice of the Massachusetts Supreme Court, his lifelong friend, Oliver Wendell Holmes. Lodge's letters to Roosevelt on the subject were persuasive. The President approved of Holmes mainly because he felt that the liberal-minded justice would be on his side as Roosevelt carried out his daring campaigns against the trusts and the malefactors of great wealth. "The ablest lawyers and greatest judges are men whose past has naturally brought them into close relationship with the wealthiest and most powerful clients," Roosevelt wrote to Lodge, "and I am glad when I can find a judge who has been able to preserve his aloofness of mind so as to keep his broad humanity of feeling and his sympathy for the class from which he has not drawn his clients."

He sought assurance from Lodge that Holmes was "in entire sympathy with our view, that is with your view and mine," before he offered him the appointment. These assurances Lodge was able to give him. Holmes was appointed and Roosevelt was overjoyed at the popularity of his choice. He was, however, to regret it before long. Mr. Holmes, as it turned out, was able to keep his remarkable mind aloof, even from the persuasions of Theodore Roosevelt.

Up till now President Roosevelt had not deviated seriously from the policy of his predecessor, but as time passed and it became necessary to have an "issue" for the 1904 campaign he began more and more to wield the big stick. The object of his attacks was the "trusts." Senator Lodge was going to find it difficult to follow his friend along this track. During the summer the Senator more than once mentioned the "heejous monsters," as Mr. Dooley called the trusts, in the many speeches he made throughout New England. At Portland, Maine, he expressed his philosophy towards the problem: —

"In endeavoring to punish trusts by removing tariff duties on any articles they happen to make, you are going to punish many other people besides, and you are going to punish, worst of all, the people engaged in these industries. . . . To undertake to destroy them and bring them down by rash legislation would be to bring on at the present time the most disastrous panic in the business world and throughout the country that can be imagined. We forget the thousands of men who are employed and at work for these trusts who are getting their living out of them and that when you wreck them you throw that labor out."

Senator Lodge was a little agitated about the direction his friend in the White House was taking. But as the summer drew to a close, a summer of intense political activity, during which Lodge and Roosevelt traveled across Massachusetts, another even more dangerous issue arose to strike alarm in Lodge's breast. As he wrote to Dear Theodore: —

Trusts, thanks to you, we can manage. . . . Tariff revision we can discuss. I do not fear it. But the rise in the price of coal we cannot argue with.

Senator Lodge was one of the first to realize that political disaster lurked in the strike in the anthracite coal fields that had begun in the spring. He sent frantic letters to the White House.

By the first week in November if the strike does not stop and coal begins to go down we shall have an overturn. I am no alarmist but the indications now on this alarm me. I care nothing for the rest. Despite . . . tariffs and trusts I believe we should hold the House and come out all right if it was not for the rising price per ton of coal which we cannot answer because it produces an unreasoning sentiment.

There were other letters, more excited, in which Lodge trembled for fear the administration might have to take the "awful step" of seizing the mines. He urged Roosevelt to do something, *not in public* of course, I know that is out of the question, but by pressing the operators." [3] He offered to do anything he could, or go anywhere Roosevelt wanted him, although he admitted he was "ineffective in such matters as coal barons." He thought there were others better

[3] Lodge's italics.

205

fitted to deal with those gentlemen than he. Roosevelt evidently agreed with him for it was Murray Crane, who had a way with coal barons as well as with ward leaders, whom he called to Washington. The President and the Governor had a long talk, during which Crane told how he as Governor had brought both sides together to settle the Boston teamsters' strike. Not long thereafter Roosevelt, practically by main force, succeeded in getting the operators and the strikers together, and the November elections were saved.

The summer of 1902 was one of the most harrying Senator Lodge had ever experienced. Not only did the coal strike give him sleepless nights, but there was dissension in the party. Eugene N. Foss, who in Lodge's words had taken over "Billy Russell's old platform of free trade in everything Massachusetts buys and protections for all she makes," was causing trouble. Foss won the nomination for Congress, which disturbed Lodge deeply, and he was now attempting to run the State Convention, threatening even to scrap Lodge's platform in favor of his own. Not in years had anyone had the temerity to question Lodge's control. But that the ambitious Foss was a real danger to party harmony there was no denying. Besides, he was an extremely wealthy man, who had made his millions in stock market speculation. Lodge thought he was "mad with pride and vanity." In the end Lodge was to drive him from the party, but in 1902 and for several years to come, Eugene N. Foss was to be a thorn in his side.

Another worry was the political ambition of his son-in-law, Gussie Gardner, who was seeking promotion from the legislature to Congress. Gardner had a scrap on his hands to win the nomination but he won 76 out of 130 delegates and, as Lodge wrote Roosevelt, "If elected as I think he will be he will be of value to you, to the party and to ever yours." Gussie lived in the Sixth District, which was also the home of George von Lengerke Meyer, one of the party's most adroit fund raisers and a member of the National Committee, who had moved to Hamilton after serving in the Massachusetts General Court. Meyer, who deserved well of his party, had political ambitions which he hoped would lead him to the Senate. It was broadly hinted that he had won his present appointment as Ambassador to Italy only through Senator Lodge's intercession and that Lodge had induced President McKinley to select him only in order to remove him as a threat to Gussie's advancement to Congress.

The Republicans, including Gussie, carried the state in November. "If you had not settled the coal strike we should have been washed out," Lodge wrote Roosevelt.

For several years Senator Lodge had been closely following the Alaska Boundary dispute. As early as January, 1899, he had reached the conclusion that "under the Russian treaty they [Great Britain and Canada] have not, as regards the Alaskan boundary question, a leg to stand on. Their whole case is manufactured." He conceded then that there might be reason to give Canada "access to the sea and a free port . . . but no territorial sovereignty." The Senator felt that such a "compromise" ought to satisfy Great Britain.

In the fall of 1899 a temporary boundary line was agreed upon, which pushed the Canadians back fifteen miles from tidewater and kept most of the disputed territory under American jurisdiction. Senator Lodge was pleased because he felt that Canada had been put in her place. When Roosevelt became President he wanted to let sleeping dogs lie, but in the summer of 1902 Sir Wilfrid Laurier, the Prime Minister of Canada, and Governor General Lord Minto intimated that the situation, which Sir Wilfrid felt was dangerous, particularly if more gold was discovered, ought to be cleared up. Roosevelt, when apprised of this, gave Secretary Hay permission to reopen negotiations.

Senator Lodge, well aware that a treaty was in the making, was anxious during the summer of 1902 lest it proceed too fast and interfere with the political situation in Massachusetts. Gloucester, the great fishing port, was in the Congressional district which Gussie Gardner wished to represent. The Senator wanted the ticklish matter of fishing rights separated from any consideration of the Alaskan boundary.

"I wrote this to Mr. Hay," he said to Roosevelt, "but I told him at the same time that it would be impossible for us to sustain the treaty unless it was reasonably satisfactory to the Gloucester people . . . I urged Mr. Hay not to sign the treaty before election. The mere knowledge that the treaty had been signed might turn Gloucester against us and cost us the Congressional district."

A treaty setting up a joint commission of "six impartial jurists of repute," three to be appointed by each side, with no seventh to act as umpire, was signed by Secretary Hay and Lord Herbert, the British Ambassador, on January 23, 1903. There were some objections to it in the Senate but, with Lodge's backing, it was ratified on February 11.

Senator Lodge immediately telephoned the White House to warn the President not to "give any intimation as to whom he is going to appoint." Secretary Hay said that the President "thought it was impossible to get the treaty through the Senate without the earnest and devoted assistance of Lodge and Turner. . . ." [4] Once it was through the Senate, Roosevelt made a gesture of inviting the Supreme Court Justices to act on the commission, but, as he had anticipated, they refused. Thereupon he named the two Senators and Secretary of War Root.

None was an "impartial jurist of repute." Indeed three

[4] Senator George Turner of Washington.

persons of less judicial temperament would have been hard to find. The press roared with critical laughter. In Canada where Lord Alverstone, the Chief Justice of England, A. B. Aylesworth, a noted Ontario lawyer, and Sir Louis Jetté, a former member of the Quebec Supreme Court, had been named to the panel there was much anger. Senator Lodge said this was "largely political," and dismissed it with his customary cynicism.

Secretary Hay, who was pleased with the appointment of Root, wrote: —

Of course, the presence of Lodge on the Tribunal is from many points of view regrettable, and as if the devil were inspiring him, he took the occasion last week to make a speech in Boston, one-half of it filled with abuse of the Canadians and the other half of it filled with attacks on the State Department. He is a clever man and a man of a great deal of force in the Senate, but the infirmity of his mind and character is that he never sees but one subject at a time, and just at present it is the acceptability of his son-in-law to the voters of Gloucester. Of course, you know his very intimate relations with the President, which make it almost impossible that the President should deny him anything he has to give him, and he insisted upon this appointment on the Tribunal.

A few days after the appointment of the three "impartial jurists" Roosevelt sent them a personal and confidential message in which he said that the treaty of 1825 undoubtedly was intended to cut off British access to the sea, and that "in the principle involved there will of course be no compromise." The President, who had been willing enough to let the matter alone a year before, was now greatly excited about it. When the British delayed the meeting he stormed and fumed and threatened to break off with Great Britain and run his own boundary line and then defend it. The tribunal finally got to London in midsummer. There were further delays by the British. Lodge stayed in London from July to mid-October, with only one or two brief visits to the Continent, before a decision was reached. After much cajoling and threatening, mainly through letters carried by Roosevelt's friends who visited England that summer, Lord Alverstone swung to the American side and the case was adjudged in favor of the United States. There were some slight concessions to Great Britain, but on the major issues involved Lodge and his partners triumphed. When the decision was reached the President wrote to Lodge: "You have rendered one of those great substantial benefits to the country the memory of which will last as long as her history lasts," and told him to hurry home. It was already late October and there "has been no ginger in the campaign."

There were reports during the summer months to the effect that Senator Lodge was being considered for the post of chairman of the Republican National Committee. This, however, was not the kind of honor which the Senator desired. He recalled the hard work during the two terms he had served as chairman of the State Committee years before, when he managed the campaign to unseat Ben Butler, and decided he wanted no part of "managing politics." He was a little upset, though, because the newspapers all said he had had no such practical experience. He wanted Mark Hanna to stay on as chairman and suggested that Murray Crane be given a place on the Advisory Committee, where, Lodge felt, he would be of "very great value."

But Mark Hanna was to die in February 1904, and in a way his death brought an era to a close. In September that ancient champion of the dignity of human rights, George Frisbie Hoar, was to go to meet his Puritan fathers, and his seat in the Senate, which he had held since 1877, was filled by Murray Crane, who had been in politics scarcely more than a decade. That spring Henry Cabot Lodge quietly celebrated his fifty-fourth birthday. He had been in Washington without a break for seventeen years. He had stepped into the temple of the Elder Statesmen.

Even Harvard had forgiven its "degenerated son." In 1904, shortly after the nomination of Theodore Roosevelt, the Senator went to Harvard to receive an honorary degree. President Eliot had not proposed it. To the end he looked scornfully at the renegade. But other members of the governing boards voted it. To Eliot, however, went the choice of words to accompany the presentation. With chill reserve he wrote: "Henry Cabot Lodge: Essayist, biographer, member in Congress at 37, now already Senator from Massachusetts, with long vistas of generous service still awaiting him." Who could miss the implications of the final clause? Were they not an unmistakable hint "to do better in the future"? President Eliot, at least, meant them as such.[5]

During Roosevelt's first years in office Senator Lodge had well lived up to his self-selected designation as "Ever Yours." He was to remain faithful to Dear Theodore for some time to come. It was with Lodge's full approval that Roosevelt announced his candidacy for a second and, as he made it clear, a final term in the spring of 1903. As soon as he had let it be known that he was seeking the nomination, President Roosevelt became deeply, almost pathologically, worried over his chances of re-election. To his closest friends he did not hesitate to say how much he feared that the country's powerful financial interests, long the backbone of the Republican Party, would do everything in their power to keep him from returning to the White House. Senator Lodge was quick to reassure him.

There had been a time when Wall Street and State Street distrusted the Wily One. But now they knew that he was

[5] According to Henry James, Eliot's biographer. See *Charles W. Eliot*, by Henry James. 1930. Vol. II, p. 99.

with them, that all his instincts were on their side, however intimate he might be with Roosevelt. Before he sailed for Europe to attend the meetings of the Alaska Boundary Commission he made inquiries to see how Roosevelt stood in the financial quarter. He quickly found that such gentlemen as Charles Jackson, "a broker and State Street man," and Gardiner Lane of Lee Higginson and Company, were admirers of Roosevelt. All they wanted to know was how the President stood regarding labor. When Senator Lodge assured them that Roosevelt was not "entirely given over to the labor side" and that he was wholly ready to "treat the labor men in the same way you would capital if they violate the law," they were greatly relieved. They promised the Senator they would pass the word on to their friends in Chicago, who were worried that in the event of a general railroad strike Roosevelt could not be depended upon.

Wherever Lodge went he found people disturbed because they feared Roosevelt was "wholly with labor, against capital." Senator Lodge, who knew his President well, became a missionary dedicated to disabusing this nonsensical theory. When Judge Fessenden of Greenfield expressed this belief "I told him there was not a word of truth in it," Lodge hastened to write his worried friend, who, at almost that very moment, was cementing his own strange new alliance with the Wall Street crowd.

President Roosevelt kept in close touch with Senator Lodge, whose strength politically was felt throughout New England, and with Murray Crane, who, silently, was becoming almost as great a power day by day. When he worried about the New York situation, where he was seeking the support of B. F. Odell, Platt's successor as boss, he urged Dear Cabot to ask Crane to come and see him as soon as possible. Lodge got in touch with the Whispering Boss, and sent him on, and then told Roosevelt that from then on all he had to do was drop a line to Dalton and Crane would be at his command. From London, in late September, 1903, Lodge, who kept in touch with politics even when abroad, sent the reassuring word that the "Wall Street situation has pretty much subsided."

Roosevelt, of course, swept the country, the magnitude of the landslide amazing even himself. He at once telegraphed to Nahant: "Have swept the country by majorities which astound me. How is Mass. legislature?" There was a good reason for him to ask the question. Senator Lodge was coming up before the legislature in January for re-election and Murray Crane was asking to be sent to take the seat of Senator Hoar. A Republican legislature was necessary. But the question amused the Wily One and he wrote to the White House: —

I could not help smiling at your inquiry. . . . Since 1856 the smallest Republican majority, which was in the year 1891, on joint ballot was forty. Last year we had thirty-one Senators out of forty. This year we shall have thirty-four out of forty, a gain of three. Last year we had one hundred and fifty-four out of two hundred and forty representatives. This year we shall have one hundred and sixty out of two hundred and forty. In other words we have gained three Senators and six Representatives. Your active mind will grasp at once the fact that the Legislature is safely Republican. There is no opposition to me or Crane.

XVI

The Dangerous Rock

SENATOR LODGE was not without his own doubts and alarms concerning his friend in the White House. It would take but little soul searching on his part to see which way to turn if the occasion should arise. Three years previously Henry Adams had warned that "the most dangerous rock on Theodore's coast is Cabot," and he had looked forward to the "inevitable shipwreck." The next four years were to tell how accurate a prophet Adams was.

When the final session of the Fifty-eighth Congress convened in December 1904, Senator Lodge, faithful to his belief in the all-importance of the Senate in the making or breaking of treaties, took his stand against the administration. This came about when the Senate received the first of the Arbitration Treaties which Secretary Hay, under Roosevelt's direction, had negotiated and which provided for the submission of certain disputes to the Convention at The Hague.

The Senate at once jumped on them and substituted the word "treaty" for the word "agreement," thus assuring that every future proposal to arbitrate would come before the Senate for individual approval before it could be sent to The Hague.

Senator Lodge fully approved of this change. President Roosevelt felt otherwise, and dictated an angry letter to Mr. Lodge on the subject. He said that the amendment made "shams" of the treaties. He urged their abandonment rather

214

than any action which might give "the impression of trickiness and insincerity which would be produced by solemnly promulgating a sham." He wanted the Senate to ratify without the amendment, his alternative being to withdraw the treaties and "simply say that the temper of the Senate is hostile to arbitration."

Senator Lodge, in the end, was saved the embarrassment of an open break with Roosevelt over the treaties when the latter did withdraw them from the Senate. Later, when Elihu Root became Secretary of State, he subscribed to the Lodge viewpoint and convinced Roosevelt that it was the correct one to take. Root negotiated a series of arbitration treaties in this way which did meet the approval of the Senate.

It was on the domestic front, however, that Senator Lodge was to find the greatest difficulty in following his friend Roosevelt with unswerving loyalty. Indeed, upon the most important issue which the Fifty-ninth Congress had to face, circumstances forced him to move far to the right of the man whom he, as much as any other individual, had helped to put in the President's chair.

True to his promise of a Square Deal, Roosevelt had, in many speeches throughout 1904 and 1905, demanded a law regulating railroad rates. In December 1905, he had told Congress he wanted "some scheme" which would bring about "government supervision and regulation of the rates charged by the railroads." He did not ask that the Interstate Commerce Commission be empowered to fix rates (that would be both "undesirable" and "impracticable") but he did urge that the Commission be allowed to establish them — "subject to judicial review" — in cases where the rates were challenged as unreasonably high.

Before sending this message Roosevelt had consulted several times with Senator Lodge, who, whatever his other sins might be, had not then been accused of being a "Railroad Senator." Any such legislation would have to be subjected to the scrutiny, and receive the approval, of men like Lodge, Aldrich, Allison, "and one or two others, who," as Roosevelt told William Howard Taft, were "the most powerful factors in Congress . . . the leaders [whose] great intelligence and power, and their desire . . . to do what is best for the government, makes them not only essential to work with but desirable to work with." Senator Lodge as always was ready with advice, although what he, the scholar and expert on foreign affairs, knew about railroad rates, a subject of which he had never made any study, is open to question.

To Senator Lodge any hint of governmental intervention in private industry smacked of dread Socialism. But, and this in his mind was more important, he feared that if rates were set by a commission New England interests might suffer. The Senator admitted that he was "very much troubled" by the whole problem. Although he agreed that a commission might "have the power to prevent excessive rates or unjust discrimination" he would not go beyond that point. Shortly after the House passed Representative William P. Hepburn's bill he had his say.

"Our railroad freight rates are the lowest in existence," he declared, echoing the good Hamiltonian sentiments of his ancestor, George Cabot of Essex. "Why should not the railroads be allowed to continue to determine them? There is no body of people — and they constitute one-seventh of our population — so profoundly interested in the prosperity of the United States as the people, great and small, who own our railroads, who operate them, who work for them. It is preposterous to suggest that the railroads of the country are hostile to its well-being and eaten up by a shortsighted selfishness which would lead them to destroy any industry or injure any locality."

216

"My own belief," he said again, "is that the natural economic forces will settle rates so far as an excess is concerned by the competition of the markets, by the play of natural forces, and by the certainty that if rates are put up to a point where it would make it profitable for someone else to come in, he will come in."

Through all of March and April the debate raged in the Senate. Senator Lodge was not destined to take a leading role in the struggle but on more than one occasion he had to stand up and argue against the measure on the passage of which his dearest friend had set his heart. In one speech in the Senate, ever mindful of the fact that he was still the scholar in politics, he commenced with a quotation from Coleridge's *Table Talk*.

"I have heard but two arguments of any weight adduced in favor of this reform bill," he said, sarcastically, "and they are in substance these, 'We will blow your brains out if you don't pass it' and 'We will drag you through a horse pond if you don't pass it' and there is a good deal of force in both."

While Lodge was summoning up the ghosts of literature and using outworn language of *laissez faire* economics of the past, Senator La Follette, who, as Governor of Wisconsin, had been the author of some model railroad legislation, was throwing facts and figures at the Senate. The Senate did not like this. Because it was La Follette's first term they felt he should not have had the temerity even to make a speech. The first time he arose, most of the Old Guard, including Senator Lodge, walked from the room.

In the course of the debate many political tricks were played by both sides. Charges and countercharges flew. When Senator Tillman, who, although a Democrat, had charge of the administration measure, justifiably felt that he had been tricked by Roosevelt, he explained his part in the secret goings-on behind the scenes and charged Roosevelt with having, in the words of Mark Sullivan, "imputed odious chicanery" to powerful Republicans.

Senator Lodge at once saw the political dangers inherent in this statement if it were allowed to go unchallenged. Hardly had "Pitchfork Ben" finished when Lodge rushed to the stenographers' room for an exact copy of his speech. Then, like the Negro in Ben Tillman's story, he got the White House on the telephone and read Tillman's words to Roosevelt. In a few minutes he was back demanding and getting the floor, and telling the excited Senate that "I took down the statement which he [Roosevelt] made to me over the telephone. . . . He said in reply that the statement which I read to him . . . was a deliberate and unqualified lie." [1] Thus, through Senator Lodge's intercession, was the first member of Roosevelt's famous Ananias Club elected to membership.

Lodge's financial and economic interests, however, lay in the corporate structures of New England and his friend Roosevelt's attacks upon the corporations and trusts must have disturbed him.[2] In the first decade of the twentieth

[1] The details of behind-the-scenes maneuvers during the passage of the Hepburn Act have often been told. Perhaps the account easiest to follow is that given by Mark Sullivan in Our Times, Vol. III, Ch. 7, pp. 191–276; a more critical account may be found in The President Makers, by Matthew Josephson, Ch. 7, pp. 210–245.

[2] Senator Lodge, at the time of his death in 1925, owned 864 shares of General Electric, 1240 shares of Union Carbide and Carbon, 2455 shares of Calumet and Hecla, 1296 shares of General Electric special, $20,000 worth of Northern Pacific bonds, $30,000 worth of U.S. Government bonds, and a lesser but substantial number of shares in the E. G. Budd Manufacturing Company, Kansas City Stockyards (pfd.), U. S. Smelting and Refining (pfd.), American Telephone, Edison Illuminating Company, Chicago Junction Railways, American Exchange National Bank, Otis Elevator.

His 864 shares of General Electric were valued then at $221,400, and his Union Carbide at $79,825.

The total value of his estate was $1,249,825, divided as follows: real estate, $153,455 (Eastern Point property, Nahant, $54,550; the Lodge villa, Nahant, $18,325; 1765 Massachusetts Avenue, Wash-

century the assertion was repeatedly made that Senator Lodge owned a slice of the General Electric Company, whose Lynn plant was not far from his Nahant home, and he was supposed to hold large interests in power sites on the Pacific Coast. General Electric was one of the huge corporations which contributed generously to Roosevelt's campaign fund in 1904. His colleague, Murray Crane, was a director and Lodge always voted tariff favors for the electric industry.

Since it was vacation time, Senator Lodge and Roosevelt were browsing in their books, the one at Nahant and Tuckernuck, the other at Oyster Bay. Senator Lodge paused in his animadversions on world politics to play literary critic. He sniffed disdainfully at Henry Adams's novel, *Democracy*, which he had not read for years but which he remembered as "extremely sordid in the view it took." In his judgment Adams's novel — in which were shown the dishonesty of powerful politicians and the dangers of party loyalty as well as a faith that democracy might somehow in the end justify itself — was a "singularly worthless" study of our political society.[3]

---

ington, D.C., $80,580); personal property (including $59,277 in Washington), $1,096,370.

Also listed among his personal property were a Stuart portrait of Fisher Ames (see Chapter I) and a portrait of Alexander Hamilton; George Cabot's commission as Secretary of the Navy from President John Adams; the Cabot jewelry; and "Mrs. Hancock's fan." He also owned between 15,000 and 20,000 books.

It is interesting to notice that in listing of shares no textile firm is mentioned. In 1910, answering a charge that he was a heavy investor in that industry, he said that "I have been amazed to hear of the gigantic profits of the New England mills, which are found in the Senate but not in the places where the mills exist." The Kansas City Stockyards was an investment of the Lawrence family of Massachusetts, members of which were among his closest friends, including Bishop William Lawrence, his quondam schoolmate and posthumous eulogist.

The listing of shares above is from the *Boston Evening Transcript* of June 4, 1925.

[3] Henry Cabot Lodge read more and wrote less as he grew older. Since his publication of his "history" of the Spanish-American War

During the Moroccan crisis in the summer of 1905 Senator Lodge was vacationing in Paris. Early in June he wrote Roosevelt that, although the immediate danger was over and he did not believe the Kaiser meant to fight, the situation was still ticklish. He wanted everything possible done to "draw France toward us," for that country should be "with us and England — in our zone and our combination" for it "would be an evil day for us if Germany were to crush France."

Later he was telling Roosevelt how much France loved the United States. He had just witnessed the ceremonies attendant upon the removal of the remains of John Paul Jones to an American battleship to be brought to the United States for permanent burial at the Naval Academy at Annapolis.

"You know," he wrote, "how I have always believed that France was our natural ally and belonged in our system and not with England.[4] The Kaiser has done more in a month to drive her toward us than twenty years of effort."

Soon, after an exchange of letters obviously written for posterity about the death of John Hay and the elevation of Elihu Root to the State Department, Lodge was advising the President that the British felt Roosevelt was under the influence of the Kaiser, a statement which both he and Henry Adams, who also was in Paris at the time, of course knew to be ridiculous. He added: "Your great work in world politics this summer will be, when the history of our time is

---

his literary output had been slim. In 1906 he was to publish his first books in seven years, two volumes of casual writings, made up from essays and speeches: A Frontier Town and A Fighting Frigate. Nothing else was forthcoming until 1910, a year of crisis in his political life, when he published Speeches and Addresses, which was just that.

[4] So given in Selections of the Correspondence of Theodore Roosevelt and Henry Cabot Lodge, Vol. II, p. 164; the disparity between this statement and the one given above is inexplicable.

written, one of your most, if not your most, certain titles to a really enduring fame."

One of these claims to fame was the peace pact between Russia and Japan; another was the Algeciras Conference, called for January 16, 1906, to settle the Moroccan question. To that conference Roosevelt sent Henry White, who had by this time been advanced to the post of Ambassador to Italy, and Samuel Gummere, Minister to Morocco. They were instructed to "keep friendly with all" but "to help France get what she ought to have."

It was only natural that President Roosevelt's dangerous intervention in a purely European wrangle should be questioned in the Senate of the United States. Both at Portsmouth and at Algeciras Roosevelt had broken more completely with the American tradition of isolationism than had any previous President. In neither instance had he deigned to consult with the Senate. He had taken things into his own hands. In such circumstances it might be expected that the Senate, led by the jealous Lodge who for so many years had propounded the Senate's right to advise and consent, would wrathfully refuse to ratify the Act of Algeciras, then in the making. But it was Senator Lodge who arose in the Senate and put that august body in its place. Consistency was not one of Henry Cabot Lodge's virtues.

On January 24, 1906, speaking on the floor of the Senate, Senator Lodge said: —

"No one, I think, can doubt the absolute power of the President to initiate and carry on all negotiations; and after a treaty has been returned to him with the ratification of the Senate, to withhold it from ratification if he sees fit so to do. There is no doubt that the Senate can by resolution advise the President to enter upon a negotiation, or to advise the President to refrain from a negotiation; but those resolutions have no binding force whatsoever, and the action of the Senate becomes operative and actually effective only when a treaty is actually submitted to it. We [the Senate] have no possible right to break suddenly into the middle of a negotiation and demand from the President what instructions he has given to his representatives."

Never before had Senator Lodge admitted the existence of such extensive Presidential powers or of such restriction on the rights of the Senate. In 1919 he was to act as if he had never spoken those words.

In this same speech Lodge made another statement which he was to live to regret. He declared that President Washington was "altogether too sensible and too practical a man to suppose that because we were not to engage in alliances which might involve us in the wars of Europe with which we had no concern, therefore we were never to engage in any agreements with any of the nations of Europe, no matter how beneficial to the world at large or to ourselves."

He had more to say, and perhaps (in 1919) to regret: —

"It is the policy of the United States to be at peace; but, more than that, the policy and interest of the United States alike demand the peace of the world, and it is not to be supposed for a moment that we are never to exert our great moral influence or to use our good offices for the maintenance of the world's peace.[5] . . . Mr. President, the phrase 'entangling alliances' does not mean that we should not unite with other nations on common questions, on the settlement of rights of commerce, as to the rights of our citizens in other countries, or in the promotion of those great and be-

[5] It was Roosevelt's and Lodge's contention that by intervening in the Moroccan question Roosevelt had held off a European war. Later historians dispute this, saying that all threat of war disappeared when Delcassé resigned in 1905. See *A Diplomatic History of the United States,* by Samuel Flagg Bemis (Revised Edition), p. 585, and sources cited *ibid.,* p. 586.

neficent objects which are embodied in international conventions."

Seldom had Senator Lodge been more nearly the statesman than on January 24, 1906, when he stood up to defend Theodore Roosevelt and enunciate a foreign policy which informed the world that, as a Great Power, the United States had come of age at last.

The Algeciras Convention was sent to the Senate shortly after it was signed on April 1, 1906. Before it was ratified, however, a reservation was added by the Foreign Relations Committee, with Lodge's quiet approval, stating that it was ratified "without purpose to depart from the traditional American policy which forbids participation by the United States in the settlement of political questions which are entirely European in their scope." Thus the spirit of George Washington was allowed to triumph after all.

In 1904 Lodge had repeatedly urged President Roosevelt to make immigration an issue, but the subject had not appealed to the President as a vital one then, and he had successfully evaded it. However, by 1906, events had occurred which made it impossible for the administration to go on ignoring what was becoming a dangerous situation.

The trouble centered in California, where Japanese children were being excluded from the public schools. The state authorities defied every effort on the part of the Federal Government to put an end to this practice, with the result that diplomatic relations between the United States and Japan were strained almost to the breaking point. President Roosevelt was forced to do something. Faced as he was with a matter of States' rights and the duty to enforce the observation of national treaties by the states, he asked Congress to provide a special Japanese naturalization bill.

Senator Lodge at the time was a member not only of the Senate Committee on Immigration, but also of an Immigration Commission especially appointed to study the whole problem of immigration laws and their enforcement. When the bills being considered by the two Houses went into conference Lodge saw his opportunity to settle the Japanese question. He had a long talk with Roosevelt, following which Secretary Root was called into conference. Shortly thereafter the clever Secretary, following Lodge's suggestions, drafted what became known as the "passport clause." This required the showing of passports by all Japanese immigrants, and the situation was so shaped as to carry also the promise of the Japanese Government to issue passports only to such classes of persons as would be *persona grata* to the United States.

With practically no publicity this important clause was slipped into the conference report. It was wholly new legislation and it strained very far the powers of a conference committee. Senator Lodge, however, had banked upon his knowledge of the political mind; he felt that none would dare raise a point against it. He was right. It became law; and, by this fertile expedient, which was wholly Senator Lodge's idea, all the political embarrassments which a separate bill might well have met were avoided. When, a few years later, Senator Lodge felt constrained to defend his public career, the passage of the passport clause was one of the topics of which he boasted the most. "I framed and helped pass the passport amendment," he crowed, which, he added, "solved our difficulty with Japan and checked the influx of Asiatic labor."

When the Fifty-ninth Congress met for its final session in December 1906, Senator Lodge was on hand with three bills. One was designed to prevent the desecration of the American flag, a worthily patriotic measure; another, which was purely political business, authorized the appointment of certain customs officers. The third was perhaps the most cynical measure presented to Congress in many a year.

Not since 1890, when he had helped write and had introduced the unsuccessful national election law known as the Force Bill, had the name of Henry Cabot Lodge been associated with any liberal or progressive domestic legislation. He now came forth as author of a bill which would forbid child labor in the District of Columbia. No latent humanitarianism caused him to take this step. He was not moved by the plight of the little children working long hours in the mills of the National Capital — for there were no mills there, as there were in Massachusetts. He was not moved to compassion by the undernourished and stunted factory children of Washington — for he could walk from 1765 Massachusetts Avenue to the Capitol itself without passing a factory worthy of the name. He was moved, instead, by fear that the very law he now proposed for the District of Columbia might, by the interdict of the national legislature, be imposed upon the working children of the forty-eight states.

In the great conflict between progressivism and reaction which had come into existence during the regime of Theodore Roosevelt there had come to the fore one Senator who was frightening in his zeal for reform. Whatever his inner motives, Senator Albert J. Beveridge of Indiana had become as ardent a reformer as he had been an imperialist, and he was now conducting what was almost a one-man crusade on behalf of such social legislation as federal meat inspection, a food and drug act, and an advisory tariff commission. Instead of being dimmed, his fighting spirit was aroused when he saw most of his reforms slaughtered in various committees, and he was determined to fight to the finish for a child labor act which he proposed to offer in the winter of 1907.

Beveridge had carried his ideas to the public. He had warned of his impending bill in at least two speeches, one of them in Senator Lodge's own city of Boston. Of course he was not alone. A national Child Labor Committee had been formed; the magazines had printed articles and stories on the grim conditions in the industries which fattened on child labor; and such humanitarians as Felix Adler, Jane Addams, and Florence Kelley had done much to arouse the public conscience against what was a national disgrace. Beveridge had made an exhaustive study of the situation and was ready to introduce a bill designed to withstand constitutional tests by forbidding child labor in all industries engaged in interstate commerce.

Senator Lodge heard about his proposed measure from Roosevelt, to whom Beveridge had written, enclosing a copy of the bill. The President was then engaged in writing his annual message to Congress. Beveridge expected that Roosevelt would support him; instead, after consultation with Lodge, he came out in favor of leaving child labor legislation up to the various states. It was then that Lodge devised his ingenious scheme. Taking Beveridge's bill as a model he composed a law applicable only to the District of Columbia. This, he reasoned, meant nothing; at least it would do no harm to Massachusetts industries. On the contrary, it would serve to salve the national conscience, without disturbing the *status quo*.

Deserted by Roosevelt and double-crossed by Lodge, the Senator from Indiana was in an angry mood and made no secret of how he felt. He vigorously attacked Lodge, who attempted to show that there was nothing original about Beveridge's measure, claiming that it had been already proposed by others. Among those whom Lodge cited was Vice President Fairbanks. A search of the record showed that this had not been the case, but even after exposure Lodge unblushingly made no apologies for his mendacity when called to account by Beveridge. The two Senators exchanged some vehement language, Lodge doing his best to ridicule Beveridge, and Beveridge answering in kind.

With consummate tact Beveridge made it appear that

Lodge was, after all, on the side of the angels, that it was apparent that the Senator from Massachusetts favored a national law. Since, he said, this was the case, he would add his bill as an amendment to the Lodge bill. The Senator from Massachusetts urged Beveridge to do nothing that might endanger the passage of the Lodge bill, and begged him, almost hysterically, not to tack on his bill. It was apparent to the Senator from Indiana that the Senator from Massachusetts was acting on behalf of big business, that his heart was not in the passage of any child labor law, and so he refused to back down. He would, as Mr. Bowers has said, rather not "stop child labor in mines, factories and sweatshops of Washington City" than endanger the chance of getting his own bill before the public.

Refusing to recede, Beveridge fought to get his own measure added as an amendment, and won. It was his only victory. In spite of one of the greatest forensic exhibitions ever offered the Senate, which lasted four days, Senator Beveridge failed to convince the Senate against the onslaughts of the opponents, who took refuge behind the cloak of constitutionalism, and the bill was killed.

Time was fast running out on the Roosevelt administration. Soon the President would have to make it clear, once and for all, whether he meant what he had said on November 8, 1904, when he had ringingly declared that "under no circumstances will I be a candidate for or accept another nomination."

Senator Lodge had first met the man who was to supplant Roosevelt in his loyalties a decade earlier when the corpulent young lawyer from Ohio had come to Washington as Solicitor General in the McKinley administration. Although, on almost his first night in the Capital, Taft had sat between Mrs. Lodge and Mrs. John Hay at a dinner party given by Senator William M. Evarts, he had never been part of the inner circle of the political elite that met in the homes of Lodge or Hay or Henry Adams. But Senator Lodge had liked him well enough. In 1897, when Lodge was pressing Roosevelt's cause for the Assistant Secretaryship of the Navy, one of those whom he approached was "Judge Taft, one of the best fellows going . . ." who readily "plunged in" and got a close friend of the President "to take hold." During the intervening years Senator Lodge had not known Taft intimately, although he had, of course, considerable contact with him at the time of the Philippine investigation.

As Roosevelt's term of office unfolded there appeared to be no reasons to suspect that he would not live up to his pledge, at least as far as 1908 was concerned. He had reiterated this to the Senate during the wrangle, in 1905, over the ratification of the Santo Domingo treaty. Senator Lodge was convinced, as early as January, 1906, that Roosevelt not only would not seek the Presidency but that he had no other office in mind. He told a correspondent for the *Buffalo Express* that Roosevelt had "passed finally and irrevocably from the region of candidate for any public office" and, since Lodge was widely regarded as Roosevelt's closest friend, his word carried weight. Certainly most of the Old Guard must have believed Roosevelt, else they would have been more cautious in attacking his favored legislation. Experienced politicians always keep their eye to the future.

In spite of the repeated protestations of Roosevelt and those who, like Senator Lodge, might be presumed to be his spokesmen, Roosevelt's admirers hoped he would again be a candidate and his enemies felt sure he was plotting the seizure of a third term. In order to clear the air of these rumors the President was advised to select his own successor. After considering a number of possibilities, of which Elihu Root was his first choice, he finally settled upon his Secretary of War, Mr. Taft. When that amiable gentleman returned from a trip around the world he was so informed. Senator Lodge, ever the practical politician in spite of his air of scholarly abstraction, preferred Root but he knew, as well as Root did, that the Secretary of State's chances of election were small. He willingly accepted Taft.

All the time, of course, Roosevelt realized the immensity of his own popularity with the rank and file, and his own unpopularity with the Old Guard. He knew that he could have the nomination easily, and probably the election; but right up to the moment of the Republican Convention he did everything in his power to keep the honor from coming his way. Of this there can be no question; whether, at the same time, he had his eye on 1912, is less certain.

Senator Lodge was chosen to preside at the convention and keep it safe for Taft. He was to go to Chicago bearing the political scars of one of the wildest gubernatorial campaigns the staid old Bay State had ever witnessed. In Boston, at the time, one John B. Moran, as District Attorney of Suffolk County, was rocking the city with his investigations of alleged graft in high and low places. In this he had the backing of Hearst's *Boston American.* A fearless prosecutor, whose personal honesty was unquestioned even by Lodge, he delighted in calling legislators and aldermen before him on graft charges. In the summer of 1906 he caused Senator Lodge some uneasy moments.

District Attorney Moran was known as a "radical" even among the Democrats. As Lodge discovered early in July, he was about to run for governor. Being of the opinion that the bigger they are the harder they fall, in his search for campaign material Moran had gone after the bigwigs of Massachusetts Republicanism. He suspected the Republican State Committee of having received contributions to its campaign chest which it had not reported. Thereupon he called Thomas M. Talbot, chairman of the State Committee, and James B.

Reynolds, an Assistant Secretary of the Treasury, before the grand jury. Reynolds was a Lodge man, who owed his appointment by Roosevelt solely to the Senator, who had known him personally for ten years as a loyal party worker. Senator Lodge, too, was called before the grand jury and vigorously questioned by Moran, who, Lodge reported, was "cheaper . . . and much worse" than William Travers Jerome, then at the height of his reputation as District Attorney of New York. Lodge and Roosevelt hated them both.

In between pleasant hours spent at Nahant reading Frazer's "delightful, brilliant . . . and charming" *Lectures on the Early Kingship* and Cicero's *Letters*, and refusing to read Winston Churchill's *Life of Lord Randolph Churchill* [6] because he disliked both father and son, Senator Lodge worried over the possible indictment of his fellow politicians. As so often happens in such investigations, in the end no indictments were forthcoming. Moran ran for governor after browbeating a recalcitrant Democratic State Convention into accepting him. It was a hard and violent campaign and, although Curtis Guild, Jr., was re-elected, District Attorney Moran piled up the highest vote a Democratic candidate for governor had yet received in Massachusetts.

Lodge was frightened by the narrow victory. He feared what the future might bring. His letters of this period are filled with worry. He wanted Roosevelt to tone down his attacks on big business and not forget the existence of "the great body of well meaning, conservative American voters."

[6] "The son I know," he wrote to Theodore Roosevelt; "I have met him several times. He is undoubtedly clever but conceited to a degree which it is hard to express either in words or figures and he was not at all sympathetic to me. I have no better reasons than these for not having read his book, but knowing the son and knowing the father I felt no inclination in that direction." Lodge described Lord Randolph as "a species of Jerome or Moran raised to the Nth power who happened to be the son of a duke." *Sel. Corr. T. R. and H. C. L.*, Vol. II, p. 232.

He found in Massachusetts that "people of moderate means not connected with any corporation" thought that perhaps it would not be too disastrous if Hearst and Moran were given a chance to "attempt their violent measures because that would bring a reaction which would put a stop to the continual agitation against property and business."

"The fact is," he said with great anxiety, "that the impression on the public mind is that all the wrong doing is on the side of capital because capitalists and corporations are practically the only things attacked in the newspapers and on the stump. Men are silent toward labor unions and assume toward them a simply defensive attitude, yet the attempted action of the labor unions has been as tyrannical as that of any trust."

In the western part of the state Senator Lodge "discussed Mr. Gompers' attitude with great frankness" but he kept quiet elsewhere because "I am conscious that to assail it would probably hurt the party and cost us many votes. . . ."

More than the unions he feared "the socialistic movement led by men of some education who make incendiary appeals to all laboring men." Grudgingly he admitted that Roosevelt, by "advocating legislation which will remove the real grounds of grievance in proper ways," had pursued the proper course, but still he was afraid that Hearst and Moran, and men like them, by "appealing to class prejudice and the worst passions," were leading the country directly to chaos.

"We have got a terrible struggle before us," he said the day after election, "to save the country from a movement which strikes at the very foundations of society and civilization."

President Roosevelt had taken every precaution to preclude a stampede at the fourteenth National Convention of the Grand Old Party, which opened on Tuesday, June 16, 1908. Senator Lodge was designated the permanent chairman. Although some members of the Taft family distrusted him, it was later proved that he had his strict instructions, and his conduct at the convention was all that Roosevelt or Taft could have desired.

In his opening speech Senator Lodge referred, as was natural, to President Roosevelt, calling him "the best abused and most popular man in the United States today." That was all the pro-Rooseveltian delegates and gallery visitors needed. For forty-six minutes cries of "Four more years of Teddy" sounded and, for a while, it appeared as if the convention might be stampeded. When the demonstration failed to subside, Senator Lodge, managing to make himself heard above the uproar, threw cold water upon the outburst by calmly announcing: —

"The President retires, by his own determination, from his high office on the fourth of March next. His refusal of a renomination, dictated by the loftiest motives and by a noble loyalty to American traditions, is final and irrevocable."

The next day the names of Cannon, Fairbanks, Hughes, Knox, Taft, Foraker, and La Follette were placed in nomination, with accompanying oratory. Again there was an attempt to stampede the convention, but, as the noise grew greater and greater, Senator Lodge again took control. He ordered the calling of the roll. It was not until Massachusetts was reached that the racket had subsided sufficiently for the reporters to count the vote. But when Massachusetts plumped its thirty-two votes for Taft the gathering realized that the nomination had gone to Roosevelt's heir apparent, and the excitement died away.

President Roosevelt was gratified at the way his friend had handled the "peculiarly delicate and difficult work at Chicago." "In point of judgment, taste and power," he told Mrs. Lodge, "it would be literally impossible to better either his words or actions."

Senator Lodge, turning down the honor of notifying Taft of his nomination, went off to Europe for his holiday, and Roosevelt, impatient now to be out of the White House, retired to Oyster Bay to plan his "scientific" hunting trip in Africa.

XVII

Skin of His Teeth

ON PATRIOTS' DAY, in the year 1910, Senator Henry Cabot Lodge sat at his desk on Capitol Hill writing a letter. Outside the window the warm mid-April sunshine glimmered on the lawn — the same lawn that Alice Roosevelt, as a child, always insisted belonged to Uncle Cabot. Today he was writing to her wandering father, but the thoughts he was setting down in his cramped and scholarly handwriting were far from springlike. He was deeply troubled because he feared that another April would see the greensward "owned" by some other Senator than himself.

"We are going to be defeated this year . . ." he wrote. "I believe we can prevent its being a bad defeat, but defeat it must be, I think."

The mood of despair had been growing on him for some time. Two months before Henry Adams had gossiped: "The Senators are scared about the next election . . . Cabot is even scared about himself." Cabot was desperately frightened, both about himself and about the future of his party. A week after his first letter he was predicting again: "To me the situation is simply this: the Republican party is on the eve of a defeat, but I do not want the Republican party destroyed or disintegrated. It is the best instrument, with all its defects, that we have to carry out what we both want to have done."

He was not quite certain where he stood, either with the President or with the ex-President. As to the latter, he knew,

234

even before 1910, that they were coming to the parting of their political ways. In 1912 Roosevelt frankly told him that this had been obvious for two years. To the end of his term, President Taft never knew how deeply he could trust Cabot Lodge. It was no secret to the friends of both that, from 1908 through 1912, when Lodge definitely broke with Roosevelt, he was playing Taft against Roosevelt, and vice versa, as he tacked back and forth across the rough waters of Republicanism in his race for political survival.

President Taft's first move towards independence of Roosevelt came shortly after his election. He decided he would select his own cabinet, with the exception of Elihu Root, whom he wanted to continue as Secretary of State. Mr. Root, however, declined the offer. Thereupon, as an obvious gesture of friendliness towards Roosevelt, the President-elect tendered the post to Senator Lodge. Had Lodge then been as prophetic of Republican disaster as he was a year later he might have accepted. Instead, on December 9, 1908, he wrote Taft declining the offer on the ground that he felt he could better serve the Taft administration in the Senate. A few weeks later he journeyed to Augusta, Georgia, where Taft was resting up for his inauguration, and had a long talk with the President-elect. Upon his return he went at once to the White House. The incredible Archie Butt, listening in as usual, reported that "he no sooner got back than he hurled discord into the Roosevelt and Cabinet camps by announcing . . . that none of the present cabinet would remain . . . that it was evidently the intention to get rid of everybody who might keep President Taft in touch with Roosevelt's influence."

At that meeting Senator Lodge warned Roosevelt that Taft had his mind made up that his administration was to stand alone, that no one would be able to call it a continuation of the Roosevelt regime. Archie Butt felt "rather disgusted" that Senator Lodge should "stir up discord between the two families," but he found some comfort in the fact that Lodge could hardly be considered one of Taft's intimates. Writing to his sister-in-law about the incident, Butt said: "Lodge is so hopelessly selfish that if the Tafts did not kowtow to him he would delight in making trouble between them and the Roosevelts; but it is my opinion that it is Lodge and not the Roosevelts, the Tafts [Mrs. Taft and the President-elect's brother] were guarding the President-elect from; but I could not say so for they [the Roosevelts] are very fond of Senator Lodge and would never brook any criticism of him."

In his biography of Taft,[1] Henry Pringle says that the "favorites at the Roosevelt court, bitter and unhappy that the reign was nearly over, continued to ride from the court of the New King and to leap from their saddles with stories of perfidy. Cabot Lodge was one of these." He then credits Lodge with having secured George von Lengerke Meyer's retention in the Cabinet, quoting John Hays Hammond's *Autobiography* to the effect that he did so to eliminate Meyer as a possible rival to Gussie Gardner. Hammond claims that Taft had already offered him the post and that he had declined it. It is doubtful if Meyer, at this late date, intended to run for Representative, although he may have had his eye on Lodge's Senate seat in 1910. As a lavish dispenser of cash for political purposes he would have been a formidable rival for the nomination. At all events, Senator Lodge seems to have acted, at this time, as almost any politician would have acted. Having turned down a post in the cabinet he was forced to keep his own fences in repair, and if he helped his son-in-law in the bargain, it was all in the family. And if this called for "sowing the first seeds of discord between

[1] *The Life and Times of William Howard Taft,* by Henry Pringle. Vol. I, p. 388.

Taft and Roosevelt," as Pringle declares,[2] that was one of the unfortunate aspects of politics which could not be helped.

Senator Lodge was at the dock in Hoboken on March 23, 1909, to see his friend off to Africa, and then he hurried back to Washington to enjoy the "rest and peace and assurance" which editor Frank I. Cobb told the readers of the *World* would be the natural reaction to the Rooseveltian discords of the past seven years. But Lodge was up to his neck in the tariff.[3] He worked in the committee room with the Republican members from early morning until six or seven o'clock in the evening, and whenever he walked out of the room he was "seized upon and talked to by persons interested in some of the 4,000 items." Before the bill came to the Senate from the House, where all tax legislation must originate, he felt, in the main, satisfied with its provisos, although he feared that duties would be retained on hides, lumber, and iron ore. At heart a strong protectionist, as representative in the Senate of the New England shoe interests he desperately wanted to put hides on the free list.

Senator Lodge also wanted to retain duties on wood pulp. His reasons are interesting. "The removal of duty would not benefit the ultimate consumer who buys newspapers or magazines one cent," he said, with an appalling disregard for the constitutional guarantee of the freedom of the press that should have brought the American Publishers' Association to its feet with anguished yells, "but it would promote the starting of new papers which had no chance of life and which only waste money in the effort to live, and it would enlarge the profits of the publishers of cheap sensational papers whom it is not desirable to help. . . ."

[2] *Op. cit.*, p. 388.

[3] Now, in the fullness of his Senatorial career, Lodge was a member of these committees: Philippines (chairman); Civil Service; Engrossed Bills; Finance; Foreign Relations; Forest Reservations; and Immigration. (*Congressional Directory*, Sixty-first Congress, 1909.)

A few weeks later Senator Lodge wrote Roosevelt: "I have never come so close to tariff making before, and the amount of ruthlessness that is exhibited on both sides surpasses anything I have ever seen."

By the time the House Ways and Means Committee had finished with its bill, which bore the name of Representative Sereno E. Payne of New York, the tariff had been revised. Unfortunately, all the revisions were upward. Meanwhile the Senate Finance Committee, under the control of Senator Aldrich, had been at work. The duties on more than 600 items had been increased. The real ruthlessness was about to begin.

President Taft — who "surprised" Lodge because "with all his great experience . . . he does not seem to have got hold of the elements of politics" — tried vainly to beat off the Aldrich attack on his tariff policies. Aldrich was the first to betray Taft when he asked, "Where did we ever make the statement that we would revise the tariff downward?" Senator Lodge was quick to take the cue. On May 8 he told the Senate, "Nobody ever pledged me to revision downward," cautiously adding, "any more than to revision upward."

It was Lodge's contention that the new tariff fulfilled the party's pledge because, in its final form, duties were lowered on 379 articles. To this statement La Follette was able to answer, with irrefutable statistics, that these 379 items were all unimportant and that the total reductions involved came only to $45,000 while the total increase through the other 600 items would amount to $10,000,000.

In the course of the great debate Senator Cummins had tried to cram into the tariff bill an income-tax amendment. The Democrats raced to his aid; the public, on the whole, applauded loudly; and the revolutionary measure seemed to be on the verge of passage. Senator Lodge was scared. "That scheme would produce so much money (apart from every other objection to the income tax, and I have some very strong ones)," he said, "that it would involve in a short time another revision of the tariff and a large destruction of protection." Lodge, who admitted the income-tax bloc had enough votes to pass it, thereupon with Aldrich and Murray Crane went personally to the President to appeal to him "to save them from the situation," as Taft put it. Taft did, by sending a special message to Congress recommending a constitutional amendment. In this he showed wisdom, as well as a knowledge of the judicial mind, for undoubtedly an income tax would have been found unconstitutional then, as the 1894 income-tax law had been. Senator Aldrich introduced the amendment which, in spite of all that Senator Lodge could say or do, became the Sixteenth Article of the Constitution on February 25, 1913.

As soon as the long, fatiguing struggle, accompanied, as Senator Lodge complained, "with every sort of nervous wear and irritation," had ended, and Congress was over for what remained of the summer, he rushed off for Tuckernuck Island. He had not been out of Washington, except for a few days after the tariff bill had passed the Senate, when he ran home to Nahant, since the middle of March. It had been wearying and he needed a rest. Alone with him on the quiet, sea-washed island was his son George Cabot Lodge, who had long since given up being his father's secretary and who was now devoting all his time to literature. The two looked forward to long hours of reading and resting in the sun and surf. They had been there but a few days when, at midnight, August 18, the younger man was stricken with what appeared to be an acute attack of indigestion. He was better the next morning and then he became worse. There was no way of getting a doctor to the isolated retreat. He suffered severely for twenty-four hours and then, alone with his father, he died.

As far as Massachusetts was concerned the dramatic political struggle of 1910 began in February when Governor Eben S. Draper called a special election in the Fourteenth Congressional District to fill the office vacated by the death of Representative William C. Lovering of Taunton. Eugene N. Foss, who had left the Republican Party a few weeks earlier, was easily persuaded to accept the Democratic nomination. With characteristic energy and hyperbole, Foss went after his election, denouncing "Cannonism and Aldrichism," the high cost of living, and the Republican Party in general, and endorsing the income-tax amendment. He was able to induce many of the leading Democrats of the state to support him. When it became obvious that he had the advantage of his opponent, a hurry call was sent to Washington for Senator Lodge. Nothing was more to the Senator's liking. He toured the Fourteenth District, lifting his coldly sarcastic voice against Foss's record as a Republican, the latter having been repudiated by his own party and become a Democrat only upon the promise of public office. His speeches got under Foss's skin, but they carried little weight with the electorate. On election day Foss swept the district.

Throughout the country this relatively unimportant special election attracted attention. It was regarded as a straw in the wind and interpreted as a stinging rebuke to Senator Lodge. His own friends thought he had stuck his neck out needlessly. Theodore Roosevelt immediately recognized the danger signals of discontent and promised Lodge that, when the proper time came, he would "hoist the black flag and fight for you without giving or taking quarter." To this he added: "Cabot, they will believe me when I speak for you, largely because I am not insincere enough to speak in the same terms for other people in whom I don't believe." Before the year was over the call was sent out for Roosevelt and his "black flag" to save Dear Cabot from disaster.

Lodge was worried to such an extent that he had given up his usual European vacation that summer. Early in the fall he established personal headquarters in the Hotel Touraine in Boston. There he set about to suppress the growing insurgency in the Republican ranks. For the past two years there had been increasingly open opposition to Lodge which came to a head when Butler Ames, a Congressman from Lowell, announced that he wanted to replace the gentleman from Nahant in the Senate. Ames was not the only aspirant. Governor Draper, who perhaps smelled defeat in the offing, and two former Governors, Bates and Guild, also were hopeful. One by one Senator Lodge summoned these worthies to the Touraine and told them that he was still "boss" of the party. With the exception of Ames they all backed down.

Although they had differed on several occasions, Murray Crane came to his colleague's aid, and worked for his success both openly and behind the scenes. During the summer Crane visited President Taft at his summer home in Beverly. While discussing the forthcoming election Crane told Taft that one of the greatest weaknesses the Republicans had to contend with was the presence in the state of Cabot Lodge.

"He has got to get ill and go to Europe," Crane said. "If we can give it out that he is ill, we might offset his unpopularity with the people, as there might be some reaction in his favor. Unfortunately he was never as well in his life."

Chuckling, the President asked, "What disease are you going to give him, Murray?"

"I don't know," Crane drawled. "He is really suffering from megalomania, but we want a simpler trouble than that. I am inclined to say he is threatened with jaundice."

Taft laughed. "He has always had that and its late announcement might cause some amusement. Better make it nervous prostration. There is an element of fatigue and overwork in that."

The jaundiced Senator did not suddenly develop a breakdown, however, but stayed on to fight. At times it began to appear as if Foss were campaigning against Lodge more than he was against Governor Draper. He turned out a vicious broadside accusing Lodge and Gussie Gardner of being two of the worst offenders in the spending of money in elections. According to Foss "this scholar in politics studied his checkbook more than works on political economy." Such jibes appealed to the electorate, which was not used to hearing the distinguished statesman subjected to this earthy kind of abuse. Lodge countered with similar charges against Foss and said the real question was, "Can Foss buy Massachusetts?" But the candidate for Governor had the advantage over the Senator. He was always one jump ahead of Lodge, and the Senator was forced into a defensive position. Foss accused; the Senator, angrily, explained.

When the situation appeared hopeless for the Republican cause Theodore Roosevelt, as he had promised, hoisted his black flag and sailed up Massachusetts Bay. His speech, made from a raised platform roped off like a prize-fight ring in the Boston Arena, was half an attack upon Foss and half a defense of Lodge. The emphasis was on the latter half. Just how much good it did the Senator in the long run it is difficult to say; but it did affect the vote on the governorship. But not in the way the ex-President had anticipated. Roosevelt's charge that it would be "scandalous" to elect Foss enraged the Democrats and Foss was well advised not to answer him. On election day Foss carried the state by nearly 24,000 votes. Although the Republicans held on to ten of the fourteen Congressional seats, the Democrats came the closest they had in years to controlling the General Court. They gained eight Senate seats and forty-four in the House. And this meant that, if there were no defections, they lacked only fifteen votes needed in joint session to beat Henry Cabot Lodge for Senator.

That same November day also saw Woodrow Wilson elected in New Jersey and Democratic governors returned in Connecticut, Nebraska, New York, Wyoming, and Taft's own state of Ohio. Congress also was to be Democratic. Senator Lodge's prediction of Republican disaster had become true.

Immediately after the election Foss served notice that he was out to rid the Senate of Henry Cabot Lodge. His first move was to try to induce an outstanding Democrat to oppose him, but when the Democrats eventually held their party caucus the man selected was Sherman L. Whipple, a Boston lawyer who was then a comparative newcomer to politics.

Governor Foss's "brazen effrontery" in attempting to dictate the state's choice of its senior Senator did not sit well with some Democrats and it furnished ammunition for the Lodge forces. But within the Republican Party there were those who would have been glad to get rid of the cold, aristocratic, and autocratic Senator Lodge. In maintaining his control of the party he had made enemies, sometimes only because of the chill affectation of his voice. Yet, from the time he had entered politics until the present, there had been no serious opposition. Now, with Butler Ames out against him and the situation in the legislature woefully uncertain, the "Kaiser of Nahant," as he was sometimes called, was destined to spend many sleepless nights before the election in the General Court in January.

Nevertheless, Senator Lodge returned to Washington shortly after the November election. While awaiting his inauguration as Governor, Foss began a state-wide tour in his campaign to unseat Lodge. With a group of barnstormers, none of whom stood high politically, and accompanied by a young woman whose task it was to enliven meetings by singing "Has Anybody Here Seen Cabot?" — to the tune of "Has Anybody Here Seen Kelly?" — they covered a lot of ground. Great crowds turned out to hear the Senator abused and his alarmed friends hurriedly sent word to Washington urging his return. Murray Crane, however, advised him not to and he replied that he would not go back to the state until January.

During the interval he made a speech in the Senate favoring tariff revision, schedule by schedule, along the lines suggested by President Taft. To this speech Foss's reply was: —

When the devil was sick, the devil a monk would be,
When the devil was well, the devil a monk was he,

and he referred to Lodge's sudden change in attitude towards the tariff as a dying Senator's "death-bed repentance." At this time Sherman Whipple made the most of Lodge's often expressed antagonism towards the movement for the direct election of Senators and said that, if he were to go up against the electorate, he would stand no chance of winning.

Then Lodge announced that on January 4 he would render an account of his stewardship at Symphony Hall.

Every seat was taken that night. Two thousand good Republicans who could not get into the large hall were jammed into Chickering Hall, where they sang "America" and other patriotic songs and listened to praise of Lodge from others' lips. Hundreds were turned away. All those who came were his friends and they were there to cheer Senator Lodge. If they had come expecting drama they were not disappointed. On the stage from which he was to speak there was no official reception committee of the

244

state's leaders. There was no presiding officer. He stood and spoke alone. He had a record of eighteen years in the Senate to account for and it took a long time. Throughout he held his admirers spellbound. One by one he counted off his achievements: his work for the Navy, for immigration, for the Philippines and Hawaii; how, of the 171 treaties that had come before the Senate in fourteen years, he had been in charge of 47; what he had done about Cuba; how he was responsible for the Panama Canal by abrogating the Clayton-Bulwer Treaty. The list was long, and it was dear to the Republican hearts to which it was addressed. When he said, "I am a Republican and a Protectionist," he was cheered to the rafters.

Those who heard him that night said they had never seen him more eloquent, nor more intensely dramatic, than when he declared: "I think I can say that I

> "Put my creed into my deed
> Nor spoke with double tongue,"

and they cheered wildly when the scholar in politics, again reverting to quotation, asked the people of Massachusetts to believe that

> "I nothing common did nor mean
> Upon that memorable scene."

Senator Lodge's apologia was well received by the Boston newspapers, most of which were his supporters, and it was likened to the great speeches of Webster and Sumner. But when the echoing applause died there was still the legislature to contend with. When the Republican caucus was held a few days later, all of Ames's supporters stayed away, as did most of the anti-Lodge insurgents. He was unanimously selected by those who attended.

The State House was jammed on the afternoon of January 17 when the two branches of the General Court met for their first vote on the Senatorship. In the Senate Lodge won on the first ballot — by a mere three votes more than was necessary. In the House, however, he received three votes less than was needed. Although he had a majority of the votes cast, under the rules of the General Court it was necessary to vote again the next day in joint session. Speaker Walker of the House, who had received four votes the first day, urged his followers to throw their support to Lodge. On the morning of the joint session the newspapers, even those most friendly to the Senator, predicted that the best he could do was to win by two votes. The chance of politics intervened, however, and he did better than that. Two Democrats deserted their candidate and openly defied annihilation by voting for Lodge. One Democrat, an old friend, stayed away from the session rather than cast his vote against the Senator. With Walker's votes thrown his way he was re-elected to his fourth term as United States Senator with five votes to spare.

With six more years in the Senate which, as he had told the audience at Symphony Hall, he loved more than he would even the Presidency if that office should ever be offered him, and with the cheers of his fellow townspeople of Nahant ringing in his ears, Senator Lodge could now turn his thoughts to statesmanship. He could put behind his parochial duties and move once again in the theater of the world — this time to oppose the Taft arbitration treaties.

Both in the United States and in England the treaties were welcomed with unexpected enthusiasm by the press and the public. Indeed, they had such widespread support that Taft, who predicted almost immediate acceptance by the Senate, urged the "peace societies" to do nothing that might stir up feeling against them. But even before they were signed an indictment against them in the first degree was being drawn up in the fertile minds of a little group of conspirators. The junto's leader was Theodore Roosevelt; its most able advocate was Henry Cabot Lodge.

We did not need to fear arbitration with Great Britain — "for neither England nor America would ever do anything adverse to the honor or vital interest of the other" — but, Roosevelt warned Senator Lodge, with either Germany or Japan questions might arise "which we could not submit to arbitration.

"If either one of them asked us to arbitrate the question of fortifying the Isthmus; or asked us to arbitrate the Monroe Doctrine, or the fortification or retention of Hawaii; or Germany's right to purchase the Danish Islands in the West Indies; or Japan's right to insist upon unlimited Japanese immigration — why! we would not and could not arbitrate."

Roosevelt knew he was aiming his shafts right at Lodge's vanity. He was angry, and he was not going to let Lodge fail him now. But, "You have just been elected to the Senate," he reminded his friend. "You were elected in a straight-out fight, in which you stood on your past; and your past forbids you to be guilty of the hypocrisy of voting for such a treaty as this."

Senator Lodge was ready for the treaties when they came to the Senate on August 4. On August 11, just one week later, Senator Lodge submitted the majority report of the Foreign Relations Committee. In that brief time he had found the means of dealing the death blow to the treaties on which Taft had set his heart. In the first place, he argued, they were unconstitutional; in the second place they were not treaties of peace at all, but breeders of war.

Senator Lodge directed his attack at Clause 3 of Article III, which provided that the Joint High Commission of

247

Inquiry might decide, in certain contingencies, whether a question was "justiciable" and, therefore, whether it was arbitrable.

But this was unconstitutional, for it deprived the Senate of its power to reject an agreement on the ground that the question was not arbitrable in the first place. Furthermore, the President had control over the formation of the Commission; the Senate did not.

Senator Lodge argued that it was unconstitutional to delegate to a commission those powers which the Constitution gave to the Senate. Even more! "We would have no power to prevent our title to the land we inhabit from being tried before a court of arbitration." Of course, no nation would at that moment raise those questions, but accepting a treaty with that clause still in it invited them to arise.

Unless Clause 3 were eliminated from the treaty, he concluded (with what Taft thought was "deficient reasoning"), the treaty would become "not what we fondly hope it will be, but an ill-omened breeder of bitterness and war."

"Absolutely sound," was Roosevelt's view of Lodge's report. He promised, "I'll back you up heartily," and throughout the summer of 1911, during which both men wrote anti-treaty articles for the *Outlook*, they exchanged friendly letters on the subject. Their old fellow Imperialist, Admiral Mahan, joined the cabal. Lodge told him that he hoped to avoid a great public debate in the Senate, for he thought that would only harm our foreign relations, but "if the President insists that the treaties must pass unamended, we shall have that debate." The President did insist, and on February 29, 1912, Henry Cabot Lodge arose in the Senate to deliver one of the most forcible speeches of his career.

The occasion was his resolution for ratification of the

treaties after acceptance of his amendments, which were to the effect that the American members of the Joint High Commission should be appointed by the President subject to the advice and consent of the Senate, and that the Senate should have the right to pass upon each case as it arose to determine whether it was an arbitrable case or not. There were, as he had said so often, some differences which should never be arbitrated, but which should be settled by force as soon as they arose.

"The greatest attribute of sovereignty," he began, "is the war power for on that power rests the peace of the country. . . . It is the duty of Congress to keep the United States so well prepared that aggression from other nations will not be invited. . . . [There is] nothing so essential to a country's peace as a well-settled conviction on the part of the rest of the world that to make war on that country would be highly dangerous and most unprofitable."

The second element in the maintenance of peace lay in the conduct of the country's foreign relations. Senator Lodge emphasized the importance of the Senate in this respect. The United States can make war without the participation of the Executive; peace without the participation of the House of Representatives; but neither without the participation of the Senate.

Although the Senate favored the essence of these treaties, as an example of the way to promote the general cause of peace throughout the world, he did not think the Senate had any intention of delegating to the Executive the treaty-making power of the Senate reserved to it by the Constitution.

He then pointed out once more those many questions which our national honor would never allow the United States to submit to an outside tribunal for arbitration, as might well happen if Article III were not eliminated.

He was not, he said, using his imagination, or asking a rhetorical question, when he asked what would happen if some great Eastern power should directly or indirectly take possession of a harbor on the west coast of Mexico and turn it into a naval station or a place of arms. Not so long ago, he continued, just such an indirect movement was begun, and was still on foot, to obtain possession of Magdalena Bay. In such a case we would intervene because it would be a violation of the Monroe Doctrine. But suppose the aggressor nation demanded the matter be taken to arbitration? This could not be prevented under the terms of Article III. A year would pass before the question could be taken up by the Commission. Meanwhile the foreign power would be strengthening its hold on its acquired territory. And even when the case came up, the Monroe Doctrine was not international law, and the foreign country would have the right to buy the territory from Mexico.

He painted other pictures of potential dangers, and, although he admitted they were hypothetical and that "today those questions to which I have alluded are peacefully at rest," he insisted that if the despicable Clause 3 were ratified all those questions would be brought to life.

"If they were raised," he said, "this treaty would be blown to the winds. That is the danger I apprehend . . . not because I fear for the United States . . . I fear it because I am the friend of peace, and . . . no greater disaster could befall the cause of peace than to make a promise in a treaty . . . which we know when we make it will not be kept. . . ."

Senator Lodge then said that these treaties did not mark the dawn of universal peace, but, properly amended, they were one step in the long march. . . . "We have girdled the globe and annihilated time with the electric current. We have brought space on the earth into subjection by the power of steam and electricity. We have entered upon the conquest of the air. But when we seek the establishment of lasting and universal peace we meet an element more elusive, more impalpable, more difficult of conquest than time or space or air, a condition more unchanged, unchanging, and unchangeable than any other in recorded history — human nature. . . . Actual peace will be, as it always has been, preserved by enlightened-men who are charged with the conduct of governments in crises which go beyond the strength of arbitral tribunals. . . . Great and lasting advances are those which have been slowly made." It was well to remember that

> While the tired waves, vainly breaking,
> Seem here no painful inch to gain,
> Far back, through creeks and inlets making,
> Comes silent, flooding in, the main.
>
> And not by eastern windows only,
> When daylight comes, comes in the light;
> In front, the sun climbs slow, how slowly,
> But westward, look, the land is bright. . . .

And with those words Henry Cabot Lodge ended his plea for isolationism on that last day of February, 1912, and those who had hoped for continued peace through international co-operation saw their dreams shattered on the Senate floor. A few days later the Senate ratified the amended treaties by a vote of seventy-six to three. President Taft, who knew how far short they fell of fulfilling the purpose for which they had been negotiated, refused to submit them to Great Britain or France. As he said, six years later, "I put them on the shelf and let the dust accumulate in the hope that the Senators might change their minds, or that the people might change the Senate; instead of which they changed me."

As a result of his speech against the treaties, Senator Lodge soon found himself in the midst of an international controversy which, in 1912, threatened to strain American relations with Japan close to the breaking point. Theodore Roosevelt really started the trouble when, in his September article in the *Outlook*, he mentioned Magdalena Bay on the coast of Lower California as a possible danger point under the arbitration treaties. No attention was paid to this particular reference until Senator Lodge revived the subject, with sensational implications, in his speech. Although he did not name the Eastern power which, he intimated, had designs on land dangerously near the approaches to the Panama Canal, it took little imagination, particularly on the part of William Randolph Hearst's editors, to recognize it as Japan.

Coming as it did from a responsible member of the Foreign Relations Committee, who presumably was in a position to receive information not readily accessible to others, the story received widespread publication. With little less than unchecked rumors to go on it was broadcast that Japan was attempting to secure a foothold upon this continent by surreptitiously buying from an American syndicate a large slice of hitherto unprofitable land on the shores of the magnificent harbor on Magdalena Bay.[4] Within a month so much had been made of this alleged Japanese plot that Senator Lodge was easily able to get the Senate to pass a resolution requesting from the President any information he might

[4] The Development Company of Lower California, originally a California corporation but at this time controlled by New England interests, owned 4,000,000 acres of land on the coast north and south from the Bay and running fifteen miles inland. The owners were reported to have approached the Oriental Steamship Company to take over this property, presumably for ultimate fortification by Japan. The State Department investigation revealed no willingness on the part of the Japanese syndicate to accept the offer. (*New York Times*, Aug. 1, 1912; *New York Tribune*, Aug. 3, 1912.)

have on the subject. This action speedily brought official denials from both Mexico and Japan.

Senator Lodge seems at no time to have had any reason to doubt the word of the President of Mexico or the Prime Minister of the Imperial Japanese Government. He had to fall back upon the supposition that if the land at Magdalena Bay fell into the hands of a private foreign concern it might very easily be passed on to the Japanese Government for military or naval purposes at some future date. The State Department examined the situation and by the end of April was convinced that no attempt had been made either directly or indirectly by Japan to acquire land in Mexico. This, however, did not satisfy the Senate Foreign Relations Committee. Senators Lodge, Root, Hitchcock, and Rayner, forming a sub-committee, decided to study the matter with a view to Congressional action. On May 2 the *New York Times* predicted that the committee's work would be of the utmost importance, for it would result in "materially extending the scope of the Monroe Doctrine."

If Senator Lodge had not been restrained by the more diplomatic and, in the matter of foreign relations, more conservative Senator Root, the resulting resolution might have been more drastically worded than it was. Senator Lodge thought it should refer unmistakably to Magdalena Bay. When faced with Root's contention that, in view of her categorical denial of evil intent, Japan might well take umbrage if the resolution were too sharply pointed in her direction, Lodge weakened. With Root's help he drafted the resolution which was accepted by a vote of fifty-one to four in the Senate. Accompanying it was a declaration stating that no evidence of activity by any foreign government had been discovered but that, since an American syndicate apparently had tried to sell the land "on the basis of its strategic value," some precautions should be taken.

The resolution, which historians have considered part of the Monroe Doctrine, and a logical modification of it to twentieth-century conditions and particularly to the Panama Canal, reads as follows: —

Resolved, That when any harbor or other place in the American continents is so situated that the occupation thereof for naval or military purposes might threaten the communications or the safety of the United States, the Government of the United States could not see without grave concern the possession of such harbor or other place by any corporation or association which has such a relation to another Government, not American, as to give that Government practical power of control for naval or military purposes.

When the President failed to accept the doctrine offered him, Senator Lodge boasted that it was the "doctrine of the Senate." Taft was upset to think that the Senate had forgotten that "I also am a part of the United States government."

XVIII

"Aspiration for Perfection"

"MY HAT is in the ring."

When Theodore Roosevelt spoke those fateful words to a reporter at Columbus, Ohio, on February 21, 1912, he forced Henry Cabot Lodge to make a decision which wrenched his very soul. It was not a sudden decision, but one which he had known for some time was inevitable.

Senator Lodge and Roosevelt had differed earlier, although amiably enough. In December, Lodge had delivered an address at Raleigh, North Carolina, on "The Constitution and Its Makers," in which he had touched upon what were to become the "burning issues" of the 1912 campaign. He not only believed, he said, that the direct election of Senators would "injure the character of the Senate," but he deeply felt that any attempt to legislate by direct vote, except perhaps in the states, was "destructive . . . retrogression," and he was fundamentally opposed to the recall of judges on the ground that such a system would rob the courts of their independence.

He was hurt to find that Dear Theodore was flirting with such radical ideas; ideas which, he knew, Roosevelt had picked up, in the words of Elihu Root, "as one might pick up a poker or a chair with which to strike." He argued patiently with his friend, but to no avail.

On February 21 Roosevelt delivered his sensational "Charter of Democracy" speech at Columbus. Cabot Lodge was shocked to read his exposition of the principles of the New Nationalism. Property, Roosevelt declared, must be made subject to human rights and government must be set free of the control of money in politics. As "weapons in the hands of the people" Roosevelt advocated exactly those things which, the Senator had warned him, struck at the heart of the Constitution — as interpreted by himself and his great-grandfather, George Cabot, before him. Initiative and referendum seemed as dangerous to Cabot Lodge as any of the proposals of Jefferson had seemed to his ancestor. And recall of judges appalled him. Senator Lodge believed, as his great-grandfather had believed, that democracy was "the government of the worst."

On February 24 Theodore Roosevelt made his "hat in the ring" statement official by announcing his candidacy for the Republican nomination for the Presidency.

Where did Senator Lodge stand now? This was the question asked in the press, which perhaps should have known the answer. But Lodge had always seemed a shifty character to the newspapers, a realistic enough characterization to justify the speculation that now took place. Lodge had no abiding affection for President Taft, as his attacks on the Knox treaties showed. This complicated the situation. Yet he belonged more surely in Taft's conservative, legalistic camp than in that of the Roosevelt who was revealed at Columbus. There was more than a witticism behind a paragraph in a letter Lodge had written Roosevelt shortly after the 1910 election, in which he had told his friend: "I am denounced as a reactionary and standpatter who is not in sympathy with the movements of the time, and on the other hand I am denounced as a dangerous radical because of my friendship with you and my sympathy with many of your views." The latter characterization must have irked him much more than the former. After all, he was an Elder Statesman now. Friendship was not everything. He made his choice. Publicly he declared: —

"I am opposed to the constitutional changes advocated by Colonel Roosevelt in his recent speech at Columbus. I have very strong convictions on those questions which, during the past three or four years, I have expressed in public with such force or argument as I could command. But Colonel Roosevelt and I for thirty years, and wholly apart from politics, have been close and most intimate friends. I must continue to oppose the policies which he urged at Columbus, but I cannot personally oppose him who has been my lifelong friend, and for that reason I will take no part whatever in the campaign for the presidential nomination."

To Theodore he wrote: —

I have had my share of mishaps in politics but I never thought that any situation . . . would have made me so miserably unhappy as I have been during the past week. . . . I could not abandon my convictions, and to come out for you, holding and known to hold the views which I have expressed, would have stultified me and made me worse than useless to you. Nor did I believe that you for a moment would wish me to do so. As for going against you in any way or supporting anyone else against you, that I could not do. There is very little of the Roman in me towards those I love best, and I hope a good deal of loyalty in my affection. . . . I shall be silent until the convention is over. I cannot tell you how much I have suffered from these harsh necessities and so I shall say no more. You, I am sure, will understand. . . .

The ebullient Roosevelt replied: —

I don't know whether to be most touched by your letter or most inclined to laugh over it. My dear fellow, you could not do anything that would make me lose my warm personal affection for you. . . . Of course you will stand by your own convictions. Now, don't ever think of this matter again.

257

Lodge kept his word. He did not speak publicly of the subject until after Roosevelt had bolted the Republican Party and the convention had renominated William Howard Taft. But he did not take the political break easily. As Henry Adams observed, he was "reduced to gloomy desperation." Of all those whose throats Theodore cut — his old friends, Cabot, George von L. Meyer, Henry L. Stimson, Gus Gardner, his own son-in-law Nicholas Longworth — it was Lodge who took it the hardest, if Adams's word may be accepted. "I think Cabot is the example of completest smashness," he confided. "You know too well my opinions of Theodore and Cabot — they date from John Hay's time ten years ago — and I've nothing to add to them, except that if Theodore has broken down from mental excitement, Cabot has broken down from mental weakness. Both are pitiable wrecks. Cabot is just plain feeble. . . ."

After Taft's renomination Lodge broke his silence. "To the best of my ability," he said at Nahant in June, "I have fought the battles of the Republican party for the past thirty years. To the Republican party I owe all that I have had in public life. With its policies and principles . . . I am in full accord. I not only believe in the policies . . . set forth [at Chicago], but I regard the declared determination of the party to stand firmly for the Constitution and for the independence of the courts, because they are vital to the maintenance of free government, as of last importance. . . ."

At the start of the Wilson administration Senator Lodge surprised many of his friends by supporting Woodrow Wilson in his determination to appear in person at the Capitol and read his opening message in person to both Houses of Congress. The scholar in politics approved the anomaly of a Democratic President reviving the custom which had been abandoned by Jefferson. The Jeffersonian Democrats in Congress objected, muttering about the "separation of powers";

to Senator Lodge it must have seemed a reversion to the ancient Hamiltonian doctrines he had always espoused. President Wilson, he may have recalled, had argued in favor of open relations between the executive and the legislative branches in his first published essay, that which young Henry Cabot Lodge, editor of the *International Review,* had accepted when Wilson was a student at Princeton in 1879.

As a member of a more or less supplicant minority it was not to be expected that Senator Lodge would take an imposing role in the legislative program of the New Freedom. The first question of importance was once again revision of the tariff. In his *The Senate and the League of Nations,* the first chapter of which is an attempt to explain that his early relations with Wilson were "without any hostile prejudice on my part," Senator Lodge dismisses this topic with these words: "Upon the questions which arose in connection with the tariff, and later regarding the bill for the establishment of the Federal Reserve Bank, I took . . . the Republican position, which I had always held, in favor of the protective tariff."

Late in September he had quietly left Washington, suffering severely from an attack of gastric ulcers. At the Charlesgate Hospital in Cambridge an operation was decided upon. It was successful, but he was not well enough to return to Washington until after the Christmas holidays.

His ill health and a subsequent European jaunt kept Senator Lodge from participating in the debates which accompanied the passage of several of the progressive measures which became law during the first term of President Wilson. Although he was not present to speak or vote he took decided stands on most of the issues and had them recorded in the *Congressional Record* by his colleague, Senator John W. Weeks.

Senator Lodge took no part in the passage of the Clayton

Anti-Trust Law, but he would have voted against it had he not been hurrying home from England at the time, September 2, 1914. The Senate was spared his utterances on the bill creating the Federal Trade Commission, but he had left word with Senator Weeks that he would have voted "Nay" had he been present.

He was absent, in Europe, when Secretary of State Bryan's "cooling-off treaties" which had been drawn up with twenty-one nations were sent to the Senate in 1914. In discussing them with Roosevelt later, he spoke of the "folly" and the "wickedness" of making treaties "which have no force and no intent of enforcement behind them." "I was away last summer," he said regretfully, "when those fatuous treaties were put through by Bryan. If I had been there I should have resisted them."

If Senator Lodge found the treaties "fatuous," he was more than willing to go along with the Democratic President when the first storm over Mexico broke in the spring of 1914. In all the Senate, for a brief period, there was no more ardent defender of Woodrow Wilson than Henry Cabot Lodge.

As a student of history President Wilson was at this time aware of the futility of attempting to establish a consistent foreign policy without first consulting the Senate. Before he laid his proposal before the Congress he flatteringly invited the Foreign Relations Committee to visit him and talk the matter over. Senator Lodge was well pleased to find a President commencing his administration so auspiciously. All along had he not argued that Presidents owed it to themselves and their country to take the Senate into their confidence? President Wilson, however, apparently did not tell the assembled committeemen all that he had in mind. At least Lodge, with the wisdom of afterthought, when he came to write about this situation years later, claimed that he did not and cited the incident as an example of the duplicity he insisted was so much a part of Wilson's character.

What Wilson asked the committee was straightforward enough: their support of his proposal to repeal the act authorizing discrimination in tolls in favor of American vessels passing through the Panama Canal. What he did not tell them was that at that very moment he was bargaining with Great Britain for her support in Mexico in return for the repeal. As he told Congress in his special message: "I ask this of you in support of the foreign policy of the administration. I shall not know how to deal with other matters of even greater delicacy and nearer consequences if you do not grant it to me in ungrudging measure."

Lodge was willing to go along in spite of not knowing why he was doing it. Obviously flattered that the President had consulted him and his committee, he spoke at great length on the question. There was opposition to granting the Presidential request, some of it from within his own party. What touched Lodge off to his gallant defense of Wilson was the inference made by Senator Bristow, a radical Republican of Kansas, that the President was being influenced by foreign and domestic corporations. That this was so Senator Lodge indignantly denied.

". . . I am sure that in dealing with it he is guided entirely by what he thinks is for the honor and credit of the United States in our relations with foreign nations," Lodge said. "I think he has the conviction that . . . the United States has fallen into an unfortunate and unhappy position, where she has incurred the active dislike of many nations and the distrust of many more, instead of the friendship and respect she once possessed. . . . He believes, I think, that prestige and influence are not to be obtained by disregarding the international obligations or by reversing policies long held by the United States simply to gratify some passing whim or some passion of the moment. I believe also that the President regards the foreign relations of the country as above party. . . . When he is dealing with foreign relations . . . if he says, on his high responsibility, to the Congress of the United States that a certain step is necessary to the good name and possibly to the security of the United States . . . I think it becomes the duty of all men, who look upon foreign relations as I do, not to try to block his path but to give him such aid and assistance in our humble way as we are conscientiously able to give. . . . I am anxious to go as far as I can in supporting my President when he is dealing with a difficult and complicated foreign situation, because the great responsibility of initiating and shaping our foreign policy must rest with the executive and cannot rest anywhere else."

No wonder President Wilson was pleased. Such unexpected support from one long noted for his partisanship was not to be ignored. He telephoned Lodge his personal thanks and later dropped him a cordial note saying he felt "honored by your confidence and your general comprehension of my motives."

Meanwhile Great Britain was living up to its part of the bargain, seeking to induce Huerta to accede to the American demands. This the Mexican General refused to do. President Wilson thereupon lifted the embargo against Mexico, thus assuring that Huerta's enemies might arm themselves; and he ordered naval vessels to stand off Vera Cruz. This brought about the "Tampico incident" when American sailors, going ashore to purchase gasoline, were arrested. When Admiral Mayo demanded a salute from the Mexicans, and it was refused, President Wilson, claiming this was but one of many instances in which Huerta had shown his contempt for the United States, asked Congressional authority to use arms if necessary to enforce the salute. Senator Lodge, brimming over with patriotism, openly sympathized with this request.

On the morning of April 17 the President called the Foreign Relations and Foreign Affairs Committees to the White House and told them that he might have to use the Army and Navy as a result of the Tampico affair. He wanted to know, according to Lodge's account, "whether we thought that he should call on Congress for authority." Lodge, as ranking Republican of the Senate group, advised him that he did not have to but that, since Congress was in session, it would be better to ask Congress for an "authorizing resolution." Wilson agreed. On Monday, three days later, Lodge and some others were again called to the White House where Wilson read them the message he was to send to Congress an hour later. "It seemed to me weak and insufficient although of course well expressed," was the Senator's reaction.

It was not the message as much as it was the accompanying resolution that annoyed Senator Lodge as he sat opposite the President in the Executive Office of the White House that April afternoon. One cannot escape the thought that the two men, the President and the Senator, were sizing each other up as they discussed it. Both were students of history, and, although they hardly knew each other (prior to Wilson's election they had met but once and then only casually at an alumni dinner at a Harvard Commencement), each, at this moment, seemingly respected the other. Lodge had his views and Wilson had his; they were not the same. We have Lodge's version of what took place: —

He [Wilson] then produced the resolution which he wished passed. It was the same as that which afterwards passed the House and authorized hostilities against Huerta by name. This seemed to me unsatisfactory, in reality a declaration of war against an individual. I said I thought we ought to speak of protection to the lives and property of American citizens as the true and international ground. Pres. said that would widen too much and lead to war. I thought it war at any event. He said that he wanted immediate action because he wished to intercept a cargo of arms for Huerta due that evening at Vera Cruz on a German ship. I suggested that he could not seize the ship without a war blockade. He said that his plan was to take Vera Cruz and seize the cargo after it was landed. I pointed out that he would then be cutting off arms from Huerta and letting them go to Villa, which would be in the nature of an alliance. He said this was due to circumstances and could not be helped.

As soon as the House heard the President read his message it received and passed the resolution. Lodge was waiting for it when it reached the Senate. According to his version objection to "the President's resolution naming Huerta was unanimous" in the Senate Committee, which, after several false starts, at last accepted a new resolution, written by Lodge with a preamble by Senator Root. "When we reassembled after the recess I saw at once the Democrats had seen the President," he said. The fight was on.

Senator Lodge's resolution, without Root's preamble and with one minor change in phraseology, was reported out by the committee. "It was something to get rid of Huerta's name . . . but without the preamble we were left to go to war in silence as to the real and only truly justifying international grounds," Lodge felt. He thereupon offered his resolution, with the preamble, as a substitute. But although he said, "I want to support the President in every possible way in this Mexican matter. I would not do one thing to embarrass him. I want to help him. I do not recognize that he is a Democratic president when we are dealing with a foreign country. I think he is the American president," his resolution was defeated by a straight party vote.

The day after the landing of American forces at Vera Cruz

Senator Lodge again saw Wilson at the White House with other members of the committee. He found him "in a state of great agitation and very much disturbed. He had never meant to have war."

"All he seemed desirous of doing," Lodge noted, ". . . was to get out of the trouble in any way possible without continuing the war which he himself had begun." The means he sought, and of which Lodge approved, was through the intervention of Argentina, Brazil, and Chile, the famous "A-B-C" mediation. "To have refused" the offer of those countries "would have been a terrible blunder," Lodge wrote in a memorandum made at the time. As a result, Huerta was driven from power, but his departure did not bring stability to Mexico.

Senator Lodge soon became, instead of a friendly critic, the most outspoken opponent of President Wilson's Mexican policy. Much of the enmity between the two men that later was to have such disastrous results stemmed from this. In his *The Senate and the League of Nations* Senator Lodge printed a peculiarly passionate disavowal of holding any "personal animosity to the President." In the course of this apologia he stated, "In all the speeches and debates I never attacked him personally or otherwise than courteously and always on public questions." This statement follows a bitter attack upon Wilson in which Lodge insisted that the only reason Wilson acted as he did against Mexico was because General Huerta "had made himself a stumbling block in Mr. Wilson's path and he had interfered with Mr. Wilson's plans, which was an unforgivable offense. . . . His egotism, so little comprehended then, was so vast that he did not hesitate to say to the world that Huerta's resistance to him must be punished. . . ."

On January 6, 1915, Senator Henry Cabot Lodge made a long and angry and critical speech in the Senate. He declared then that Wilson's refusal to recognize Huerta was merely personal vindictiveness on the part of the President of the United States, who, less than a year before, Lodge had said alone should make the foreign policy of the United States. "The President is a man accustomed to obedience," he said. The President deeply resented General Huerta's refusal to abdicate when Wilson asked him to. "This was animosity," said Senator Lodge, "not a policy."

Between 1914 and 1916 the gulf between Wilson and Lodge widened. Upon his return from Europe after war broke out in August Lodge told Roosevelt that he would no longer remain silent about Mexico and, in the same breath, said that Wilson's attitude towards preparedness was "pitiful." That autumn and early winter his private remarks about Wilson were caustic. He was all for having a Congressional investigation to find out what the condition of our national defenses was and when the administration objected he said, "Wilson and Bryan go beyond anything we have ever had, and there are certain persons who I think were pretty inefficient in the past." A few days after writing that he dropped in for a visit with his old friend, Henry Adams. Although he was growing feeble and old, Adams's observations were still as keen as ever. "This morning Cabot . . . fulminated against Woodrow Wilson as usual, for Cabot raves against that great man. . . ." Lodge continually sneered at Wilson for his desire "to be the great pacificator and settle the war in Europe." Before the end of 1915 he was calling Wilson a "humbug."

Senator Lodge was particularly bitter over Woodrow Wilson's Ship Purchase Bill. This administration proposal was to the effect that the government should, at least during the European crisis, buy up merchant ships and operate them. The "socialistic" implications of the bill made Lodge's blood boil but most of his violent assaults upon it were made as usual on loftier grounds. He scented a German plot and even suspected that Wilson, while declaring for neutrality "in fact as well as name," was pro-German.

"The ship purchase bill," he told Roosevelt, ". . . is one of the most dangerous things internationally — I say nothing of its viciousness economically — which could be imagined. The plan is to buy the German ships. If this is done and the Allies refuse to recognize the transfer of the flag, which France and Russia certainly will do . . . we shall find ourselves with Government-owned ships afloat which the Allies regard as German ships and therefore good prize and which are liable to be fired on and sunk. In the case of a private transaction this would not be very dangerous, but when it comes to dealing with Government-owned ships . . . they bring us within measurable distance of war."

He warned his friend that "this incompetent Administration may flounder into war, just as they blundered and floundered into bloodshed at Vera Cruz."

An amendment which Senator Lodge offered barring the purchase of ships belonging to any belligerent was defeated in the Committee on Commerce. Later he offered it to the Senate. Lodge and his anti-administration colleagues knew that with such an amendment the bill stood far less chance of passage. Nevertheless the opponents were in the minority and Wilson was bringing pressure to pass the bill. The only way left open to assure its death was by a filibuster and, from early in January to the fourth of March, "this policy of resistance," as Lodge (who once had maintained the Senate's right to vote was greater than its right to debate) called the filibuster, went on with unabated fury in the Senate. Leading it were Senators Gallinger, Root, and Smoot, all vigorous Republicans; at times they had the aid of seven Democrats, who slid over, so they said, in order to clear up the filibustering mess and make way for other important legislation. In the end the bill was kept from passage and it was to be another year before the administration could obtain qualified Congressional approval for government purchase of merchant ships.[1]

Although Lodge was a more ardent supporter of Wilson's stand on neutrality than he gave the impression of being in his posthumously published *The Senate and the League of Nations*, he felt at the same time that the administration was stupidly unrealistic in its attitude towards national military and naval preparedness. The administration had no more outspoken a foe on this score than Lodge's son-in-law Gussie Gardner, who demanded, early in the autumn of 1914, that the United States should start at once to prepare for war.

On December 2, 1914, Senator Lodge made startling charges as to the alleged inefficiency of the Army and Navy and, by inference, blamed this on the President.[2] His letters of the period bristle with angry references to the topic of national defense. One needs only to glance through the pages of the *Congressional Record* to see how often he warned his colleagues in detail of what he considered our woefully inadequate state of preparedness. At no time, however, did he predict our becoming involved in the European imbroglio. He based the need for national preparedness more on the trouble with Mexico than on anything else.

During the debate on the National Defense Act of 1916, he argued in behalf of a regular standing army of 250,000 men.

[1] Senator Lodge was absent from the Senate when the United States Shipping Board Act passed the Senate, but his colleague, Weeks, said that he would have voted "Nay." *Congressional Record*, Vol. 53, pp. 12824–12825.
[2] At least none of the instances of incompetency which he cited on December 2, 1914, went back of Wilson's administration. (*New York Times*, December 3, 1914.)

"Is that in any measure due to the Senator's apprehension of greater trouble than we have with Mexico?" Senator Stone asked.

"No," replied Lodge, ". . . it is not due to that, still less to any apprehension of war with any first class power."

The reason we needed 250,000 men was for "ordinary protection," he said without further elaboration.[3]

All his sympathies, however, lay instinctively with the Allies and he knew that, if we must be drawn into the conflict, it would have to be on their side. Like everyone else he followed the course of the war with a good deal of trepidation. But politically his one great aim at this time was the same as it had been during the only other Democratic administration he had known since he had been in Congress: if we must have war let it come under Republican leadership. Then it had been Cleveland and Spain; now it was Wilson and God knows what.

In the very speech in which he had championed President Wilson on the repeal of the canal tolls act in such generous language he had served warning. "I believe in government by parties and party responsibility," he had said. "I have for many years fought the battles of the Republican party, alike in days of sunshine and in days of storm and darkness. If life and strength continue, I shall to the best of my ability oppose President Wilson if he is a candidate for re-election and the party which he leads. The allurements of political advantage appeal to me as strongly as they can to any man. But when the relations of my country with other nations are involved I cannot yield to them. My politics has always stopped at the water's edge."

[3] Lodge introduced a number of preparedness resolutions. See *Congressional Record*, Vol. 53, pp. 4427, 5935, 9749, 10251. Their contents range from a warning by Rear Admiral Bradley A. Fiske of the unprepared state of the Navy to a request to print in the *Record* a paper on the sources of nitrogen compound.

That was as far as he would go; farther, perhaps, than he may have been expected to go. After all, he was a politician and a party man; and he never let anyone forget it. "To thwart the purposes or discredit the policies of the official head of a political party is legitimate political warfare," he said. "To discredit or break down the President of the United States upon a question of foreign policy is quite another thing, never to be undertaken except for very grave reasons. In the one case we overthrow a party leader and political chief within the arena where the American people alone sit in judgement, in the other we break down and discredit the representative of the whole country in the great forum of the nations of the earth and paralyze his future power and usefulness in that field where he and he alone can declare and represent the policies, the honor, and the dignity of the United States."

And so Senator Lodge was bending every effort to over-throw the party leader and political chief, to thwart his purposes and discredit his policies. He was looking forward to 1916. Perhaps by then Theodore Roosevelt would have been brought back into the fold. He would be a good man, a strong man, to have in the White House in these dangerous times. They had been through one war together; they could go through another. And, if not Roosevelt, it did not really matter, except that it must not be Woodrow Wilson at any cost.[4]

[4] On February 8, 1915, he wrote: "I cannot believe there is the slightest possibility of Taft receiving the Republican nomination." He felt the "masses of the Republican party" felt the same and said: "They have a very good chance to win the next time and they are bent on turning Wilson out. They know they cannot do it with Taft." (*Sel. Cor. T. R. and H. C. L.*, II, 454.) That he hoped it might be Roosevelt may be deduced from a letter he wrote to Charles G. Washburn on May 24, 1915, after the conclusion of the Roosevelt-Barnes libel suit: ". . . It is a very great victory for Theodore and, contrary to the belief of sanguinary friends of Mr. Wilson, I think it is a fortunate

Senator Lodge expected we would be drawn into the war and did not fear it. But Wilson was doing his best to ruin the country's reputation by his weak policy on preparedness. When, in the summer of 1915, he began to take a realistic view and sent for reports from the War and Navy Departments, Senator Lodge snorted, "He is the Commander-in-Chief . . . he has been two years in office, and now is sending for reports as to their condition. It seems to me, an old-fashioned person, that the President as Commander-in-Chief ought to know about the Army and Navy as soon as he enters office."

During the winter Senator Lodge accepted an invitation from Union College at Schenectady, New York, to deliver the Commencement address on June 9. The scholar in politics took a great deal of pride in those speeches he was asked to give at such exercises, and always endeavored to make them polished literary products from which he excluded, as much as was humanly possible, all partisanship. His speech at Union was no exception. He gave much thought to its preparation. He entitled it "The Maintenance of Peace."

"What can we do in the larger sense toward securing and maintaining the peace of the world?" he asked the Union College graduates. "This is a . . . difficult question, but turn it back and forth as we may there is no escape from the proposition that the peace of the world can only be maintained as the peace and order of a single community are maintained, by the force which unified nations are willing to put behind the peace and order of the world. Nations must unite as men unite to preserve peace and order. The great

thing for the Republican party and will help more than anything else to bring us together. The overthrow of Barnes removes one of the conventional cries of the Progressives and as seven Republicans were on the jury I think that Theodore will be more than ever ready to unite with the party to which he belongs. . . ." (*Washburn Papers:* American Antiquarian Society, Worcester, Mass.)

nations must be so united as to be able to say to any single country, 'You must not go to war'; and they can only say that effectively when the country desiring war knows that the force which the united nations place behind peace is irresistible.

"In differences between nations, which go beyond arbitrable questions, peace can only be maintained by putting behind it the force of united nations determined to uphold it and prevent war. No one is more conscious than I of the enormous difficulties which beset such a solution or such a scheme, but I am certain it is in this direction alone that we can find hope for the maintenance of the world's peace and the avoidance of needless wars. Even if we could establish such a union there might be some wars which could not be avoided but there are certainly many which might be prevented."

Wars cannot be stopped by "language, by speech-making, by vain agreements which no one could carry out," he told the graduates, who may hardly have dreamed at that moment that within two years they would go marching down the road to war themselves. But still there was a way.

"It may seem utopian at this moment to suggest a union of civilized nations in order to put a controlling force behind the maintenance of peace and international order; but it is through the aspiration for perfection, through the search for utopias, that the real advances have been made. At all events, it is along this path that we must travel if we are to attain in any measure to the end we all desire of peace on earth. It is at least a great, a humane purpose to which, in these days of death and suffering, of misery and sorrow among so large a portion of mankind, we might well dedicate ourselves. We must begin our work with the clear understanding that our efforts will fail if they are tainted with the thought of personal or political profit or with any idea of self-glorification; we may not now succeed, but I believe that in the slow process of the years others who come after us will reach the goal. The effort and the sacrifice which we make will not be in vain when the end in sight is noble, when we are striving to help mankind and lift the heaviest burdens from suffering humanity."

"That's a capital speech of yours," said Theodore.

Congress was not in session and a long, restful summer at Nahant and Tuckernuck stretched ahead. There could be no European trip, what with the war on. Senator Lodge would read and study, play around a bit, perhaps, with the state campaign. In December he would need all his strength to renew in Congress his fight with the administration over preparedness for war.

On the evening of September 27, after a quiet dinner, Nannie Lodge was suddenly taken ill. Sturgis Bigelow, the Senator's faithful friend and his family physician, was a house guest. He at once recognized the symptoms of a severe heart attack. Dr. Lawrence Cusick of Nahant was called at once. But there was nothing either of them could do. Just after midnight she died. Two days later Bishop William Lawrence, the Senator's old schoolmate and lifelong friend, conducted the simple Protestant Episcopal services at Christ Church, Cambridge, where Cabot and Nannie had been married forty-four years before. Henry Cabot Lodge was to face the climax of his career alone.

XIX

Amblings to Disaster

IN HIS message to Congress in December 1914, President
Wilson had repeated the substance of his proclamation of
neutrality and set himself squarely against a policy of preparedness. To do more than enlarge the National Guard,
he told the lawmakers, "would mean . . . that we had lost
our self-possession, that we had been thrown off our balance
by a war with which we had nothing to do, whose causes
cannot touch us. . . ."

How quickly the fallacy of his isolationism was to be borne
in upon him! First there was the British blockade, which
shut off Germany almost completely as a market for American foods and munitions. Next there was Germany's reply
to the blockade — the submarine that was turned loose
against the Allied lifeline.

A nation whose exports of munitions alone rose from
forty to three hundred and thirty million dollars in the first
year of the European conflict, and whose principal private
bank was passing out daily orders for $10,000,000 worth of
goods for the Allies, could hardly expect long to escape involvement. The danger of getting hurt grew day by day
as each side, Germany and the Allies, began disregarding
all the ancient rules of international law. Great Britain, so
used to ruling the seas, extended the list of contraband to
exclude practically all the goods her enemy needed to im-
port; worse still, she detained American ships in her ports

and opened American mail. Germany, on her part, was sending torpedoes into any ships that came within range of her periscopes, without stopping to see if anyone aboard happened to be an American citizen.

Both sides cavalierly ignored the letters of protest that were sent after each incident, from the desk of William Jennings Bryan, the Secretary of State. Then, on May 7, 1915, the British liner *Lusitania,* bound from New York to Liverpool, was torpedoed off the Irish coast with the loss of 1150 lives, 114 of whom were Americans who had disregarded the published warnings of the Imperial German Embassy not to travel on "vessels flying the flag of Great Britain."

At least once during the ensuing weeks, when the "rights" of Americans to travel on belligerent ships were being discussed, Senator Lodge was called to the White House for consultation with President Wilson. He believed the purpose was to sound him out as to how he would stand if the United States should break off relations with Germany, an act which he favored just as soon as a case against Germany could actually be proved by identification of a submarine.

But within a year the Senator had become disgusted with what he considered President Wilson's flabby policy of meaningless words. In March 1916, the *Springfield Republican* reported that he had called Mr. Wilson's administration the worst in the country's history, with the possible exception of Buchanan's. President Wilson was well aware that Senator Lodge bore him no love and suspected him of being willing to do anything in his power to discredit his administration. In January of that year he had written a friend: "I think you cannot know to what lengths men like Root and Lodge are going, who I once thought had consciences but now know have none. We must not suffer or twist ourselves as they do, or use their insincere or contemptible methods of fighting; but we must hit them straight in the face, and not mind if the blood comes."[1] On the last day of March those conscienceless men, Root and Lodge, lunched with Theodore Roosevelt, Robert Bacon, and Leonard Wood, and over the cigars and coffee laid preliminary plans to bring the Republicans and the Progressives together in the holy cause of driving Woodrow Wilson from power.

That winter both the President and the Senator accepted invitations to speak before the first annual assemblage of the League to Enforce Peace which was to meet at the Mayflower Hotel in Washington on the twenty-seventh of May, only a few days before the Republican Convention was to convene. The night of the great meeting arrived and found the two scholars in politics on the same platform. President Wilson had not released his speech in advance and there was much speculation as to what he would say. Senator Lodge spoke first. It was a historic speech.

"The limit of voluntary arbitration has, I think, been reached," he said once more. "I think the next step is that which this League proposes and that is to put force behind international peace, an international league or agreement, or tribunal, for peace. We may not solve it in that way, but if we cannot solve it in that way it can be solved in no other. . . .

"The way in which this problem must be worked out," he said, "must be left to this League and to those who are giving this great question the study which it deserves. . . . I know how quickly we shall be met with the statement that this is a dangerous question . . . that no nation can submit to the judgement of other nations. . . . I know the difficulties that arise when we speak of anything which seems to involve an alliance.

"But I do not believe that when Washington warned us

[1] *Woodrow Wilson: Life and Letters,* by Ray Stannard Baker. Vol. V, pp. 126–127.

against entangling alliances [2] he meant for one moment that we should not join with the other civilized nations of the world if a method could be found to diminish war and encourage peace.

"If our aspirations are for that which is great and beautiful and good and beneficent to humanity, even when we do not achieve our end, even if the results are little, we can at least remember Arnold's lines: —

> "Charge once more, then, and be dumb!
> Let the victors, when they come,
> When the forts of folly fall,
> Find your body by the wall."

President Wilson, who had already said that he prayed to God that if "this conflict has no other result, it will at least have the result of creating an international tribune and producing some sort of joint guarantee of peace on the part of the great nations of the world," went this night a little farther than Senator Lodge.

It was his belief, he said, that the people of the United States would want, at the war's end, a universal association to preserve the freedom of the seas and to "prevent any war begun either contrary to treaty covenants or without warning and full submission of the causes to the opinion of the world." A few days later, he spoke of his willingness to join an alliance "which will unite the peoples for keeping the peace of the world on the basis of universal justice. Therein is liberation; not limitation."

The seed of the League of Nations had been sown and no less a scatterer than Woodrow Wilson was Henry Cabot Lodge.

[2] He said "entangling," apparently; but the scholar in politics knew better and in his published version of the speech he has changed it to "permanent alliances," which is the phrase Washington used in his Farewell Address. It was Jefferson, in his first Inaugural, who spoke of having "entangling alliances" with no nations.

It was no world-minded Senator from Massachusetts who headed the Massachusetts delegation to the Republican National Convention at the Coliseum in Chicago early in June, 1916. Here the decision was to be made that would, he confidently expected, drive the dreadful Wilson from public life. To whom this great honor might go he, of course, did not know. It might be Charles Evans Hughes, the brilliant former Governor of New York and now an Associate Justice of the Supreme Court; it might be Theodore Roosevelt, brought back penitent to the fold; it might be Senator John Wingate Weeks, whose name Lodge would offer to the Convention; and it might even be Henry Cabot Lodge of Massachusetts.

Immediately after the adjournment of the opening session the Committee on Resolutions met and elected Senator Lodge as chairman. This was an important and, as it turned out, momentarily unpleasant post. Although the sins of the Wilson administration were crying for rectification, to thousands of women throughout the United States the one and only issue was equal suffrage for women. The suffragists and antisuffragists were at Chicago in force. They stormed the open meeting, the suffragists all decked out in yellow sashes and yellow hatbands, hissed their opponents roundly and all but broke out in a memorable hair-pulling match. Luckily the leaders restored order before the chairman's whiskers were scattered to the Chicago winds.

The astute Republican leaders were glad of the women. Senator Lodge's committee could play at fighting a desperate battle over the wording of the suffrage plank, while the real purpose of the delay was to gain time for an agreement between the Republican leaders and the leaders of the Progressives, who were meeting at the same time, also in Chicago. The latter had high hopes of naming Theodore Roosevelt, but Senator Reed Smoot had thrown their camp into consternation by telling them that the Republican Party would take "anyone but Roosevelt." The Progressives were still rushing around in confusion, seeking a compromise candidate, when the Republicans reconvened.

"Lodge," said the *New York Times* the next day, "is the first man in the memory of many an old convention-goer who ever read a platform that the convention heard. Mostly the platform passes in a roar of conversation . . . but Lodge read amidst tense silence. Every eye was upon him. Every ear was his. Not a word was missed." Cheers met his venomous assertion that "we believe that peace and neutrality, as well as the dignity and influence of the United States, cannot be preserved by shifty expedients, by phrase-making, by performance in language, or by attitudes ever changing in an effort to secure votes or voters." Milder cheers approved: "We believe in the pacific settlement of international disputes, and favor the establishment of a world court for that purpose." [3] Cheers, too, met the planks declaring for preparedness and national defense and Lodge's incisive criticism of the administration's Mexican policy. And there was polite Republican applause for the planks on labor that were a direct sop to the Progressives.

When Lodge started to read the words declaring in favor of woman suffrage the galleries broke into wild acclaim. Alice Roosevelt Longworth, who was to be one of Senator Lodge's most intimate friends until his death, "with a mischievous twinkle in her bright eyes" urged the galleries to "get up and show yourselves and cheer. It's your moment of victory." They rose, they cheered, but Lodge's clear voice cut through. With a loud, explosive "but" he went on to

[3] The League to Enforce Peace, through Nicholas Murray Butler, had begged Lodge to present a plank endorsing its specific international program. His ears still ringing with President Wilson's May twenty-seventh speech, Lodge stubbornly refused, and substituted grudgingly this practically meaningless plank.

read the modifying clause which said the Republican Party "recognized the right of each state to settle the question for itself."

"Mrs. Longworth," the *Times* reporter noted, "laughed herself into convulsion as her suffragist friends hurriedly sat down, applauded until her hands were sore, and hurled gay taunts at them." A few years later there was to be no more vocal a camp follower of the Battalion of Death than she.[4]

Meanwhile the confused Progressives had received an amazing letter from their "chieftain," Theodore Roosevelt, which read in part: —

. . . I deeply appreciate your loyalty to me and the position in support of me which you have taken. But it would be an injustice both to you and myself not to regard that loyalty to me as fundamentally a loyalty to the principles you and I represent . . . the Progressive National Committee . . . pledged ourselves to leave nothing undone to reach an honorable agreement with the Republicans in order to achieve the end we have in view.

In view of the conditions existing I suggest the name of Senator Lodge of Massachusetts. He is a man of the highest integrity, of the broadest national spirit and of the keenest devotion to the public good. . . . He has not only a wide experience in public affairs, but a peculiarly close acquaintance with the very type of questions now most pressing for settlement. He has consistently fought for preparedness, preparedness for the Navy, preparedness in fortifying the Panama Canal, preparedness in upbuilding

[4] Two years earlier a group of suffragists had "blacklisted" Senator Lodge as one who should be kept out of public office on the ground that he opposed "humanitarian measures of legislation." Stung, he claimed to have carried the so-called "phossy-jaw" bill through the Senate in the Sixty-fourth Congress (a measure forbidding the manufacture of the old-fashioned sulphur matches, which were disagreeable to consumers and deathly dangerous to those who made them). He also boasted he had worked for the "opium bill," the Mann "white slave" Act, and, of course, his famous District of Columbia Child Labor Act. "I know of no humanitarian measure of this character I have not supported," he said. (*New York Tribune*, October 5, 1914.)

the Army. He has been on the whole the member with the largest vision and the most intelligent devotion to American needs we have had on the Foreign Affairs [sic] Committee during this generation. . . . In addition he has been one of the staunchest fighters for different measures of economic reform in the direction of justice. . . . I, therefore, urge upon you favorably to consider his name and report on it to the Conferees from the Republican National Convention, and if you do not agree with me in this respect nevertheless to transmit this telegram to the Republican conferees and to request them to place it before their Convention. . . .

The Progressives listened to the letter in a daze. As Claude Bowers has put it: —

Why Lodge — in Heaven's name, why Lodge? He had been a consistent reactionary all his life; had hated the Bull Moose Movement with all the venom that went with his hostility; had made speeches furiously assailing the Progressive program and had them published as Senate documents and distributed at the public cost. There was scarcely a line in the Progressive platform that was not, to him, as the red banner of the picador to the bull. It was incredible — and yet there it was — the letter! [5]

There it was, but it did Senator Lodge no good. True, his name was transmitted to the Republican Convention, over which that great and good poker player, Warren Gamaliel Harding, presided. But there the suggestion of Henry Cabot Lodge as a compromise candidate fell, as Claude M. Fuess has remarked, "like a feather on a block of granite." [6] On the third and crucial ballot Senator Lodge received only seven votes. He might draw what satisfaction he could from the fact that his colleague, Senator Weeks, whom he had nominated, received only three votes. Governor Charles Evans

[5] *Beveridge and the Progressive Era*, by Claude G. Bowers; 1932, p. 488.

[6] *Calvin Coolidge, the Man from Vermont*, by Claude M. Fuess; 1940, p. 158.

Hughes, who was acceptable to both Senator Lodge and Theodore Roosevelt, was then nominated by acclamation.

"The first duty of the Republican Party in the coming campaign," Lodge told the Convention, "is to drive from power the administration and the party which have so gravely injured us at home and so deeply discredited us abroad."

Senator Lodge, who would for the first time that fall be running for Senator under the system of popular vote which he despised, started carrying out his part of the duty at the annual clambake of the Dorchester Republican Club at Nantasket Point on August 19. "It is easy to set down fine words when there is nothing in them," he said. "After the awful disaster of the *Lusitania* the President . . . used the memorable phrase, 'Too proud to fight.' The country responded next morning. It was not a friendly response. So he changed. And we had a great note on 'strict accountability' and it, too, remains a phrase. There has never been a reparation or even an apology for the Americans drowned or killed on the *Lusitania*. We are left with phrases — nothing but words."

On October 27 Senator Lodge spoke to a large gathering of Republicans in the shoe-manufacturing city of Brockton and the next morning what he had to say was splattered all over the front pages of the nation's newspapers. He had created one of the great sensations of the campaign and, in doing so, had made Woodrow Wilson his enemy for life.

With little more to go on than what amounted to backstairs gossip, Senator Lodge told his Brockton audience of a dramatic play of forces within the administration: "After the note [protesting the sinking of the *Lusitania*] had been read to the cabinet and agreed to by all the members, Mr. Wilson added the postscript which I have not seen, because it mysteriously disappeared. In this postscript President Wilson informed the Imperial German Government that the words 'strict accountability' and other strong phrases . . . were not to be taken seriously, and ended by agreeing to refer the whole matter to arbitration. This, of course, pleased Mr. Bryan, but it did not please the other members of the cabinet, who threatened to resign and expose the whole thing. The postscript was removed, and Mr. Bryan resigned."

The very same edition of the *New York Times* which prominently displayed Lodge's garbled charges contained denials of his version from cabinet members presumably in a position to know the truth. Undeterred by the hornets' nest he had stirred up, the Senator, whose swing of the circle had brought him to the Boston suburb of Somerville, repeated his charges the next night. This time he said the information had come to him from a Dr. Charles H. Bailey of the medical faculty of Tufts College, who had heard it from former Assistant Secretary of War Henry C. Breckinridge while they were both riding on a train heading eastward from San Francisco four months before.

"This simply throws an additional light upon the shifty character of this administration in its foreign policy," Lodge said.

"Anyone who quoted me to Senator Lodge as reported is a scoundrel," Mr. Breckinridge telegraphed the *Times,* which editorially referred to Lodge's charges as a "puerile partisan falsehood. . . . It is possible that Mr. Bryan proposed a modification of the *Lusitania* letter, which was rejected," the newspaper added. "If that is true, it is not the least discreditable to President Wilson and Mr. Lodge knows it." And that is about what really had happened. Bryan wanted to inform Germany that the United States would willingly arbitrate the matter on the principle of the Bryan treaties. The State Department thought this inconsistent and so told Mr. Wilson. He agreed. The instruction which Bryan had prepared to send Ambassador Gerard was suppressed.

President Wilson, who was at Asbury Park, New Jersey, then sent a telegram to Walter Lippmann in New York,[7] which slapped Senator Lodge right across the face: —

. . . Let me say that the statement made by Senator Lodge is untrue. No postscript . . . was ever written or contemplated by me except such changes as I myself inserted which strengthened and emphasized the protest. It was suggested, after the note was ready for transmission, that an intimation be conveyed to the German government that a proposal for arbitration would be acceptable, and one member of the cabinet spoke to me about it, but it was never discussed in a cabinet meeting, and no threat of any resignation was ever made for the good reason that I rejected the suggestion after giving it such consideration as I thought every proposal deserved which touched so grave a matter. It was inconsistent with the purpose of the note. The public is in possession of everything that was said to the German government.

On November 1 Lodge issued a retraction: —

The President of the United States has denied that there was any postscript to the *Lusitania* note and we are all bound, of course, to accept the President's denial just as he makes it.

"We wonder," said a *Times* editorial writer, "what his grandfather [*sic*] George Cabot, pacing up and down the Federalist Preserve of Elysia, thinks of the behavior of his grandson and biographer. Can you imagine George Cabot or Harrison Gray Otis spreading stage-coach tittle-tattle at second or third hand as political or Gospel truth?"

It was all right for the *Times* to spoof, but a great and historic damage had been done. Senator Henry Cabot Lodge had accused the President of United States of playing

[7] A Jonas Lippmann, a campaign stump-speaker for the Democrats, had queried President Wilson as to the truth of Lodge's charges. The answer was sent to Walter Lippmann of the *New Republic*, a friend of the President, by mistake. It was released to the press at Asbury Park.

a shifty game, a game which might have endangered not only the prestige of his country, but also the rights and perhaps the lives of his people. President Wilson, stung to the quick, had called his attacker a liar. He had struck him straight in the face and had not minded if the blood came. A stubborn and proud man, Wilson could never forget. A stubborn and angry man, Lodge would never forgive.[8]

The ill-tempered quarrel did little damage to Senator Lodge's campaign for re-election to the Senate. On November 8, while the country waited to hear from California and some Eastern newspapers were announcing a victory for Justice Hughes, he was elected over Mayor Fitzgerald by a substantial margin. One can imagine his chagrin when the final returns from the whole nation were counted and Woodrow Wilson was safely elected for another four years.

Between the time of the conventions and the elections Congress had remained in session and had passed several important acts. Among them was the Federal Farm Loan Bank Act, designed to improve the agricultural credit situation. Only five Senators voted against it. One was Senator Lodge. The next important piece of legislation was the Jones Act which, at long last, granted to the Philippines what was practically a territorial status. Senator Lodge, declaring that the act left the United States responsible for the islands but with no power over them, voted against its passage.

Those were the last of the Wilsonian domestic policies to come before the Congress — the end of the New Freedom. Congress adjourned on September 8 and the "lame duck

---

[8] Senator Lodge's own version of this unhappy episode, which does him little credit, may be found in *The Senate and the League of Nations*, p. 32 ff. The reader should also consult *The True Story of Woodrow Wilson*, by David Lawrence, p. 145 ff., for the Wilsonian version. A complete and apparently impartial contemporary account may be found in the pages of the *New York Times* between October 27 and November 2, 1916.

session," which met between December 4 and March 4, had no matters of significance before it. The United States was traveling fast down the road to war, and Woodrow Wilson, with all the power at his command, was trying to stem the descent and bring about peace on earth once again.

In January 1917 a minor incident occurred which helped widen the breach between President Wilson and Senator Lodge. Both were invited to address the celebration of the 100th anniversary of the Church of St. John in Washington. According to Senator Lodge the President informed the committee in charge that he would not appear on the same platform with Lodge. When advised of this by the embarrassed committee, the Senator offered to withdraw; but Dr. Roland Cotton Smith, the rector of the church and an old friend of Lodge, would not allow him to do so. The President did not attend; Lodge made his speech; and only a few persons in Washington were aware of what happened.

Such was the relationship between the President and the Senator when Mr. Wilson appeared before the Senate on January 22. His purpose in addressing "the council associated with me in the final determination of our international obligations" was to disclose to the Senate "without reserve the thought and purpose that have been taking form in my mind in regard to the duty of our Government in the days to come when it will be necessary to lay afresh and upon a new plan the foundations of peace among the nations."

It was in this speech that Woodrow Wilson set forth his belief that the mission of American democracy was to show the people of the world the way to liberty. The great service which the United States could perform in a warring world "is nothing less than this, to add their authority and their power to the authority and force of other nations to guarantee peace and justice throughout the world. Such a settlement cannot now be long postponed. It is right that before it comes this Government should frankly formulate the conditions upon which it would feel justified in asking our people to approve its formal and solemn adherence to a League for Peace. I am here to attempt to state those conditions."

Senator Lodge, his eyebrows raised in a diabolical arch, listened intently as this President set forth the things he felt were necessary to secure a lasting peace. Already on the side of the Allies, the old war hawk trembled as Mr. Wilson called for a "peace without victory" on the grounds that a dictated peace "would be accepted in humiliation, under duress, at an intolerable sacrifice, and would leave a sting, a resentment, a bitter memory upon which the terms of peace would rest, not permanently, but only as upon quicksands."

With the rest could Senator Lodge be in disagreement — the right to self-determination, the freedom of the seas, disarmament, and a league of nations to administer the peace? In the light of his address to the graduates of Union College, in the light of his speech before the League to Enforce Peace, wherein he had corrected the historical misinterpretation of Washington's isolationism, it would hardly seem possible. And yet, eight days later he was to stand for nearly two hours in the Senate and tear to pieces President Wilson's great humanitarian plea.

Senator Lodge's speech, delivered more than two months before the United States entered the war against Germany, was the opening gun in the Senator's three-year battle against Woodrow Wilson and the world principles for which they both stood.

He began his lengthy peroration by paying his chill respects to the President for having recognized "the duties imposed upon the Senate by the Constitution in regard to our foreign relations." Although he refused to believe the President's message was "epochal," as it had been hailed in the press, he had to admit it was "highly important." He then began his assault.

President Wilson's vision of ending the war before either side could claim a victory seemed a strange proposal. "It seems to me incredible," he said, "that people who have made such awful sacrifices . . . should be content to forgo the prospect of victory, in the hope of bringing the war to an end, with everything left just as it was." It seemed strange to people in the United States as well as among the belligerents. In such a result "they might well think that all their efforts and losses, all their miseries and sorrows and sacrifices, were a criminal and hideous futility. Both sides have been inspired by the hope of victory; both sides are still so inspired."

He had no patience with Mr. Wilson's generalities. "We must deal with things as they are," he said; "we must uncover realities" — and he proceeded to be "realistic." Of the principle of self-determination he asked: "Who is to decide whether the principle is recognized under the different governments of the world with whom we are to form the League for Peace 'supported by the organized major force of mankind'? If the recognition of this principle is to be essential to the lasting peace which we are to support . . . what is to be done about Korea, or Hindustan, or Alsace-Lorraine, or the Trentino, or the Slav Provinces of Austria, or the Danish Duchies? Does the government of Armenia by Turkey, with its organized massacres, rest on the consent of the governed, and if it does not are we to take steps to remedy it, or is Turkey to be excluded from the league, or is the league to coerce Turkey to an observance of our principles?"

As to the freedom of the seas: this was an entirely new doctrine and if a serious attempt was made to enforce it we, and those nations which might sign the covenant with us, would surely be involved in every war which might occur between maritime nations.

Forgotten, now, was his Senate resolution of 1910 which had suggested the use of the combined navies of the world as "an international police force for the preservation of universal peace"! Abandoned was his theory that the peace could be maintained by force. In such a league as the President proposed, peace would be difficult of accomplishment. Should one member refuse to abide by the league's decision, war would result, and the United States alone would have to keep on hand 500,000 armed men as its share of the police force. Moreover, these American troops would be ordered about by the league — not by the United States. And who would run the league? If it were set up as Mr. Wilson proposed, the majority membership of little nations would do the ordering.

Although Senator Lodge claimed he had no "superstitious regard" for the policy established by Washington and advanced by Monroe, he summoned forth the spirits of those worthy Presidents. Washington, he recalled, had set forth his policy under conditions not unlike those that now exist; and the wisdom of his stand had been demonstrated for more than a century. We "should not depart from it without most powerful reasons and without knowing exactly where the departure would lead."

In the past the wily Senator had learned about conjuring up a dismal picture of future calamity. He had used the trick effectively in his successful fight against the treaties in 1911, when he had constructed hypothetical cases to show how the machinery then proposed might fetch disaster to the United States. He knew, then and now, that the answers to the element of fear which he had created would never catch up with his original charges. Now he asked the Senate to assume that a league had been created, one which "must deal with questions of vital interest and go beyond the limitations of voluntary arguments" and, in Mr. Wilson's words, be "supported by the major force of mankind."

"China and Japan, we will say, acting upon the principles of the brotherhood of man which this league is to embody, come before the representatives of the league and demand for their people the right of free emigration to Canada, Australia, and New Zealand, which now practically exclude them. . . . Suppose the league decided that the people of China and Japan ought not to be deprived of the right to migrate anywhere, and that Canada, Australia, and New Zealand, backed by England, decline to accept this decision. The league will then proceed to enforce its decision, and we shall find ourselves obliged to furnish our quota to a force which will compel the admission of Asiatic labor to Canada. Are we prepared to make war upon Canada in such a case as this, our quota of the forces of the league perhaps being under the orders of a Japánese commander in chief?

"Let us turn the question the other way. Suppose the Asiatic powers demand the free admission of their labor to the United States, and we resist, and the decision of the league goes against us, are we going to accept it? Is it possible that anyone who wishes to preserve our standards of life and labor can be drawn into a scheme veiled by glittering and glancing generalities, which would take from us our sovereign right to decide alone and for ourselves the vital question of the exclusion of Mongolian and Asiatic labor? These are not fanciful cases drawn from the region of the imagination. They are actual, living questions of the utmost vitality and peril today. In them is involved that deepest of human instincts which seeks not only to prevent an impossible competition in labor but to maintain the purity of the race. Are we prepared to make any agreement which would put us in such a position as that? Before we give our adhesion to a league for peace let us consider all these contingencies. . . ."

He then turned upon the advocates of Peace at Any Price

who clamored "with passionate demand" that we should immediately join a league of peace, warning that "they too, if they persist, will meet the day when words are vain, when there is no help or shelter in language, and when they must face relentless, unforgiving realities." He was not unwilling, he said, to use the power and influence of the United States for the promotion of peace. Indeed, there was nothing he had so much at heart, *but* we must remember that it is better to "bear the ills we have than to fly to others that we know not of." And he had four concrete measures to offer. They were adequate national preparedness; the rehabilitation of international law at the close of the war; the extension of the use of voluntary arbitration "within necessary and natural limits"; and the general reduction of the arms of all nations.

He earnestly urged full support of Senator Borah's resolution committing the United States without reserve to the policy of Washington and Monroe, "whose statements are as clear as the unclouded sun at noonday and are not reflections of double meaning words under which men can hide and say anything or nothing. . . . There is no lurking place for a league for peace 'supported by the organized major force of mankind' in the sentences of George Washington and Thomas Jefferson. . . . Let us beware how we take any steps which may precipitate this country and the people who are to come after us, and whose inheritance it is, into dangers which no man can foresee. . . ."

The Senator's great speech, which was a summation of all that he had learned in nearly a quarter of a century of rapt devotion to the foreign policy of the United States, was smothered by the crash of events.

Two days after its delivery President Wilson, irked by Germany's renewal of submarine warfare in direct violation of the agreement of May 4, 1916, severed diplomatic relations with the Imperial German Government. A month later the people were startled when the State Department released the Zimmermann note showing Germany's efforts to stir up Mexico against the United States. On March 12 the President took the law into his own hands and issued an order authorizing the arming of merchant ships. On March 16 and 17 three American ships, homeward bound, were attacked without warning and sunk without a trace. Nothing could now stem the tide. President Wilson with heavy heart called the Congress to meet in special session on April 2. When it gathered on that fateful day he delivered his War Message. In it he declared that he had "exactly the same thing in mind now" as he had in mind when he addressed the Senate on January 22.

"A steadfast concert for peace," he said in solemn tones, "can never be maintained except by a partnership of democratic nations. No autocratic government could be trusted to keep faith within it or observe its covenants. It must be a league of honor, a partnership of opinion. Intrigue would eat its vitals away, the plotting of inner circles who could plan what they would and render account to no one would be a corruption seated at its very heart. Only free peoples can hold their purpose and their honor steady to a common end and prefer the interests of mankind to any narrow interest of their own. . . ."

Then, after declaring it was not the German people but rather German autocracy against which he asked America to fight, he said: "It is a fearful thing to lead this great peaceful people into war. . . . But the right is more precious than peace, and we shall fight for the things which we have always carried nearest our hearts, for democracy, for the right of those who submit to authority to have a voice in their own governments, for the rights and liberties of small nations, for a universal dominion of right by such a concert of free peoples as shall bring peace and safety to all nations and make the world itself free."

That was the heart of his message. Those were America's war aims on April 2, 1917. He asked for a declaration of war within a month. It was given four days later.

The "perilous" and "vacillating and shifty course" which Senator Lodge said Wilson had pursued, and which, upon another occasion, he was to call "our amblings to disaster," had brought us war, at last. Once again Senator Lodge was to speak pious words about the necessity of standing behind the President who, he said, was no longer a party leader, but the commander in chief of a country at war. This conciliatory mood, however, was to be short-lived. There was to be no more bitter nor any more outspoken critic of the President's conduct of the war than Senator Lodge.

Senator Lodge took to heart the advice given him by Theodore Roosevelt, who was boiling over with personal hatred for the President because Mr. Wilson had stymied Roosevelt's vainglorious idea of raising an army of Rough Riders and leading them to Berlin. "Of course," the thwarted Colonel said, "be very careful never to antagonize Wilson on any point where he is right. But it is imperatively necessary to expose his hypocrisy, his inefficiency, his rancorous partisanship, and his selfish eagerness to sacrifice all patriotic considerations to whatever he thinks will be of benefit to himself politically."

Roosevelt even told Senator Lodge that, "if our people were really awake," Wilson "would be impeached tomorrow." We do not have Lodge's answer, but that the two men were in accord in their hatred for Wilson in the early months after our entrance into the war is apparent from even a casual reading of their letters. Senator Lodge, publicly and privately, blamed all the confusion and delays attendant upon a great nation's entering its first major war since 1865 upon President Wilson and his appointees. Because ships and arms did not spring up overnight, Wilson was to blame. And yet, in spite of the fact that the President would not "allow any Republicans if he can help it to have a post of any importance," by August 1917 even Lodge had to admit: "Still, we are moving, although slowly."

But it was not long before Senator Lodge was wailing, "We are in real danger of losing the war right here in Washington." After reading his complaints one cannot help thinking back to his condemnation of the Copperheads of the Civil War as expressed in his own *Early Memories.* Perhaps that is unfair, but still, the record shows he missed no chance to attack the administration which was responsible for the conduct of the war, and especially the Commander in Chief.

As the war months wearily passed Theodore Roosevelt became the leader of the anti-Wilson junto, which, with a mixture of patriotism and partisanship, schemed and plotted to wrest control from the President. They concentrated their efforts towards repudiating Mr. Wilson at the polls in November 1918. Senator Lodge was as vocal as anyone. In March he let loose a blast in the Senate condemning the "delays and failures in the prosecution of the war." A month later he was preaching, through the columns of the *Boston Evening Transcript* and elsewhere, that "nothing is more dangerous than this effort . . . to confuse the President with the country."

One thing which struck terror to Senator Lodge's conservative heart was the apparent friendliness of the Democratic President towards the Russian Revolution. "On the whole," Lodge complained, "I am inclined to think that the despotism of disorder is worse than the despotism of order, because the despotism of disorder, as we see it in Russia, is leading to the dissolution of the country and to the destruction of all moral sense among the people. They will not even fight to preserve their country and their race, and there does not seem to be a body of men among them who are ready to fight to maintain both liberty and order, which is an appalling spectacle."

Early in September Senator Lodge was horrified by signs that President Wilson was about to sanction a negotiated peace. He would not give Mr. Wilson credit for having any humanitarian motives. After delivering a campaign speech in Boston he said that he hoped his remarks would "help make it difficult for Wilson to betray the United States and the Allies by negotiating a peace with Germany with a view to the German vote in this country." It was a snide, and self-revealing, remark.

It was at this time, incidentally, that he first became really aware of a "very able, sagacious man of pure New England type" named Calvin Coolidge, the Lieutenant Governor of Massachusetts who was candidate for Governor that year. They had first become acquainted in 1916 when the shy and silent Calvin had visited Washington in 1916 for the first time in his life, shortly after becoming Lieutenant Governor. The Senator had entertained him and given him advice. Although poles apart in temperament, education, and social background, the Yankee and the Brahmin hit it off well enough together and they remained friendly until Calvin Coolidge forged ahead of Lodge as a political power in the Bay State. Just then Lodge liked Coolidge because, as he told Roosevelt, he was "in thorough sympathy with your views and mine. . . ."

Towards the end of September President Wilson traveled to New York where he asserted that the creation of a league of nations was "in a sense the most important part of the peace settlement itself."

To Albert J. Beveridge, who had reverted to his early

status of jingo, this was "a call to arms for a defense of American nationalism." Others of the anti-Wilson cabal thought it gave them an outstanding issue for the campaign that had only a little more than a month to go. Theodore Roosevelt, in a moment of rare caution, warned his allies not wholly to reject a league of nations, but to concentrate upon the idea that such an organization was "probably chimerical."

Then came Germany's wireless appeal to Wilson for peace terms, closely followed, on October 6, by Austria's suit for a peace based upon President Wilson's Fourteen Points. The President's prestige soared to new heights as America saw the end of war in sight. As of that date even the most sanguine Republican would not wager on the election of an anti-administration Congress in November. Senator Lodge, however, went into action with a loud demand that President Wilson refrain from replying to Germany. In all the United States there was no more outstanding advocate of the On-to-Berlin school than Senator Lodge, who demanded that hostilities should not cease until the Allies had won a complete victory and unconditional surrender on German soil.

On October 13 Germany accepted the "terms laid down by President Wilson in his address of January 8 and in his subsequent addresses as to the foundation of a permanent peace." It was Roosevelt who gave the reaction of the anti-Wilson clique — it was "dangerously near to treacherous diplomacy." Senator Lodge followed him with an interview, which was thoroughly condemnatory of Wilson's conduct, and in which he urged that there should be no peace discussion with the enemy. "The only thing now is to demand unconditional surrender." And the terms of this should not be dictated by the President — they should be left to Marshal Foch and the generals of the armies. Within a few days, he soon boasted, he had received "hundreds of letters and tele-grams from all over the country supporting all I said or did."

On the wide political front, almost to the end of the campaign of 1918, internationalism was far less the burden of oratory on either side than might be supposed. For one thing, President Wilson's dictum that "politics is adjourned" for the duration had been taken more or less seriously by the country as a whole. Politicians were content to stick as closely as possible to local issues. And so, in the midst of war, the people's own selfish interests remained the paramount issues. Wartime taxation, wartime food restrictions, wartime price regulations, wartime wages (and, in the West, under the impetus of the Non-Partisan League, government ownership) were much more immediate worries. And these could be blamed upon the "inefficiency," even the "dishonesty," of the administration, while one inferred that relief from these grievances would only come if the opposition were to win. Politics in a democracy, as Mr. Wilson discovered, is never adjourned.

The campaign became one in which the Republicans claimed they could prosecute the war more efficiently and speedily than the bungling Democrats, thus forcing the Democrats onto the defensive, with claims for credit for the national successes as their best weapon. In the midst of this wrangle (there were also Prohibition, woman suffrage, and farm legislation to add to the domestic confusion) nobody sought to educate the electorate to one important fact: that upon the choice of Senators in November lay the kind of peace that would soon be arranged. President Wilson, however, had this very much in mind when, on October 25, he issued his now famous appeal to the nation to return to Congress a Democratic majority. Only in this way, he said, could the uninterrupted continuance of the administration's policies, and a unified and solidly supported control of the peace negotiations, be assured. He asked a vote of confidence to prove to the Allies the popularity of his program. In this message — so dangerously mistaken, as it turned out — he admitted that the Republican Congressmen were loyal, but still they were against the administration, and such party opposition would create grave obstacles in the conduct of foreign affairs.

The Lodge-Roosevelt junto was delighted. National Committee Chairman Will H. Hays, Theodore Roosevelt, Senator Lodge, and all the other Republican leaders, and some disgruntled Democrats who had long nursed grudges against Mr. Wilson, shouted with joy. The bars were down. Politics had reconvened. President Wilson himself had done the trick. War was openly declared on the administration.

Between President Wilson's well-meaning but ill-advised request for a vote of confidence and the suddenly important elections there stretched an interval of ten days. This was time enough for the Republicans to launch disastrous attacks upon the Democratic Party and its leadership, but hardly time for the administration to propagandize effectively its program for the coming of peace. On election day, when thirty-seven Senatorial contests were settled, the Democrats gained one seat and lost seven, thus giving the Republicans a majority of two in the Senate. An analysis of the elections shows that not one of the Senatorial contests was fought on a discussion of which policy the United States should pursue in the making of a lasting peace.

To Senator Lodge, however, the election was a repudiation of Woodrow Wilson. Did he, perhaps, think then of what he had said the month before the election of 1898 when President McKinley was asking for the return of a Republican Congress: "If we give a victory to his political opponents, we say not only to the United States but we say to the world . . . that the people of the United States repudiated the result of the war and repudiated the man . . . who is now leading us back to peace . . ."?

Woodrow Wilson refused to admit repudiation. He was not to be swerved from his course by the results of the elections. Although he realized that the loss of the Senate could only be considered as a vote of lack of confidence and that, as a result, he was placed at an international disadvantage, he was determined to carry through the plans on which he had set his heart. On November 18 he announced that he would go to Paris to negotiate the peace.

When the President's mysterious adviser, Colonel Edward Mandell House, had gone abroad to ferret out information for his chief, Senator Lodge had said: "I dread Colonel House going abroad. This is what you call secret, furtive diplomacy." He dreaded even more Woodrow Wilson's journey. The President might think he was seeking those "open covenants of peace openly arrived at" which he had spoken of on January 8, 1918, when he had laid down his Fourteen Points. But Lodge knew better. President Wilson was on his way to sell out American Sovereignty forever.

The Peace Commission which the President appointed, with himself at the head, consisted of Robert Lansing, the Secretary of State; Colonel House; Henry White, Lodge's old friend; and General Tasker H. Bliss. When Senator Lodge saw the list he snorted, "The President has appointed himself four times and Henry White." Mr. White was the only Republican on the commission.

To Senator Lodge the President's ignoring of the Senate in selecting his Commissioners of Peace was unforgivably insulting. It has often been said since 1918 that if President Wilson had included Senator Lodge among the commissioners the Treaty of Versailles and the League of Nations might have met a far different fate at the hands of the Senate than they did. Lodge might then have been persuaded to revert to his earlier opinions of an international league for peace. He might then have found in the words of Washington and Monroe some further substance for the interpretation he had given them before Woodrow Wilson advocated the League. His vanity assuaged, the dignity of the Senate maintained, he might well have rid his soul of its jaundice — and changed the course of history.

But Woodrow Wilson ignored him. Senator Lodge stayed home, to plot the destruction of Woodrow Wilson and whatever treaty he might bring back from the Palace of Versailles. As the President sailed, Henry Cabot Lodge was already scheming at Theodore Roosevelt's sickbed, laying his ingenious net to ensnare Wilson's great dream. For Senator Lodge, in the words of Frank Cobb, hated Woodrow Wilson "as only a small-minded man can hate a great man." Whenever he thought of the unsmiling Presbyterian in his black coat, treading the floor of the council chamber, his blood turned to bile. Ovid's description of Envy, which John Quincy Adams once applied to Randolph of Roanoke, applied with equal force to Senator Lodge: —

His face is livid; gaunt his whole body;
His breast is green with gall; his tongue drips poison. . . .

XX

With Umbrageous Words

THEODORE ROOSEVELT lay in his bed in the Roosevelt Hospital suffering from inflammatory rheumatism throughout most of the autumn of 1918. Through his window on November 11 came the hysterical sounds of a city celebrating the Armistice. He was suffering intensely, yet he was not so sick but that his friends might visit him. Towards the end of November Elihu Root and Henry White sat at his bedside, discussing the terms of peace that were soon to be fixed at Paris. Cabot Lodge was too busy with the affairs of state in Washington to come to New York. But he sent Theodore frequent notes. As soon as the revenue bill was disposed of he would come over, he said, and they would have a long talk. Henry White hurried back to Washington to prepare for his last great adventure in diplomacy. He was to sail with Wilson early in December.

Roosevelt, dying, hated Woodrow Wilson with an implacable hatred. The grizzled Root would not let his feelings towards the President color his mind: he wanted a moderate peace, and he believed in some kind of international institution to guarantee the future peace; he and Colonel House had agreed on that in August. Former President Taft, now reconciled with the man he never forgot to call "Mr. President," was for a league of nations now, as he always had been. Of all the old allies of the ailing Colonel, Lodge alone shared his bitterness.

Senator Lodge had known Henry White for nearly a quarter of a century. They were both of that little clique of intellectuals who had hovered around Henry Adams and John Hay in the nineties. White had always been a Republican. On more than one occasion Senator Lodge had been able to do him a favor. Now he was going to ask a favor of Henry White. As White busied himself with his packing Senator Lodge talked long and earnestly. Peace, he told Henry White, must be determined by the United States and her allies. And it must be imposed upon Germany, who must be forced to accept the terms, however harsh. The first and controlling purpose of the Peace Conference, he went on, must be to put Germany in a position where it would be "physically impossible" for her ever "to break out again upon other nations with war for world conquest."

There were some other things he wanted Ambassador White to remember. Among them were the complete restoration of Belgium and the assurance of her future independence. In order to assure this, and some other things, the Senator was quite willing to make the United States a part guarantor of any European settlement to be arrived at in Paris. He then told White that he favored large indemnities, that Germany must be forced to pay "at least a portion of the cost of the war which she precipitated and for which she alone is responsible."

Venturing next to speak for the entire American people, Senator Lodge told Henry White: "Nothing would so protect us from war in the future as the separation of the German empire into its chief component parts." Another thing the "American people would like to see," he added, would be to have the Turkish government "entirely out of Europe. . . ." Then there was the question raised by the third of Mr. Wilson's Fourteen Points: his "general interdiction" of economic barriers must never be interpreted so as "to interfere with discriminating tariffs or reciprocity treaties."

Thus far he had not expressed himself concerning the League of Nations, but when he reached it he was explicit: —

"The League of Nations to preserve and enforce peace presents a conception which must appeal to every right-thinking man, but like many other general ideas when we pass from theory to practice the terms and details are vital. It need only be said . . . that under no circumstances must provisions for such a league be made a part of the peace treaty which concludes the war with Germany. Any attempt to do this would not only long delay the signature of the treaty of peace . . . but it would make adoption of the treaty, unamended, by the Senate of the United States and other ratifying bodies, extremely doubtful."

Senator Lodge incorporated all that he had said to Henry White in a lengthy memorandum which he handed to the Peace Commissioner on December 2, 1918. The memorandum, he said, represented the view not only of the Republican Party, but of the whole American people. He then suggested that Henry White lay this remarkable document before Clemenceau and Balfour, and certain other European statesmen, all of whom Lodge knew, who would be at Paris. He asked this not so much to enlighten them on the terms of peace as to let them know "what I believe to be the real feeling of the people of the United States and certainly the Senate of the United States. This knowledge may in certain contingencies be very important to them in strengthening their position."

When Woodrow Wilson sailed for Paris, Henry Cabot Lodge believed that the President carried in his back a knife stuck there by his enemy. Henry White, however, was an honorable man. He knew that there was no available consensus, Republican, Democratic, or American, on the subject of the League, or even of the terms of the peace. His duty, as he saw it, was to "serve a large purpose in his old diplomatic role of mediator" and help to bring "discordant American minds together." He locked the paper in his case and showed it to no one.

A fortnight later Senator Lodge came to New York and had two bedside conferences with Theodore Roosevelt. On consecutive mornings, they discussed for several hours the peace treaty then in the making and the "league of nations" which, they had every reason to expect, Woodrow Wilson would insist upon incorporating in it. Although they did not know what form the covenant would take, their friend Root had had several conferences with Colonel House, and they may be supposed to have acquired a good general idea to go on. With Mrs. Douglas Robinson, the sick man's sister (whose guest Senator Lodge was), joining in the conversations, they laid down general rules for defeating the League when it should be reported to the Senate. Senator Lodge later described these meetings: —

"The draft of the Treaty was not then before us, but we fully discussed the League of Nations in all its bearings. We were in entire agreement. The position that I have taken, and now take, had his full approval. The line I have followed in the Senate and elsewhere is the one he wished to have followed." [1]

Mrs. Robinson afterwards recalled that Dear Theodore and the Wily One, on those occasions, thought up certain reservations to the League which Senator Lodge would propose in the Senate. "I do not mean," she explained, "that definite clauses in the league were definitely discussed, but many contingencies of the document, contingencies which

[1] He made this statement in his debate in Boston with President Lowell of Harvard in March 1919.

304

later took the form of definite clauses, *were* discussed, and the future attitude toward such contingencies more or less mapped out."

It was a council of war. The whole broad strategy which Lodge, as Captain of the Battalion of Death, carried out in the Senate with miraculous fidelity was planned almost to the last detail even before the League of Nations had been reduced to terms on paper by the statesmen in Paris. Whatever league the President might bring home, they were ready for it. Whatever form it took, by reservation and amendment they would harry it to its death.

With this deep purpose in his mind, Senator Lodge returned to Washington. A few days later Theodore Roosevelt was well enough to journey to his home at Sagamore Hill, Oyster Bay. There, still grieving over the death behind the German lines of his son Quentin, he spent the Christmas holidays. On January 6, 1919, an arterial embolism brought his turbulent life to a close. A friendship which since 1884 had lasted over that roughest of roads which is politics was ended. To Senator Lodge fell the burden of carrying out the duty pledged by two vain and aging men. He had loved Theodore Roosevelt as a brother, and he was not to fail him in this trust.

On the day that Senator Lodge returned from the council of war the *Boston Evening Transcript,* which was to be his most faithful supporter in the months to come, predicted that the Senate was about to engage in "one of the great debates in the history of popular government." For, as Lodge told the *New York Sun* a few weeks later, the League (or, as he put it, anti-internationalism) was about to become "the biggest Republican issue since the Civil War."

Senator Lodge on December 19 informed the Senate that on the twenty-first he would deliver an address on "the question of peace and the proposed league of nations."

Senator Knox, not even waiting for President Wilson to arrive in Paris, had already opened the debate, declaring, among other things, that "the practicability of such a league . . . is, to say the least, most doubtful if indeed it be not altogether chimerical at this period of civilization." Senator Lodge carried on from there. In his very last letter to Theodore Roosevelt he said that his long speech, which he interrupted debate on the revenue bill to deliver, "was intended chiefly for the benefit of the Allies." It was intended also for the benefit of the absent President. It was a warning. He began, as might be expected, by reasserting the right of the Senate to advise and consent, stretching that constitutional provision to mean that the Senate might, if it so desired, give advice — even if it were not requested.

President Wilson had been in Paris but a week when the Senator spoke. The plenary sessions there had not yet begun, but Senator Lodge was ready to sow seeds of suspicion. "The plan seems to be to project upon the Senate," he said, "the most momentous treaty ever made without any information of the steps which led to it or as to the arguments and conditions which brought about its adoption. This scheme, which is indicated by all the facts known to us, rests upon the theory that the Senate, although possessing the power, would not and could not dare to reject a treaty of peace.

"We cannot compel information," he continued in his haughty way, "but we are abundantly able to make our opinions known not only to the President but to the Allies, who have a very clear and even acute idea of the power of the Senate in regard to treaties. They must know that the Senate can and often has rejected treaties. Others the Senate has refused to ratify and held without action. Many others have been vitally amended. The Allies should not be kept in the dark as to the views of the Senate."

Senator Lodge recalled how, in 1898, he had seen "a treaty of peace bitterly opposed and ratified, after the exertion of the most powerful influences, with only two votes to spare.

"But if a treaty of peace might not be rejected," he warned, "it can be debated and amended, and I can conceive of extraneous provisions wholly needless for a peace with Germany being unwisely added, provisions which would surely be stricken out or amended, no matter how many signatures might be appended to the treaty. Protracted opposition and amendments mean long delays, and delay is only less fortunate than rejection. All these untoward results can be avoided if the Senate frankly expresses its view beforehand on certain leading points for the consideration of the Allies and of the President himself."

Nothing could be much clearer than that. "Extraneous provisions" could only mean the League of Nations. And he had shown just what "untoward results" might occur if the Peace Conference — and Mr. Wilson — did not pay heed to Senator Lodge.

Although Lodge's speech was published in the Paris newspapers and he was undoubtedly informed of its context by his faithful secretary, Joseph Tumulty, President Wilson made no effort to communicate with the Senate. He had already made it clear that in his opinion the creation of a league should be the basis of the Treaty and he was now busy seeing that his scheme was carried out. Wilson, idealist though he may have been, was no innocent American sheep among the wolves of Europe. He was hardheaded, a Scotch-Irish Presbyterian, and he was used to direct dealing. No man was ever more determined that his righteous cause should have its way. The week after the opening of the conference he had won the British, the French, and the Italians over to the principle of the League; with his legal advisor, David Hunter Miller, he had drafted a covenant, and he had conferred with his fellow commissioners. On January 25, exactly a week after the official opening of the conference, the seventy delegates approved the resolution for the creation of a League of Nations as an integral part of the Peace Treaty.

While President Wilson was drafting the original Covenant, back home one strong voice was raised in its favor in the Senate. It was the voice of a brave and angry Republican, Senator Porter J. McCumber of North Dakota, who declared that the time to adopt "restrictive or preventive measures is now, and not some indefinite time in the future . . . today, when the awful horrors and consequences of war are apparent to every heart — and not when those horrors are forgotten and only the military glamor and glory remain to influence the sentiments of humanity. . . . How can you in one breath approve the alliance to make war to save the world and in the next breath condemn an alliance to save the world by the prevention of any savage or brutal war which might threaten it?" How far different his sentiments were from those of Senator Beveridge, who wrote to Lodge, after his peroration against the League, that the future of the party was in his hands "more than in those of any other man," and that the party's prospects would be "seriously, perhaps fatally injured by the acceptance of Mr. Wilson's international plan, or any variation of it." [2]

One by one the attacks were made. Senator Borah, who believed with a deep and personal honesty that internationalism in any form would lead only to world domination and the "destruction of the national spirit," served notice that he would fight to the bitter end against any league of

[2] Beveridge, who had previously neither liked nor trusted Lodge, now thought him "a tremendously big man, and gentle and courageous"!

any kind. Of course, the League had its defenders, like John Sharp Williams of Mississippi, who felt that the hand of God Himself was behind it. But the attacks were louder than the defense — even though the attackers or anyone else in America had not yet seen a draft of the Covenant.

The news that came from Paris was neither reassuring nor plentiful. President Wilson had clamped down a strict censorship. Senator Lodge, however, was kept reasonably well informed by his friend Henry White, who sent him many cablegrams and letters during the early weeks of the conference. White looked upon the League as a necessary experiment and he was by now convinced that it should be incorporated in the Peace Treaty. He attempted by logical persuasion to modify Lodge's harsh views. When he read the Senator's December 21 speech he was vexed, but being a tactful man his comments to the Senator were written softly: Lodge ought to realize that the idea of a league was spreading and that it would do the Senator no harm if he paid some consideration to views other than his own. Furthermore, he said, he had Wilson's assurance that the President desired no such league as Lodge was conjuring up, "whereby our army and navy would be placed under the orders of a combination of powers, or any orders but our own." There was, wrote the Ambassador, a "good deal" to be said for the League. But Senator Lodge was in no mood to be convinced. He would not take Wilson's word for anything; he was worried about the Army and Navy; and what about the Monroe Doctrine?

On January 8 Ambassador White sent Lodge a startling telegram warning him of the "steady westward advance of Bolshevism." It "thrives only on starvation and disorder," he said, and already it had engulfed Russia and Poland and was threatening Germany. He urged Senator Lodge to throw all the weight of his influence behind President Wilson's request for $100,000,000 to feed starving Europe. Lodge's reply was hardly that of a generous man. Herbert Hoover, who was to administer the funds, was not yet a member of the Republican Party. Lodge did not want to see all that money in Democratic hands. Particularly did he feel that there was "a very strong feeling in this country against giving food or money to the Germans. . . . I believe our expenditure will be carefully limited to those people who were either our allies or our friends." He was much more interested in hurrying things up at Paris. He could not understand why a simple thing like a peace conference was taking so long. "Delay," he told White, "helps the Germans."

The good Ambassador kept Lodge fairly well up-to-date, but of course even he did not know everything that was going on. Lodge quickly began to suspect that White had been taken into the enemy's camp. White was too tactful to write him, as he did William Phillips, that Wilson "is really a wonderful man [who] has established the combination of President and Prime Minister to an extent I should never have believed possible. . . ." He did, however, write Lodge of the great receptions accorded Wilson everywhere he went in Europe; but what was more important, he said everything he could to persuade Lodge that the League was inevitable and that it "would be useless . . . to make a point of postponement until after the other matters, with which the Peace Conference will have to deal, have been settled. . . ."

When Henry White learned that Lodge had amended the $100,000,000 relief bill to exclude Turkey, Bulgaria, and German Austria from its provisions, he sent a rather annoyed cable of protest. This aroused Senator Lodge to reply testily that the bill had passed, but that he had a feeling Hoover wanted to spend the money without much regard to the wishes of Congress. He then quickly passed on to more important matters: "It seems pretty clear here that the League of Nations is going to be a voluntary association, and the idea of putting force behind it is abandoned. If they do put force behind it" — Lodge threw out the threat — "I think it will be ill received here by the country generally and I do not believe it could pass the Senate." This elicited a detailed reply. White took up specific problems, but the really important statements were: —

I can only repeat once more that no member of this Commission has the slightest intention, or ever has had, of allowing our army and navy to be placed in a position in which it can be subject to the orders of any international body, nor, as far as I have learned on the part of anyone, of abandoning or modifying the Monroe Doctrine.

That letter was dated February 10. Four days later the result of the long night sessions of the League of Nations Commission, which President Wilson had dominated as chairman, was ready to be presented to the delegates. As President Wilson said when he read it to the assembled representatives of half the civilized world: "A living thing is born. . . . It is a definite guaranty of peace. It is a definite guaranty by word against aggression. . . ."

The next morning Senator Lodge read in the newspapers for the first time the living charter of that "evil thing with the holy name" against which he had already set his heart and mind.

President Wilson sailed for America. As his ship cut through the winter fog, Senator Lodge was thoroughly aware of the truth expressed by his former secretary and lifelong friend, Louis A. Coolidge: "He knew very well that the citizens of Massachusetts, both Republicans and Democrats, were almost unanimously favorable to the terms of the League as they were brought over here by the President of the United States." Not long before Lodge himself had written: "We have got to take our share in carrying out the peace, which is really a part of the war." And yet he was awaiting President Wilson with anger and hatred.

President Wilson's ship ominously was headed for Boston. Already from Paris the President had sent a request to postpone discussion on the League until his arrival, and he had invited the members of the House Committee on Foreign Affairs and the Senate Committee on Foreign Relations to dine with him at the White House on February 26. This had made little difference on the home front. In the Senate, days before his arrival, Senator Poindexter had opened debate on the League with a violent comparison of that proposed body with revolutionary Russia. Senators Borah and Reed, the insurgent and Democratic isolationists, had added their scornful words. Senator Lodge had restrained himself, but he was by no means friendly.

"As he is the President of the United States," he wrote, "of course I accepted the invitation to the dinner. I should not have thought of doing otherwise. I also felt, as a gentleman and man of honor, that having accepted the invitation to dinner I should comply with his request not to discuss the terms of the League as set forth in the draft of the committee, until after the dinner. The President, however," he went on, bitterly, "does not seem to look at it in the same way, and is going to land in Boston, my own city, and there address a great mass meeting which is all arranged for while I am reduced to silence because I wish to observe what I think is required of an honorable man."

However much Senator Lodge may have resented President Wilson's choice of "my own city" as a port of debarkation, there was nothing he could do about it. President Wilson had not chosen Boston as a studied affront to Senator

Lodge. The arrangements had been made long before in accord with a standing promise. When he left Paris he did not intend to speak. He decided to do so en route, when it was brought to his attention that he was expected to make a public appearance. After all, he was the first President in history to leave the United States to take part in great councils on the shores of Europe; he was at the height of his popularity; and, as President of the American people, he could hardly ignore their expressed desire to pay him homage.

Furthermore, as far as Massachusetts was concerned, there was a strong sentiment in favor of the League. Its people were for it, and so were its political and intellectual leaders. Former Senator Murray Crane was as avid for the League as Senator Lodge was antagonistic. Even Governor Calvin Coolidge was not then against it. President Lowell of Harvard was to do valiant battle in its behalf. Boston gave the President a tumultuous welcome.

In his address at Mechanics Hall President Wilson, to a great extent, respected his own interdiction against discussion; but in another way he issued a challenge. Although he spoke in generalities and avoided any reference to the sulking Senator, there was no escaping the meaning of his words, or the identity of the man to whom they were addressed.

". . . America is the hope of the world," he said proudly. "And if she does not justify that hope results are unthinkable. Men will be thrown back upon bitterness of disappointment not only, but bitterness of despair. All nations will be set up as hostile camps again; men at the peace conference will go home with their heads upon their hearts, knowing they have failed — for they were bidden not to come home from there until they did something more than sign the treaty of peace. . . . Any man who thinks that

America will take part in giving the world any such rebuff and disappointment as that does not know America. I invite him to test the sentiments of the nation."

There was more: "We set this nation up to make men free and we did not confine our conception and purpose to America, and now we will make men free. If we did not do that all the fame of America would be gone and all her power would be dissipated. She would then have to keep her power for those narrow, selfish, provincial purposes which seem so dear to some minds which have no sweep beyond the nearest horizon. I should welcome no sweeter challenge than that. I have fighting blood in me and it is sometimes a delight to let it have scope, but if it is challenged on this occasion it will be an indulgence.

"Think of the picture, think of the utter blackness that would fall upon the world. America has failed. America made a little essay at generosity and then withdrew. America said, 'We are your friends,' but it was only for today, not for tomorrow. America said, 'Here is our power to vindicate right,' and then next day said, 'Let right take care of itself and we will take care of ourselves.' America said, 'We set up a light to lead men along paths of liberty, but we have lowered it — it is intended only to light our own path.'"

The dreadful prophecy moved the minds and hearts of the hundreds who heard it that night, and the millions who read it the next morning. In the chill soul of Henry Cabot Lodge the words kindled no fire. He was unmoved, withdrawn, waiting. Already he and Senators Knox, Penrose, and Smoot had met in conference, planning concerted opposition, although they had agreed to say nothing openly until after the White House dinner. Lodge's only comment was, "To think of his talking like that in my home state!"

The dinner was a gala affair held in the state dining room.

At the table, where Mrs. Wilson was the only woman present, the conversation avoided the matter that was on the minds of the thirty-six diners; but afterwards, when Senator Lodge had escorted Mrs. Wilson from the table, and all were gathered in an oval around President Wilson in the East Room, the grave topic was reached.

"The President answered questions for two hours about the draft of the constitution of the League of Nations, and told us nothing," Lodge jotted down shortly afterward. "He did not seem to know it very thoroughly and was not able to answer questions. . . . He was civil and showed no temper. We went away as wise as we came."

Others who were present did not take quite as critical an attitude. Congressman John Jacob Rogers,[3] for instance, said that the President was never "so human or so attractive" as he was that night, and that he answered every question, "easy or difficult, as fully as possible and with apparent candor." But those who went to the dinner favoring the League left it still in favor; those who were opposed departed still in opposition.

Two days later Senator Lodge was ready to open fire on the League. Supported by Senator Knox he demanded that the peace be the first consideration and that the League be put aside until later, if ever. The United States, he said, must never be drawn by "any glittering delusions, through specious devices of supernational government, within the toils of international socialism and anarchy."

He then drew together the arguments already made by himself, Borah, Reed, and Poindexter — those gentlemen whom former President Taft said he "would not trust overnight." He spoke in measured tones, often sarcastically, but without raising his voice in passion or anger. Perhaps his most telling argument against entering a League was the

[3] Representative Rogers was an opponent of the League of Nations.

future difficulty of agreeing to interpretation of the terms of the Covenant, there being no Supreme Court to pass upon them. He wanted to know if the Covenant safeguarded the Monroe Doctrine — and strongly implied that it did not. Then there was the matter of immigration. This was and must remain purely a domestic issue, not something for an "international league" to consider. He wondered, too, about America's position in the League — would she not have but one vote to England's five? After all, each of England's self-governing dominions would have a vote. And then there was that most perilous commitment, Article 10.[4] This Article, with its guaranties against aggression and which Woodrow Wilson was later to say was the very heart of the Covenant, seemed to Senator Lodge to be "a very grave, a very perilous promise to make." He wanted the American people long to consider Article 10 before making the promises which he said it called for. He painted a picture of our Army and Navy and the flower of American youth being continually called forth to war to protect someone else's back yard.

Softly Senator Lodge said he was "not now contending" that all the provisions of the Covenant should not be accepted. "What I ask, and all I ask, is consideration, time, thought. . . . We cannot reach our objects by a world constitution hastily constructed in a few weeks in Paris in the midst of the excitement of a war not yet ended." Let us make the peace first. He ended his exhaustive analysis of the League: "That which I desire above everything else, that which is nearest to my heart, is to bring our soldiers home. The making of a League of Nations will not do that.

[4] Article 10. Guaranties Against Aggression. The Members of the League undertake to respect and preserve as against external aggression the territorial integrity and existing political independence of all Members of the League. In case of any such aggression or in case of any threat or danger of such aggression, the Council shall advise upon the means by which this obligation shall be fulfilled.

. . . What is it that delays the peace with Germany? Discussions over the League of Nations; nothing else."

Senator Lodge's speech was a remarkable combination of objections to a document not yet before the Senate, and at the same time an almost demagogic appeal to the war-weariness of the nation. Into it he had put most of the lessons in political persuasion which he had learned in the forty years he had been a politician.

From that time the assault upon the League was to be steady and telling. The Republicans took the lead, although some wistful Democrats were merely waiting their chance to follow. Senator Knox, who called the League "a plan to strangle and crush us," and Senator Sherman of Illinois, who likened it to a "Pandora's box of evil," were among those who, within the next few days, let loose a flood of oratory against the League and its sponsor. In the meantime Senator Lodge, having spoken his piece, was busy behind the scenes.

Early on the morning of Sunday, March 2, he received a visit at his home from Senator Frank B. Brandegee, that brilliant, high-strung Connecticut Yankee who had led the "cross-examination" of Wilson at the February dinner. Brandegee had been disturbed by the lengthy defense of the League uttered in the Senate the day before by Senator McCumber and was brimming over with a clever scheme he had evolved. Sitting there in Lodge's library, he told the gentleman from Massachusetts that some declaration should be made, without delay, "to the effect that a League of Nations such as it was understood was to be proposed, and the outlines of which had been given through the press"[5] could not pass the Senate.

[5] Lodge puts it this way in *The Senate and the League of Nations*, p. 118; he infers, with characteristic unfairness, that the League Covenant was some sort of mystery; the first draft of the charter, already approved by the Peace Conference, had been published and his own speech of February 28 quotes extensively from it verbatim.

When Brandegee further suggested that they get the signatures of "more than one third of the Senate" to the statement Senator Lodge was, in his own words, "very much struck by the proposition. Brandegee had no difficulty in convincing me of its essential and even vital importance." The two conspirators hastened to the home of Senator Knox who agreed to draft the resolution.

Throughout Monday Senators Lodge, Knox, Brandegee, and Albert B. Cummins of Iowa scurried through the corridors and offices of the Capitol securing signatures — Harry S. New, George H. Moses, J. W. Wadsworth, Jr., W. G. Harding, William E. Borah, Boies Penrose, Hiram Johnson, Walter E. Edge, Truman H. Newberry, Medill McCormick, Albert B. Fall — until thirty-eight names were appended to the document.

"We did not think it desirable to ask any Democrats to sign," said Lodge. "We knew there were Democratic Senators opposed to the League, but we did not wish to involve or embarrass them. . . ."

At two minutes past midnight Lodge arose in the Senate and one reporter said his hand was shaking as he held the resolution.

"Mr. President," he said, "I desire to take only a moment of the time of the Senate. I wish to offer the resolution which I hold in my hand, a very brief one: —

"'. . . *Resolved* by the Senate of the United States in the discharge of its constitutional duty of advice in regard to treaties, That it is the sense of the Senate that while it is their sincere desire that the nations of the world should unite to promote peace and general disarmament, the constitution of the league of nations in the form now proposed to the peace conference should not be accepted by the United States; and be it *Resolved further*, That it is the sense of the Senate that the negotiations on the part of the

318

United States should immediately be directed to the utmost expedition of the urgent business of negotiating peace terms with Germany satisfactory to the United States and the nations with whom the United States is associated in the war against the German Government, and that the proposed league of nations to insure the permanent peace of the world should then be taken up for careful consideration.'

"I ask unanimous consent for the present consideration of this resolution."

Senator Lodge knew, and afterward cynically admitted, that the introduction of the resolution was "clearly out of order." His only fear was that no Democrat would object to its introduction, thereby allowing it to come to a vote and be defeated. He took that chance — and won. Senator Swanson of Virginia objected. With great relief, Lodge, as soon as Swanson had spoken, said, "Of course, I recognize the objection." He then read the names of the signers, more than one third necessary to defeat a treaty, into the Record and left the hall.

"The plan worked out beautifully after Senator Swanson's objection," he chuckled. "Our purpose, however, had been served. The declaration went out to the world."

The *New York Sun* joyfully exclaimed: —

Woodrow Wilson's League of Nations died in the Senate to-night. Henry Cabot Lodge, Senator from Massachusetts, who has bitterly opposed a League of Nations on the terms drawn up by President Wilson, read the death warrant of the League.

To this unprecedented challenge President Wilson gave stern answer. In a speech in the Metropolitan Opera House, standing next to Mr. Taft, he told the world that when the Treaty was brought back the "gentlemen on this side will find the Covenant not only tied in it, but so many threads of the Treaty tied to the Covenant that you cannot dissect the Covenant from the Treaty without destroying the whole vital structure."

On the way back to Paris, Wilson said to Ray Stannard Baker, his friend and biographer, that there was no use in his offering any amendments to the League. "No matter what changes are accepted," he said with foresight, "they will only ask for more. The Republicans will make it an issue in any event."

The Lodge-Knox-Brandegee "round-robin" strengthened President Wilson's determination but in Paris it spread discontent among the leaders of other nations. Realizing that an important segment of American opinion was no longer behind the President, the Europeans were now in a position to bargain. As William Allen White put it, Mr. Wilson was reduced to "trading the substance of European demands for the shadow of American ideals."

Senator Lodge, who was soon to be recognized as the ablest of those who, in Mr. Wilson's words, espoused a "doctrine of careful selfishness, thought out to the last detail," was not then or later among the "irreconcilables," as those who, like Senator Borah and Senator Johnson, would have no part of the League in any shape or form were known. Those bitter-enders had no fear of adverse public opinion. On the other hand, Senator Lodge cared about it a great deal. He wrote to Beveridge that he "could not agree we are against any League at all"; indeed Lodge felt, early in March, 1919, that such an irreconcilable position would "drive away support." Uncertain of just how far he would go, Senator Lodge lacked the courage of Borah, and was not ready to indulge in an open fight; he put his faith, as Mr. Bowers has said, in "the finesse of the diplomacy of dissimulation."

From Paris, Henry White continued to feed his old friend information, which Lodge refused to digest. "We certainly did not go into the war for any material gain of our own,"

White wrote, "and I have not the slightest doubt on two points — first of all, that unless we form part of any League of Nations which may be set up, there will be none; and, second, we can only revert to the old and final method of settling international disputes, namely, war. . . ."

Lodge listened, but he was not willing to be convinced. He wrote again and again, repeating his earlier objections to the League. When White, almost in exasperation, pointed out plainly that in the light of the best evidence Lodge was wrong — even when White recalled how "our late dear and lamented friend, Theodore Roosevelt, used to say that he always tried to get the best that he could obtain . . . instead of holding out for perfection" — Lodge refused to be moved.

In what was a desperate and wholly unauthorized effort to reconcile the President and the Senator, White finally cabled Lodge to send him, not generalities, but the "exact phraseology of amendments modifying the League which Senate considers important." Senator Lodge, resting up in Boston for his widely heralded debate with President A. Lawrence Lowell of Harvard University, so used to intrigue himself, at once suspected a plot. Had not Wilson inspired the cable from White? It was an unkind, unjust suspicion. White was not conspiring with the President to learn the opposition's strategy; he merely desired the information so that he might be in a better position, if the chance arose, to persuade the President to change his course. Even Root, to whom Lodge showed the telegram, was suspicious; Brandegee and Knox were, too. Lodge's cabled reply was cold: —

. . . The President expressed no willingness to receive any communication from the Senate while that body was in session. If he wishes now to have amendments drafted which the Senate will consent to, the natural and necessary course is to assemble the Senate in the customary way. Manifestly I cannot now speak for the Senate or consult its members, nor can they consult with each other, nor can the President consult them while they are at their homes in 48 States.[6]

Thus Henry White failed. As Allan Nevins has pointed out, failure was inevitable: —

. . . Lodge was utterly incapacitated for understanding a great deal in the situation of Europe and the world which White, from his vantage point in Paris, comprehended perfectly. Naturally a man of narrow vision, strong in national feeling and weak in international instincts, Lodge had little perception of the vital need for the League, little knowledge of the tremendous difficulties of making peace, little sense of the unavoidability of compromise and give-and-take in Paris. He did not see, as White did, that the old nationalist fears, the traditional arrangements for defense and offense, the habit of looking suspiciously at every international agreement, must be given up. The old road had led to disaster. A new one must be found — and it would require courage, imagination, generosity. . . .

In the welter of partisan discussion of the League nothing attracted as much attention as the March debate in Symphony Hall, Boston, between Senator Lodge and President Lowell. The Armistice was but a scant four months old. The veteran combat divisions of the British, French, and American armies were still keeping their armed watch on the Rhine. No peace with the Central Powers had yet been signed. The citizen soldiers in the United States had not all been returned to their homes, the mothers and fathers of the nation were waiting to know what the sacrifices of 1917 and 1918 had brought. No wonder 72,000 persons sought tickets to the debate. Had there then been the radio, nearly every set in the nation would have been tuned in that night. As it was, 3500 privileged citizens were jammed into Sym-

[6] Wilson had angered the Republicans by refusing to call a special session of Congress before he went to Paris for the second time.

phony Hall, and correspondents from all the leading newspapers were on hand. Governor Calvin Coolidge presided.

Senator Lodge appeared more gaunt and gray than usual as he attacked the Covenant. His objections were familiar: specific exclusion of the Monroe Doctrine, of immigration, and of the tariff from the jurisdiction of the League, which, of course, should not be established as a part of the Peace Treaty. He brought most of his fire to bear upon Article 10. But the most effective weapon which Lodge used was innuendo. In one breath he "hoped" that in Paris there could be arranged a League in "proper form, properly prepared, free from doubts, excluding what ought to be excluded." In the next breath he prayed that the American people might be spared having to "go through a dark tunnel of umbrageous words, with nothing to see at the end but the dim red light of internationalism." Skillfully he played upon the emotions when he cried out that nothing mattered except to "impose the reparations, build up the barrier states, put the monster where it cannot spring again, and bring the soldiers home."

President Lowell's logic contrasted with the Senator's emotional appeal, his vision with Lodge's innuendo of an unknown and dreadful fate. After reading the Covenant's rough draft, which is all that then existed, word for word, Lowell admitted that it lacked much and that amendments might be desirable, yet he devoted most of his time to an eloquent plea to save the substance of the League as the world's greatest hope for unity and peace.[7]

Against that the aging Senator cried: "I am an American. I never had but one flag, and I am too old to learn to

[7] Dr. Lowell challenged Lodge to state whether he would vote in the Senate for an amended League, and to say what amendments he wanted. Lodge evaded the issue by saying he *supposed* he would support the League if changed to suit him — but he would not say what changes he demanded.

love another, an international flag," and won the louder applause.

There was no official judge of the debate. Newspaper polls taken after the meeting indicated that opinion was almost equally divided. Most of the press felt that both Lodge and Lowell were in near enough agreement so that the two schools of thought could easily iron out their differences and insure adoption of the League.

Calvin Coolidge said, "Both men won."

A people, unanimous in their hope that the war for democracy should not have been fought in vain, were being divided. The scheme for defeating the League which was hatched at Theodore Roosevelt's bedside was developing rapidly. Although Senators Borah and Johnson wanted no part of the "diplomacy of dissimulation," it became ever more apparent as the spring of 1919 wore on that Senator Lodge's plan to insist upon hamstringing reservations would be followed by all of Wilson's opponents. Even Taft and Lowell lent their support to this policy. In mid-April, the latter men cabled President Wilson: —

Friends of the Covenant are seriously alarmed over report that no amendment will be made specifically safeguarding Monroe Doctrine . . . without such amendment Republican Senators will certainly defeat ratification, because public opinion will sustain them. With such amendment treaty will be promptly ratified.

In April 1919, the Republicans won a great victory in Paris. To men like Taft and Root, who were able to rise above partisanship, the victory was obvious. Working almost beyond human endurance, President Wilson, by the sheer force of his own idealism, wrought a new Covenant for the League of Nations which he had every reason to believe he could send safely to the Senate. Nearly all the objections

324

that had been raised against the first draft had been recti-fied in the new version. The right to withdraw from the League after two years was now assured. Article 15 had been so amended as to allay the fears of those who, like Senator Lodge, had raised the bugaboo of immigration. The 22nd Article had revised the conditions under which mandates might be imposed.

Most, if not all, of these changes had come from sugges-tions originating from Republican sources. An analysis of the Covenant shows that four of Elihu Root's suggestions had been fully adopted and three partially recognized. Six of the points raised by Charles Evans Hughes had been ac-cepted by the conferees. And all of the concrete proposals set forth by Senator Lodge and William Howard Taft had been written into the Covenant.

In all his speeches and pronouncements Senator Lodge had stressed above everything else the need for recognition of the Monroe Doctrine. Even this President Wilson had achieved, if almost at the risk of breaking up the conference. The French had been loud, and logical, in their objections. But by sheer magic President Wilson — the man who "failed at Paris"! — won them over one midnight when he delivered "an extempore speech of witching eloquence." When the League Covenant was written into the Versailles Treaty its 21st Article read: —

Nothing in this Covenant shall be deemed to affect the valid-ity of international engagements, such as treaties of arbitration or regional understandings like the Monroe Doctrine, for secur-ing the maintenance of peace.

While President Wilson, "utterly beaten, worn out, his face quite haggard . . ." struggled on in Paris, Senator Lodge bided his time. On April 28 the revised Covenant was pub-lished. If President Wilson had expected a favorable reaction from the Republicans, he was disappointed. What he had predicted to Mr. Baker on his trip to France came true. When Senator Lodge saw the revised form, with Article 10 still intact and Article 21 added, he was struck with fear that some of the reservationists would rush into print claiming a victory. He at once conferred with Senator Charles Curtis of Kansas. The following morning the two majority leaders of the Senate telegraphed every Republican Senator: —

We suggest that Republican Senators reserve final expression of opinion respecting the amended league covenant until the latest draft has been carefully studied and until there has been an opportunity for conference.

In accordance with his own instructions — which he later had the effrontery to call a "strictly non-partisan telegram" — Senator Lodge said nothing, except: —

"I am not prepared to make a statement in regard to the new draft at this moment, because I desire to examine it carefully and compare it with the former draft, and also to confer with my colleagues, for it is obvious that it will require further amendments if it is to promote peaee and not endanger certain rights of the United States which should never be placed in jeopardy."

With the exception of Senator Charles L. McNary of Oregon, the entire body of Republican Senators accepted the Lodge muzzle. The independent Oregonian expressed exactly the reaction Senator Lodge had feared. "In my opinion," he said, "the Covenant has been amended to meet all the legitimate objections raised against it." But the *New York Tribune*, anticipating a contest in the Senate to amend the revised draft, editorially called it "a great hoax." The Monroe Doctrine clause was "plainly a fraud . . . a package covered with gold foil." Article 10 was still as "iniquitous" as ever.

After despatching his telegram Senator Lodge and Senator Borah, who was opposed to the League in any shape or form, had what the latter called an "entirely satisfactory" conference. He felt he was immune from Lodge's interdiction and issued a blast against the treasonable Article 10. To Senator Beveridge, Lodge wrote that he and Borah, at the meeting, had agreed "as to the amendment line," and that the important thing now was to assure Republican control of the Senate. Thus early did the two schools of opposition join.

Senator Lodge knew as well as anyone that the great problem was political. As Mr. Beveridge put it, the League had become a party issue: "No power can prevent that." Chairman Will H. Hays, Lodge, Borah, all knew it, and as they awaited Wilson's return with the Treaty of Peace they were active in reuniting the Republican factions for the all-out drive against "Wilson's League" that was then in the making.

On the same day that he had sent his "strictly nonpartisan" telegram to the Republicans, Senator Lodge had addressed a letter, written in partisanship and composed in ignorance, to the Italians of Boston. In it he wholeheartedly condoned Italy's claim to the seaport of Fiume over the disposition of which President Wilson and the Italian delegates at the conference had just had their serious disagreement. Lodge, who claimed he had read all the histories of Dalmatia and therefore knew what he was talking about, said that Fiume was as vital to Italy as New Orleans was to the United States. In spite of some exasperated efforts on the part of Henry White to put him straight historically, geographically, and morally, the scholar in politics insisted he needed no correction.

Looking out upon the American scene, Senator Lodge found things were not to his liking. Among the articulate —

the "preachers of sermons," college professors, editors — there was almost unanimous approval of the League as its Covenant then stood. From George Harvey he learned at first hand that the bankers and capitalists were literally unanimous in their advocacy. He told all this to Borah on the day of their memorable meeting. The massive Idaho isolationist thought Lodge was right in his judgment of conditions. For this reason Borah, according to Lodge, agreed to support "any amendments or reservations which I and those who agreed with me should offer, although, of course, so far as he was concerned, after having voted for the amendments and reservations in the belief they would make the treaty better and the League safer, on the final vote he would vote against acceptance of the treaty by the Senate."

In Senator's Lodge's hands the legislative front was safe. But there was work to be done elsewhere. This fell to Senator Brandegee and to George Harvey, the journalist. The latter brought Henry Clay Frick, the Pennsylvania multimillionaire, into the fold; Senator Knox persuaded Andrew W. Mellon to open his pocketbook. Senator Brandegee's Washington home became the headquarters of the cabal, which poured out uncounted thousands of dollars, some of which were raised by Senator Medill McCormick, to educate the public, through all the available outlets of organized propaganda, to distrust the League.

President Wilson, although still in Paris, was forced to call Congress to meet in special session on May 19 in order to get the appropriations bills passed before the end of the fiscal year. On May 20 Senator Johnson introduced a resolution calling upon the Secretary of State to produce "forthwith" a copy of the Peace Treaty, which had been submitted to the Germans only a few days before. While debating this Senator Lodge announced that no executive sessions would be held, but that the Treaty would be laid before the country without any secrecy. "Pitiless publicity" was the phrase he used.[8]

A few days later he launched into a severe attack upon Article 21. He had now discovered objections to the article that had been amended in Paris in answer to his own demands. The Covenant dared to call the Monroe Doctrine an "international engagement"! It never was an international engagement or understanding, he cried. "It is all ours; and now it is carried into this league of nations. It is already interpreted by England, although it is wholly our affair, and it is to be determined in the future by the League of Nations." Senator John Sharp Williams, one of the keenest students of international affairs ever to sit in the Senate, said that Senator Lodge's "objection to the exclusion of mention of the Monroe Doctrine increased to virulence when he was faced with the inclusion of it."

Virulence was the word. There were virulent attacks upon the President for keeping the unsigned Treaty a "secret," and great excitement when Senator Lodge and Senator Borah charged that copies of the Treaty existed in this country, although none had been sent to the Senate. There was virulence when Senator Knox introduced his new resolution, which would cut the League from the Treaty. In the debate that followed Senator Reed raised the issue of race and color, saying that the League would place all mankind under the rulership of the blacks; Senator Sherman the next day had discovered that it was the Pope who would rule.

Senator Lodge soon found that he could not hold the Senate in line for the Knox resolution. Somewhat distressing,

[8] Cf. Chapter XIII, ante: In 1898 Lodge insisted the Peace Treaty, then under consideration, be debated in *secret* session. At the same time he demanded the election of a Republican Congress so that the world would not think America had repudiated the results of the Spanish-American War and the Republican President who "led it victoriously and is now leading us back to peace."

too, was the appearance of Chairman Hays, who had arrived in Washington at Lodge's invitation, and who said that the Republican Party was for "a League of Nations," when it was apparent that most of the Republicans were against the League, either totally or in part. Senator Lodge tried without success to forward his proposal to insert a qualifying resolution which Root had suggested, stipulating that ratification by the Senate should not be effective until the Senate's reservations were accepted by the other powers. But these were both minor matters.

On June 28 a defeated Germany signed the Peace of Versailles. The next day President Wilson sailed home. There he was to encounter as bitter intrigue and as adamant opposition as any he had met in Paris. On July 9 he arrived in New York. The great city warmly welcomed him, but that evening in Carnegie Hall, where Senators Reed and Johnson were addressing a mass meeting, his name was hissed. In Washington, Senator Lodge waited.

XXI

The Great Debate

PRESIDENT WILSON entered the chamber of the United States Senate on July 10, 1919. Amid the cheers of the crowded galleries and the more restrained applause of his official family and the Senators of the forty-eight states gathered there, he delivered into their eager hands the Treaty of Peace. The Chairman of the Senate Committee on Foreign Relations, Henry Cabot Lodge, escorted him to his seat.

"The stage is set, the destiny disclosed," the President said. "It has come about by no plan of our conceiving; but by the hand of God who led us into this way. We cannot turn back. We can only go forward, with lifted eyes and freshened spirit to follow the vision. It was of this that we dreamed at our birth. America shall in truth show the way. The light streams upon the path ahead, and nowhere else."

His words had hardly faded away and the door closed behind him when Senator Lodge moved to refer the Treaty of Peace to the committee which he headed. The motion was carried. The light upon the path ahead flickered and grew dim.

When the Treaty, with its fatal Covenant of a League of Nations, was dropped in the maw of this committee, it became, for the time being, the property of seventeen men. Ten were Republicans. Of these ten, six were old members — Lodge, McCumber, Borah, Brandegee, Fall, and Knox; four had been appointed at the start of the Sixty-sixth Congress — Harding of Ohio, New of Indiana, Johnson of California,

331

and Moses of New Hampshire. With the exception of McCumber all had signed the "round robin," placing themselves on record as opposed to the League of Nations as it had been hammered out on the forge of Versailles.

The seven Democrats were headed by Gilbert M. Hitchcock of Nebraska. He was an able Senator, but as a parliamentary tactician he was no match for the wily Lodge. The others were John Sharp Williams, that amazing Mississippian who could achieve lucidity whatever the circumstances, Swanson of Virginia, Atlee Pomerene of Ohio, Key Pittman of Nevada, Marcus A. Smith of Arizona, and John K. Shields of Tennessee.

When the Treaty was placed at the mercy of these gentlemen it seemed as if there were little that could be said, either for or against the League of Nations, that had not already been said with passion and at great length. But Senator Lodge had promised "pitiless publicity." He proceeded to keep his promise. The Treaty itself was to be singularly immune from attack, but the Covenant was to shrivel under the burning light of Senatorial inquisition.

Hardly had the document been started on its way to the committee room when the strategists went into action. At Lodge's beck there gathered around him in the Senate cloakroom Senators Borah, Brandegee, Fall, and one or two others — the leaders of the several groups who before long were to be maneuvered into rejecting the League by voting first one way and then another.

The essence of the Republican strategy was clear: each article would be separately considered, ridiculed, attacked until the American people had been given a picture of the League as a devouring creature bred in infamy, ready now to demolish all the ancient rights of Americans, subject them to all the whims of foreign rulers, and bring about greater and more terrible wars.

In a series of a dozen or more conferences, held at Lodge's home, at Alice Roosevelt Longworth's, at Senator Knox's, and elsewhere, the Republican lines were laid. The great danger which they faced was that the solid Democratic phalanx and the pro-League Republicans would join forces. By gaining parliamentary control, they would be able to dictate the terms of ratification and defeat the projected crippling reservations and amendments. At these meetings, however, this danger was hammered home to the so-called irreconcilables. They were not asked to desert their principles when it came to a final vote, but they were shown the necessity of voting, in the early stages of the game, with the Lodge conservatives, thus assuring a necessary Republican majority in favor of the reservations which Senator Lodge would soon propose, and against those which the Democrats undoubtedly would set forth as substitutes.

The Borah-Johnson group, determined in the end to bring total defeat to the Treaty, accepted the idea. Both sides, the irreconcilables and the reservationists, were also agreed upon another point: the tactic of delay. They shrewdly realized that the American people were not yet wholly "educated" to the dangers of the "evil thing with the holy name." The campaign of propaganda was already taking effect, but the longer it continued the safer the anti-League forces would feel. Since the Senate could not vote on the Treaty until the Foreign Relations Committee reported it out, it was agreed to keep it there as long as possible. The Republican majority of the committee assured this.

The committee was already packed against the League by the Republican leaders. When four vacancies had occurred as a result of the 1918 elections, they had been filled with three irreconcilables: Senators Johnson, Moses, and New. The fourth place went to Senator Harding, a middle grounder. Later Senator New joined the Lodge group. Senator Moses was chosen instead of Senator Frank B. Kellogg, who had seniority, presumably because the latter had refused to sign the "round robin" and had spoken in favor of the League. When Senators Williams and Hitchcock challenged Lodge to deny that the Republicans had deliberately filled the committee with anti-League Senators, the gentleman from Massachusetts refused to answer.

Although the Republicans dominated the committee, Senator Lodge found himself in a delicate position — a position that was to have a great bearing upon the final outcome of the great debate.

He had his strategy. The irreconcilables had theirs. Together they would introduce into the Senate certain amendments which they were certain the Democrats would reject. If this failed, they would then insist upon reservations so crippling that the Democrats would be forced to vote against ratification.

Senator Lodge, who put his trust in reservations which would change the face and body of the League but which would still leave it in the Treaty for what it was worth, was at the mercy of Borah, Johnson, and Moses. They could dictate, or they could withdraw. They held the ultimate power.

Throughout July, while the Treaty was being read by the committee, the debate on the League, both within and without the Senate, continued violently. It had its defenders as well as its detractors, but the latter seemed to make the most noise and garnered the most publicity. Nearly everything that was said had been said before. Senator Lodge was steadily in the limelight as he seized every opportunity to embarrass the administration.

Shortly before the Treaty had been sent to the Senate he had written Henry White: —

If the President adheres to his position that we must ratify the treaty without crossing a "t" or dotting an "i," my best judgment

334

is that he will fail. The treaty will be sent to him with reservations, and then it will be up to him to hold it back. I am giving a good deal of time and thought to it.

In the heat of the Washington summer Lodge was devoting long hours every day in the committee room. He did not know, he said at this time, "what the final judgment of the people will be," but, as the summer slid along, he was sure that the hostility to the League was growing. He felt that if by any chance the League was adopted it would be "a sorry day for the country in years to come. . . ."

He attacked the Wilson administration for the Shantung settlement; he harried the President to produce copies of an alleged secret treaty made between Japan and Germany before the Armistice was signed. In mid-July two gentlemen who favored the League, James G. Macdonald and Allen T. Burns, visited him. As they discussed the Treaty in the committee room the Senator reached for a copy of the general arbitration treaty with Great Britain negotiated in 1911 by President Taft. He pointed out the reservations and amendments made by the Senate.

Exultingly Lodge remarked, "And President Taft never saw fit to return the treaty to Great Britain!" Mr. Burns later said that Lodge then declared, "We shall deal with the Versailles Treaty in the same way. If President Wilson does not see fit to return it to our Allies, that is his responsibility." Then, "with a snap of his jaw and a bang of his fist," the Senator said, "That is the way to handle such treaties!"

The very next day Senator Moses, in a Senate speech, opposed ratification of the entire Treaty, which, he said, would be "infinitely worse for us than even the League of Nations, bad as it is." Senator Lodge thought that Mr. Moses had made one of the most effective arguments yet against the League.

By July 31 the committee, which had spent two full weeks

reading the 87,000-word treaty into the records, felt the time had come when it could use some help in dotting the "*i*'s" and crossing the "*t*'s." On that day the first open hearings were held. From then until late in the autumn a steady procession of witnesses, some with relevant testimony to offer and others with none, filed through the room.

Among them were representatives of small nations — Albania, Egypt, Hungary, Ireland,[1] and Persia — who had not been invited to Paris, and who added to the growing public confusion and distrust of the League. Later other and more important witnesses were to be heard.

Under the questioning of the Senators, led by Lodge, much embarrassing information was obtained. It was pretty well shown that President Wilson had been annoyed and displeased with the Shantung settlement, and the inference, at least, was left that something had been "put over" on him. A month later, after several heated debates, Senator Lodge moved the adoption of an amendment designed to transfer the former German rights in Shantung from Japan to China. The Lodge motion was carried in the committee by a party vote of nine to eight, McCumber voting against.

[1] Although Senator Lodge had upon one occasion in 1914 deplored the tendency of certain members of the Senate to treat of foreign affairs with little more dignity or foresight than they would a harbor appropriations bill, he was not above injecting local politics into the grave matter of the Treaty of Versailles. In May members of the American Commission for Irish Independence had gone to Paris demanding a hearing. Early in June the Foreign Relations Committee passed a resolution requesting the American delegation to secure a hearing for de Valera and others. When Henry White objected to this on the grounds that Irish independence had "nothing to do with the making of peace," Senator Lodge replied: "Neither did the Monroe Doctrine come within the jurisdiction of the Peace Conference." Although Lodge admitted the Irish matter did not concern the Peace Conference he justified his interest in it: "You know what the Irish vote is in this country. As far as I can make out they are bitterly opposed to the League, and the fate of the Democratic party in the Northern States is in their hands. They are having great meetings and all pronouncing against the League. Cardinal O'Connell presided at one of these meetings in Boston. . . ."

At various times in the next few weeks, many witnesses were called to show the alleged existence of disagreements among the American delegates to Paris [2] and much pertinent testimony was spread upon the record. But much that was hardly pertinent to the Treaty of Versailles was also spread. In obtaining the latter, Lodge played his part, thus adding to President Wilson's growing dislike, which eventually reached the point where mentioning the name of the Senator from Massachusetts to the President was, as Senator Hitchcock said, like waving a red flag at a bull. Senator Lodge's bringing of William C. Bullitt before the committee, with his documented recital of President Wilson's quarrels with Secretary of State Lansing, which Lansing, out of deference to the President, was in no position either to affirm or to deny, did nothing to draw Senator and President closer together.

Early in August Norman H. Davis, who had been in Paris as a financial expert, was called before the committee. In reply to a question by Senator Knox as to whom else the committee might summon as an expert, Mr. Davis answered, "President Wilson." Lodge's reply was heated: "The President has never offered to come before this committee. He only sent a telephone message saying he would be glad to have the committee come to the White House. We have called for paper after paper and he has not sent one." The President, of course, had publicly offered to appear before the committee in his speech of July 10.

As the grim heat of August settled down upon the Capital, Senator Lodge prepared to make his first speech since the Treaty had been submitted to the Senate. On August 12 he spoke for two hours.

[2] Among those called at one time or another were General Bliss, Henry White, Colonel House, of the American Peace Delegation. They were requested to appear. Senator Borah moved that they be subpoenaed, but his motion was defeated. Senator Lodge was among those voting for the motion.

Taking first things first, Senator Lodge took up the preamble of the Covenant and compared it unfavorably with the preamble to the Peace of Paris, whence had stemmed the Holy Alliance. One after another he assailed the various Articles of the Covenant. As usual he poured forth his strongest words in assault upon Article 10. Grim was the picture which he painted of what would happen if, at any time, the United States failed to live up to the letter and spirit of the Covenant. We would be dishonored! The League would crumble into dust! Nothing would be left but a legacy of wars!

His speech was a long, and bitter, renunciation of the League, delivered in spirit and language but little different from the words he had uttered before. But the galleries, crowded with representatives of women's organizations and a contingent of veteran Marines from Château-Thierry, who had just passed in review before the President, hung on every word. The Senator was frequently interrupted by applause, as when he said it was impossible to isolate the United States and that our part in the war had disposed of any charge of selfishness that might be leveled against us.

"You may call me selfish, if you will, conservative or reactionary, or use any other harsh adjective you see fit to apply," he cried, "but an American I was born, and American I have remained all my life. I can never be anything else but an American, and I must think of the United States first, and when I think of the United States first in an arrangement like this I am thinking of what is best for the world, for if the United States fails the best hopes of mankind fail with it. I have never had but one allegiance — I cannot divide it now. I have never loved but one flag and I cannot share that devotion and give affection to the mongrel banner invented for a league. . . .

"Are ideals confined to this deformed experiment upon a

noble purpose, tainted, as it is, with bargains and tied to a peace treaty which might have been disposed of long ago to the great benefit of the world if it had not been compelled to carry this rider on its back?

"We all share these aspirations and desires, but some of us see no hope, but rather defeat, for them in this murky covenant. For we, too, have our ideals, even if we differ from those who have tried to establish a monopoly on idealism. Our ideal is our country. . . .

"We would have our country strong to resist a peril from the West, as she has flung back the German menace from the East. We would not have our politics distracted and embittered by dissensions from other lands. We would not have our country's vigor exhausted, or her moral force abated, by everlasting meddling and muddling in every quarrel great and small, which afflicts the world. Our ideal is to make her even stronger and better and finer, because in this way alone, as we believe, can she be of the greatest service to the world's peace and the welfare of mankind."

The shouts of the Marines echoed through the Senate as he finished his dramatic peroration. Not for years had the Senate heard such loud applause. When Senator Williams replied to the Senator from Massachusetts he was hissed.

Two days after his long denunciation of the League, Chairman Lodge asked President Wilson for a public conference, and received an immediate acceptance. The date was set for 10 A.M. on Tuesday, August 10, in the East Room of the White House.

President Wilson, who already had held private conferences with several Republican Senators and had learned from them that, by acceptance of reservations, he might save his League, was in a stern, uncompromising mood when the Senators marched in. Already he had been thinking of taking his fight to the people. He was not, even then, a well man.

It was hardly in that spirit of "accommodation" which he had often said was an essential in the conduct of public affairs that he read to them from a prepared statement: —

"Nothing, I am led to believe, stands in the way of the ratification . . . except certain doubts in regard to the meaning and implication of certain articles of the Covenant of the League of Nations, and I must frankly say that I am unable to understand why such doubts should be entertained. . . . There was absolutely no doubt as to the meaning . . . in the minds of those who participated in drafting them, and I respectfully submit that there is nothing vague or doubtful in their meaning."

Senator Lodge, who had been insisting that the Covenant was not "made in America," questioned the President closely as to other drafts in an effort, it seems, to prove that the League was the evil creation of British minds. On the whole, the conference was a failure. Wilson was unbending. He had set his mind upon the League as it stood in the Treaty and was unwilling to have it changed. His supporters, however, did not think he could have done otherwise. Among them was the *New York Times*, which said: —

If the President's interpretation . . . of the treaty . . . and his straightforward replies to the questions of the Senators have not removed from their minds all reasonable doubts and misgivings, then evidently nothing can . . . and the country will be forced to the conclusion that their objections do not lie in the treaty or in the League covenant, but somewhere outside. If that be true, then the people must deal with the Senatorial obstructionists, for the President has exhausted the resources of reasoning and exposition.

Shortly after the conference the committee adopted fifty amendments to the Treaty.

August ended as it had begun, in a welter of Senatorial words against the Covenant of the League. On September

3, President Wilson started on his brave but fatal tour which, he hoped, would swing public opinion behind him. In the next three weeks he was to travel 8000 miles, participate in a dozen great parades, and deliver forty-four speeches. As he began his historic trek he was met with apathy, but, as he proceeded, the warmth of his receptions increased. He swung through Missouri, Iowa, Minnesota, to the Northwest. Then he moved down the Pacific Coast to Southern California. He was on his way home, with but half a dozen speeches left on his schedule, when, in Kansas, he broke down.

The Foreign Relations Committee waited a week after his departure from Washington before it brought in its reports, two full months after it had received the Treaty.

Lodge had written to Beveridge a short time before: —

But the votes to defeat the treaty squarely are not there, for the simple reason that the League is tied onto the treaty of peace, and we cannot get votes to separate them. I am not arguing the right or wrong of it, but telling you what the situation is. My business was to unite the Republicans, and they are united now on strong and effective reservations. Any that go on will be effective, and Mr. Wilson's maneuver will be without result. . . .

There, in a nutshell, was the reason why the Treaty had lain so long in committee. But now it was out. Everything, it appeared, was at last under control. A reporter asked Senator Lodge if he had any reply to make to the President's castigations of his opponents, and Lodge replied with a smile: "No, there is nothing to say at this time, except that the treaty situation is better now than it has been for months. I can say that reservations will be adopted before the treaty is ratified."

Between September 10 and September 15 the committee presented three reports. The majority report, written in part by Senator Lodge, caustically answered the charges of delay with the comment that, in forty-five days (not counting holidays and the time it took to print the report), the committee had considered what it had taken the Peace Conference six months to accomplish. It then attacked the President's "autocratic" methods. Attached were forty-five proposed amendments and four reservations which, it was obvious, the President would never accept.

The minority report, signed by the Democratic members, dismissed all amendments, opposed all reservations, and urged ratification of the Treaty with the League as it now stood. Senator McCumber presented a remarkable separate report, which chided the majority for substituting irony and sarcasm for argument, for paying too little attention to the Treaty itself, and for proposing amendments which would isolate us from the rest of the world and keep us from consummating "the duties for which the war was fought."

Attached to the majority report was this reservation: —

The United States declines to assume, under the provisions of Article 10, or under any other article, any obligation to preserve the territorial integrity or political independence of any other country, or to interfere in controversies, or to adopt economic measures for the protection of any other country . . . against external aggression or for the purpose of coercing any other country . . . and no mandates shall be accepted by the United States . . . except by action of the Congress. . . .

The three other reservations covered the Monroe Doctrine, withdrawal from the League, and domestic questions.

As October approached Senator Lodge found himself in a difficult position. His business, as he had said, was to unite the Republicans. It was not an easy task, holding the two wings in line. A great deal of pressure was brought to bear upon him from both sides. He had to restrain the overzealous, he had to prod the reluctant, he had to soothe those who stood in between. Particularly vehement were the irreconcilables, who never knew just how much to trust his leadership. In the closed committee room they addressed him with violence more than once, and heckled him in words, so he plaintively complained, which "no man of my age should be obliged to hear."

He fought stubbornly and, as various amendments which he and Senator Fall had introduced were defeated in the Senate, the wisdom of his strategy became more apparent. The votes on these showed how the land lay. In their defeat the majority had been composed of about forty Democrats and between fourteen and eighteen mild-reservationist Republicans. The minority had also been split between about twenty "organization Republicans" and some twelve or thirteen irreconcilables. Thus three Republican groups — reservationists, mild-reservationists, and irreconcilables — must be brought together to assure the success of any motion.

As October sped along, further amendments were defeated and Lodge's motion to strike the Shantung articles from the Treaty was lost. This made it clear to all Republicans that the time had now come to do what the Wily One had long since told Jim Watson they would do — accomplish by reservations what could not be done directly.

Lodge himself wanted the Treaty and the League destroyed. But his position as majority leader, the official medium between all the Republican Senators, committed him to caution. And, also, like most of the others of his political faith, he wanted to make the League an issue in the 1920 Presidential campaign. Until Wilson's dangerous illness precluded the possibility, Lodge was unconvinced that the President would not seek a third term. Nineteen hundred and twenty was always in the forefront of his mind. He cared more about the political regeneration of his party, and the maintenance of his own leadership, than anything else. Among his close friends there were many who thought that he saw himself as the Republican standard bearer. This, they said, explained why he fought so hard, and worked so valiantly at the tremendously difficult task of keeping the various factions in line.

The irreconcilables, on the other hand, were less obsessed with the politics of the situation. Senator Johnson, at least during his speaking tour which he undertook to counteract Wilson's, may have thought of himself as Presidential timber, but Borah and Moses and the others wanted nothing more than to kill the Treaty. Thus they could afford to be firm. They had little to lose and everything to gain.

Such was the situation as the amendments were beaten down in October. The Foreign Relations Committee now turned to the task of framing reservations — fourteen of them. Ten were added to those originally proposed, although the language was somewhat softened. These bore Senator Lodge's name. Although he was not the author of all of them, he willingly let them be known henceforth as the Lodge Reservations. On October 23 Senator Lodge said that the reservations would have the same value as amendments.

In the meantime President Wilson's illness, following his collapse on September 26, had robbed the Democrats of leadership. Alarming stories about his physical and mental condition spread throughout the country. Although his mental condition then was perhaps not as serious as the alarmist press said, there was no denying the fact that he was incommunicado in the White House, that none saw him from day to day except Mrs. Wilson, his physician, perhaps his secretary.

Shortly before the reservations were to come up for a final vote Stephen Bonsal, who had been an interpreter at Paris for Wilson, visited Senator Lodge at the request of Colonel House, who was having no more luck than anyone else in reaching the side of the sick President. Bonsal had several talks with the Senator from Massachusetts, during one of which Lodge penciled on a copy of the Covenant certain mild changes, running to less than one hundred words in all. He intimated that if President Wilson would accept these changes the Treaty could be ratified. Bonsal rushed the document to Colonel House, himself ill in New York, who forwarded it to the White House. There was no answer. House always felt that Mrs. Wilson had destroyed the memorandum, which was in Lodge's writing and signed with his name; or at least that she had prevented it from reaching her husband. It was Bonsal's belief that, when Lodge heard nothing from the White House, he took the silence as a personal affront, his hatred for Wilson increased, and his determination to defeat the Treaty stiffened.

Others at this time suspected that Lodge was on the point of "surrendering," or that he was, at least, willing to reach some kind of agreement with the Democrats which would save the League. Senator Hitchcock never had this feeling. "I admit," he told Bonsal, "that in some of my unofficial cloakroom talks with Lodge he expresses views which even to me seem reasonable, but when I ask him to get down to cases and state what changes he would suggest, his face hardens. I think he would like to induce me to offer changes and concessions. Of course, by my instructions, although, owing to the President's illness, they are somewhat out of date, I am precluded from doing so. So my conviction deepens that whatever may have been his purpose two months ago, today Lodge has decided to beat the Treaty and the Covenant — if he can."

Senator Hitchcock said that to Bonsal on November 18. The next day a letter came from the White House, over Wilson's signature, which Hitchcock read to the Democratic Senators at a conference which was held just before the

Senate assembled to vote on Senator Lodge's resolution of ratification: —

> . . . I assume that the Senators only desire my judgment on the all-important question of the final vote on the resolution containing the many reservations of Senator Lodge. On that I cannot hesitate, for, in my opinion, the resolution in that form does not provide for ratification, but rather for nullification of the treaty. I sincerely hope that the friends and supporters of the treaty will vote against the Lodge resolution of ratification. I understand the door will then probably be open for a genuine resolution of ratification. I trust all true friends of the treaty will refuse to support the Lodge resolution.

That day there were three votes on the Treaty. One was for the Treaty with the Lodge Reservations. The Democrats, loyal to their leader, joined with the irreconcilables to vote this down, 55 to 39. Another was for the Treaty with the five reservations which Senator Hitchcock had proposed.[3] This, too, the Senate rejected, by a vote of 51 to 41. On the third vote, which was for the Treaty as it stood, the reservationists, as Lodge had predicted, joined with the irreconcilables to defeat it, 53 to 38.

As the final vote was taken, Senator Lodge turned to Senator Swanson and said, "The door is closed."

Closed, yes, but not yet locked. The immediate reaction to the Senate's rejection was almost nationwide consternation and regret. If the *Transcript* rejoiced, if Senator Borah called it the greatest victory since Appomattox, there were many millions of people throughout the country who felt, with another editor, that the Senate "under the bankrupt

---

[3] (1) The right of Congress to authorize, or forbid, use of American forces for League sanctions; (2) the Monroe Doctrine; (3) equality of voting power with Great Britain, including her Dominions; (4) right of withdrawal; and (5) exemption of domestic issues from League jurisdiction. These were, of course, in the Lodge reservations.

leadership of Henry Cabot Lodge" had done a shameful thing.

Soon a demand for some kind of compromise swept the country which even Senator Lodge could not ignore. The Democratic leaders were correct in their belief that public opinion demanded further consideration of the Lodge Reservations. The Treaty was not yet dead. When Senator Lodge visited Boston within the fortnight following the final vote he found that "a situation had developed . . . which was caused by the continued assertion of the friends of the League that the reservations had been added and the defeat of the treaty brought about by disputes between the two parties on what were merely verbal differences. . . ." Although he said this belief was false, he came to the conclusion that "it was most desirable to make an effort, at least, to come to some agreement between the two sides; that is, between the opponents of the reservations and of the treaty and those who favored accepting the League substantially as it was offered. . . ."

The special session of Congress ended with the vote on the Treaty. The new session met on December 1. It was Senator Lodge's contention that the President must withdraw and then resubmit the Treaty, which would throw it again into the hands of the Foreign Relations Committee. This scheme, however, was blocked. Lodge then announced that he would "stand pat" on the reservations, a warning that he was in no compromising mood. When Senator Underwood attempted to form an official bipartisan committee of conciliation, composed of ten Senators, Lodge at first stood solidly in the way. The middle-grounders, angered at his obstruction, were reported to have warned Lodge that they would ignore his leadership if he did not hasten a compromise, talk of which now filled the press, and that they would move over to the Democratic side.

347

When the Democrats gathered on January 8 to celebrate Jackson Day they received a message from the White House. "Personally, I do not accept the action of the Senate of the United States as the decision of the nation," the President said. He was not averse to "reasonable interpretations" accompanying the act of ratification, but he warned: "We cannot rewrite this treaty. We must take it without changes which alter its meaning, or leave it, and . . . face the unthinkable task of making another and separate kind of treaty with Germany." If the Senate would not ratify, then "the clear and single way out" was to submit the question to the voters of the nation — to make the next election "a great and solemn referendum. . . ."

This political solution did not sit well with the Democratic politicians,[4] and the pressure for compromise continued. Senator Lodge, however, accepted the President's electoral challenge, and took the stand that it was the President who was unyielding, not himself. But he was forced into a position of at least appearing to be willing to talk with the other side. Several Democrats thereupon visited him on January 15, two days after President Wilson had called the first session of the Council of the League of Nations, which had come into being through the ratification of the Treaty by enough of the Allied Powers to put it into effect.

The meeting resulted in several conferences between Senator Lodge and Senator Hitchcock, which a few other Senators attended. Rumors soon spread throughout Washington that Senator Lodge was again on the verge of "surrendering." Undoubtedly he had been brought around to the point where he was willing to make some kind of compromise agreement with the Democrats. But in reach-

[4] They were well aware that the great mass of Irish-American, German-American, and Italian-American voters were opposed to the League.

ing it he had worked himself into a difficult position which, in the end, was disastrous.

Learning of his intentions the irreconcilables — Borah, Johnson, Knox, McCormick, Sherman, Poindexter, Brandegee, and Moses — haled Lodge before them and laid down the law in unmistakable language. For nearly an hour they argued with him, telling him to stand firm, and warning him that if he did not do so they would drive him from his post as party leader. They threatened to reorganize the Senate. "You won't be majority leader a day longer," they said.

Lodge was desperate. He said he could resign his position. They said they would give him no chance to resign. "We will make it a public exhibition," they threatened. He bowed to their threats and thereafter refused to compromise at all on the reservations on Article 10 and the Monroe Doctrine.

Senator Johnson later declared that on the day of that stormy meeting, which took place in his office with sixteen bitter-enders present, "we were right at the entrance of the League of Nations." But, he said, those sixteen men "called the thing off through the then leader of the Republican party in this chamber — Lodge."

Several more meetings of the so-called conciliation committee, which was composed of Lodge and New, representing the Republican regulars, Kellogg and Lenroot, representing the middle-grounders, and five Democrats, were held. President Wilson then told Senator Hitchcock that he was willing to accept the reservations that had been prepared bearing Hitchcock's name. These were closely akin to the Lodge Reservations, even in phraseology. But they were Democratic reservations — not Republican. That was their only essential difference. Senator Lodge explained it: "The Democrats are simply trying to make some change, great or small, so that they may say the reservations are theirs." Neither the Republicans nor the Democrats — neither Lodge nor Wilson — were willing to run the risk of giving the other side any chance to claim the victory.

The conferences ended on January 30, four days after Senator Lodge had said, "There can be no compromise of principle."

There had been none, nor was there to be any. There was no move in this direction from President Wilson. On February 9 the Senate voted to reconsider the Treaty and referred it once more to the committee. The next day it was reported back, with a new set of reservations adopted as a result of the bipartisan conferences.

There followed a month of oratory, arguments, bickering, quibbling, during which the petulant Wilson charged the reservationists with being nullifiers. Early in March the Borah contingent forced Senator Lodge to accept an amendment to the latest draft of the reservations, across the face of which Wilson scrawled the single word "Disapproved." On March 19 the Treaty came up for vote.

On that fateful day, twenty-three Democrats deserted President Wilson and joined with thirty-four Republicans to ratify the Treaty. Twenty-four Democrats remained faithful and joined with fifteen irreconcilables to vote against ratification. The fifty-seven Senators who voted for the Treaty, with its amendments and reservations, were not enough to win. Sixty-four votes were needed to complete the Constitutional two thirds. The Treaty had failed again. This time the door was closed — and locked.

That afternoon when Senator Lodge returned to his home he was met at the door by Corinne Roosevelt Robinson, the sister of his old friend. He "went into his library with a very heavy brow," she later recalled. "He said, 'Just as I expected to get my Democrats to vote with my Republicans on going into the League, a hand came out of the White House and drew back those Democrats, and prevented our going into the League with reservations.' "

But his own daughter did not think that he had ever meant to do that. She said: "My father hated and feared the Wilson league and his heart was really with the irreconcilables. But it was uncertain whether this league could be beaten straight out this way, and the object of his reservations was so to emasculate the Wilson league that if it did pass it would be valueless and the United States would be honorably safeguarded. My father never wanted the Wilson league, and when it was finally defeated he was like a man from whom a great burden was lifted."

Heavy-browed or lighthearted as Lodge might be, the ultimate defeat of the Treaty of Peace and the League of Nations was his. He could not disown it if he would. And that he never tried to do. Before his death he wrote his own version of the long and desperate struggle, but he did not live to see it in print. "Lodge from his grave," Mark Sullivan wrote in 1926, "is still emitting undying hate against his rival in the shape of a book conceived as a self-justification but unable to avoid being partly an *apologia pro vita sua* and partly a last thrust of malevolence."

In 1915 Lodge had wanted a League of Nations. When it came, it was the gift of a Democratic President, the gift of a man whom his closest friend deeply hated and for whom he himself had built up a hatred equally intense. For that reason, and because he wanted to bring back his party into power, he fought to the bitter end.

XXII

This Is the End

THE AUTUMN of 1919 had seen much unrest in the nation. In Boston the policemen went on strike. Out of this situation there arose a new national figure in Calvin Coolidge.

Immersed though he was in the fight against the League, Senator Lodge had watched what was going on in "my city" with close attention. He feared that "if the American Federation of Labor succeeds in getting hold of the police in Boston it will go all over the country, and we shall be in a measurable distance of Soviet government by labor unions."

Governor Coolidge, braced by Murray Crane, took his famous stand on the side of law and order. When Lodge came to Boston to attend the Republican State Convention, which renominated Coolidge, he was loud in his praise of the Governor's stand. At this convention, however, he came into a headlong collision with Crane. From the beginning the former Senator had been one of the League's stanchest supporters. He had not changed his attitude now.

Murray Crane, even then a sick man, threw his challenge at Lodge. The latter tried to force the convention towards an anti-League stand. But Crane, still powerful in party councils, won. In a midnight meeting of the bosses he forced an endorsement of the League to be written into the Republican platform. The rebuke to Lodge did not go unnoticed. The two party leaders had openly split.

Now, in March 1920, with the League nothing more than the "shattered hulk" that Lodge called it, all attention was turned to the approaching national conventions, forerunners of that "solemn referendum" which President Wilson had asked.

In the Republican ranks four men stood out as possible Republican candidates: Leonard Wood, whose campaign was to be managed by Senator Moses, the irreconcilable; Senator Hiram Johnson; Governor Frank Lowden of Illinois; and Senator Warren G. Harding. The so-called Senate cabal, of which Lodge, the party leader, was an intimate member, generally favored Harding.

Around Thanksgiving time, however, Lodge had talked with Governor Coolidge, whose name had already been mentioned as a Presidential possibility, and had said he would like to present his name to the convention. He also told Frank Stearns, Coolidge's closest mentor, that he was "for the Governor, not merely as a favorite son, but really for him for the nomination for the Presidency of the United States." On November 26 he told the *Transcript* that he favored Coolidge, thus becoming the first prominent Republican to endorse him.

By early spring, however, Lodge's ardor had cooled. Coolidge, in his laconic way, had not encouraged the campaign in his behalf, and had issued no statement indicating whether he was seeking the office or not. Lodge rather suspected that Coolidge thought his chances at the convention limited. He did not, however, turn his back on the Governor, although his sympathies appeared now to be with General Leonard Wood, who regarded himself as heir to the Theodore Roosevelt tradition.

In March the *Herald* announced confidently that Senator Lodge would present Coolidge's name at Chicago in June. But those "on the inside" knew that he was trying hard to escape the rash commitment he had made four months earlier. It was not strange that he should try to do so. Coolidge, as everyone knew, was to all intents and purposes Murray Crane's man. And Crane, even after the March defeat, was still fighting for the League.

On the twelfth of that month Senator Lodge, surrounded by members of his family and a few close friends, quietly celebrated his seventieth birthday in the library of his Massachusetts Avenue home. He was now an old man, an elder statesman indeed. But age sat lightly on him. He had enjoyed the fight against Wilson and it had not aged or wearied him. He looked forward to the coming convention. Who knew but that perhaps it would be the last he would attend? Certainly at none of all those others where he had played a great or small part had he ever occupied the prominent place in the spotlight that was to be his in June.

In the inner Republican circle, Lodge was maneuvering with all his old-time wile to steal the show. He had little difficulty in wresting the temporary chairmanship from Beveridge. Once that was accomplished he set out to make himself permanent chairman. Not only did he want this for its power and prestige but, once in the chair, he would be relieved of having to nominate Coolidge. Lodge was assured of the post when the Senate junto picked Jim Watson of Indiana to head the platform committee. National Chairman Hays was also from Indiana. The post Lodge coveted would have to go to another state. Lodge knew, when he left for Chicago, that the post would be his.

As temporary chairman he delivered the keynote speech. Mark Sullivan, who heard it, said it was filled with "waspish malice." A *Boston Herald* reporter said that it set forth the issue of the coming campaign, which could be summed up in one word — Wilson. To H. L. Mencken, sitting in the press section, the speech was "bosh," but it was bosh "de-

354

livered with an air — bosh somehow dignified by the manner of its emission. The same stuff, shoveled into the air by any other statesman on the platform, would simply have driven the crowd out of the hall, and perhaps blown up the convention then and there. But Lodge got away with it because he was Lodge — because there was behind it his unescapable confidence in himself, his disarming disdain of discontent below, his unapologetic superiority."

As permanent chairman Lodge ran the convention to his liking. "He presided over the session from a sort of aloof intellectual balcony," wrote Mencken, "far above the swarming and the bawling of the common herd. He was there in the flesh, but his soul was in some remote and esoteric Cathay. . . . It was delightful to observe the sardonic glitter in his eye, his occasional ill-concealed snort, his general air of detachment from the business before him. For a while he would watch the show idly, letting it get more and more passionate, vociferous, and preposterous. Then, as if suddenly awakened, he would stalk into it with his club and knock it into decorum in half a minute. I call the thing a club; it was certainly nothing properly describable as a gavel. . . . Supporting it was the Lodge voice, and behind the voice the Lodge sneer. That voice seemed quite extraordinary in so slim and ancient a man. It had volume, resonance, even a touch of music; it was pleasant to hear, and it penetrated that fog of vaporized humanity to great depths. . . . His delight in the business visibly increased as the climax was approached. It culminated in a colossal chuckle as the mob got out of hand, and the witches of crowd folly began to ride, and the burlesque deliberations of five intolerable days came to flower in the half-frightened, half-defiant nomination of Harding — a tin-horn politician with the manner of a rural corn doctor and the mien of a ham actor."

Mencken, the philosopher, wondered then — and we may still wonder — how one as superior as Lodge, as little given to the "puerile hypocrisy" of denying his superiority, how one of such breeding, background, traditions, and learning, could allow the ineffable Harding to get the nomination. There was, indeed, a profound irony in the role he played, and Mencken, certain that it could not have escaped the gentleman from Massachusetts, often detected him "snickering into his beard as the obscene farce unrolled itself before him."

One by one the names of the various aspirants for the nomination — among them Calvin Coolidge — were presented with the usual ghastly oratory to the convention. On the first ballots Senator Lodge voted for General Wood. When, after consultation with Senator Smoot, Chairman Lodge concluded that Wood and Governor Lowden were deadlocked, Lodge, openly disregarding the preponderance of "Noes," adjourned the convention until the following morning.

That night, on the fourth floor of the Blackstone Hotel — in that famous "smoke-filled room" — the Senate cabal, with Senator Lodge present throughout the weary hours, sat in conspiracy. They were picking their man. Lodge had already deserted the cause of the governor of his own state. Earlier that week he had said to Henry L. Stoddard: "Nominate a man who lives in a two-family house! Never! Massachusetts is not for him!" Coolidge's biographer is certain that if Lodge had stuck by the man from the two-family house his prestige and influence were such that Coolidge would then and there have been chosen. But Coolidge was Crane's man, and Crane had fought, with all the power at his command, to drive the implacable Senators of the resolutions committee to pledge their party to the League of Nations. Rather than chance losing his control of the Massachusetts machine to

Crane, Lodge cynically chose Harding, and voted for him the next day.

Once Harding — whom Senator Medill McCormick called a man "of ripe experience, of deep learning, and of great power" — was safely nominated, Lodge called for nominations for Vice President. He had already been approached by the Oregon delegation, which had asked him to let his name be offered for that post. But Lodge had coldly declined.[1] The cabal had settled on Senator Lenroot of Wisconsin. They felt that he, like Harding, was one of them and therefore to be trusted. Once Lenroot's name was seconded Senator Lodge left the hall. Judge Wallace McCamant, a delegate at large from Oregon, resenting the autocratic attitude of Lodge and the other Senators, then placed Calvin Coolidge in nomination for "the exalted office of Vice President." A weary convention, barely listening as other names were offered, shouted "We Want Coolidge!" He was nominated on the first ballot. When he went to Marion, Ohio, to notify Harding of his nomination, he used the occasion to deliver a withering blast against the League and all forms of "internationalism."

Senator Lodge, although disappointed, was a stanch Republican and supported Calvin Coolidge throughout the campaign that resulted in the election of Warren G. Harding and Calvin Coolidge over James M. Cox and Franklin Delano Roosevelt.

In a way, Senator Lodge's career came to an end with the election of Harding. His great fight was done. He had beaten the League and played an important part in naming the man who, in leading the country back to "normalcy," interpreted his election as a complete repudiation of the League. Calvin Coolidge may have said, "I doubt if any

[1] Had he accepted, he would have been nominated — and become President on Harding's death!

particular mandate was given in the last election on the question of the League of Nations and if it was the preponderant issue." Harding felt otherwise, and those who had made his Presidency possible also felt otherwise. A World Court? Pious words, uttered by that poker player who had taken Senator Albert B. Fall into his cabinet, brought about no entrance of America into the World Court. Peace with Germany? It became a separate peace. Europe went its way; America went its way. The Harding era descended into scandal. Senator Lodge never once raised his voice in protest. His day of leadership was done.

In 1922 it became necessary for Senator Lodge once again to go before the people of Massachusetts and ask them to return him to Washington. His power had so lessened that, in his campaign, he had to call upon Calvin Coolidge to come to his aid. The Vice President responded, for he, too, was a good party man. He went to Pittsfield, in the heart of the country which had always been faithful to Murray Crane. Coolidge spoke well for the aged Senator. On their way home Lodge stepped from the train to buy the newspapers. "Coolidge Receives Ovation," the black type read.

Lodge, still slim and immaculate and dignified at seventy-two, crumpled the paper and turned to the man beside him.

"Look at this, will you?" he snorted. "*Coolidge* receives ovation, and it was *my* meeting!"

He tore the paper to shreds and tossed them from him and boarded the train.

But there were those in Massachusetts who still respected the old man. There were the Irish, who remembered his attacks upon perfidious Albion and upon the League which had spurned de Valera; there were the Italians, who remembered what he had said about Fiume. There were enough voters to whom the name of Henry Cabot Lodge was as familiar as the look of their daily paper.

"I wish they would accept me as an institution or a monument for this one time," he said to a friend. "They will never have another chance to do it . . ."

On election day he received the desperately meager plurality of 7354 votes. His total vote was 50,000 less than that cast for the Republican candidate for governor. But they were enough to send him back to the Senate, which had listened so long to the old, commanding, harsh voice of the gentleman from Massachusetts.

Lodge was growing perceptibly old. The cynicism which always had been so much of his character was becoming more marked. Those who had listened to his long, scholarly oration in December 1920 at Plymouth, where the three hundredth anniversary of the landing of the Pilgrims was being celebrated, found his words a "masterpiece of sophistication and disillusionment."

Calvin Coolidge and his friends took control of the state machine away from him, although he struggled hard to keep his hold upon it. He was made to realize that his race had been run.

On the night of August 1 Warren Gamaliel Harding died. A newspaperman telephoned the Lodge home at Nahant. Lodge, sleepy-headed, came reluctantly to the telephone. "Sir," said the reporter, "I am sorry to disturb you, but word has just come through that President Harding has died. . . ." He was about to ask if the senior Senator from Massachusetts cared to make a statement, when the harsh voice cut through: —

"My God! That means Coolidge is President!"

But he drew closer to the new President as the days passed and for a time was even friendly with him. After all, Coolidge was of his own beloved party. On several major issues Lodge, however, refused to go along. Lodge was pledged to the Bonus Bill for veterans of the World War. He had consistently voted for every bill that had ever come before him to set or increase pensions for veterans of America's wars. In fighting for the Bonus Bill he was not inconsistent. He even voted to pass this bill over Coolidge's veto. For his defiance of Coolidge he won new enemies throughout the country. He never apologized for his action; he was, indeed, proud of it. Lodge also opposed Coolidge on the World Court issue and, as might have been expected, on the Japanese Exclusion Act, which Coolidge thought was "unworthy of America."

As the 1924 convention drew near there was much talk in the newspapers of a rift between the President and Senator Lodge. Publicly they met on open terms, although Lodge probably had never forgotten what Murray Crane had said when Lodge turned up at the ceremonies notifying Coolidge of his nomination as Vice President: "He has no business here — he is not wanted." It was still true.

When the Republicans met at Cleveland to nominate Coolidge for President, Lodge was pitiable. The familiar trim, slim figure seemed to sag. His room at the hotel was so wretched that he had to seek refuge with his former secretary, Louis A. Coolidge. He was out of everything. He was just another delegate with a single vote. He felt then to the full the ingratitude of politics. He was deeply hurt. His only consolation was that his old Senate colleagues, Brandegee, Jim Watson, Charlie Curtis, were out of it all too.

When Representative Theodore E. Burton, sounding the keynote, demanded "a Republican majority in the next Congress made up of members tried and true who will stand united," men stood up in the galleries, remembering his vote on the Bonus Bill veto, and shouted, "Down with Lodge!" and "Put Lodge out!" They waited until the tumult died down and then, when their voices could be heard, they shouted again, "Put Lodge out!"

He sat there in the hall, not on the platform, for he was

not even a member of the lowliest committee, and those who saw him said he was as unmoved as a stone.

After the convention he returned to Nahant. There was the sea to watch, his book on the Senate and the League of Nations to write, to let the animus out of his cramped soul. There were memories, of course, of Henry Adams, dead since 1918; of Theodore; of the books he had written and the books he had meant to write . . . of Nannie, who had been so dear and close, so great a help to him in that beloved library on Massachusetts Avenue. . . . There was his bright young grandson, who bore his name, to talk with, to plan the future with. . . . And there was the sea, restless like himself, and imperious also. . . . Thirty-one years in the Senate, so much history to look back on! That awful, desperate fight with Woodrow Wilson, whose funeral he had refused to attend, and all that went before. . . . Had he been right? Was the victory really his?

Late in July he was taken ill and removed to the Charlesgate Hospital in Cambridge. He rallied quickly and in August was back at Nahant. There he remained until the trees turned and the sound of approaching winter could be heard as the surf rolled in. On October 20 he was operated upon. On November 9 he suffered a stroke. At 11.14 o'clock that night Henry Cabot Lodge died.

The Commonwealth of Massachusetts, by order of its General Court, placed a statue to his memory on the grounds of the State House. But there are those who feel that his real memorial was not a piece of bronze, but the surge of death that roared across Europe in the autumn of 1939, the catastrophe that we call the Second World War, and that he helped cause it himself, that he started the dreadful grotesquerie that day when he sat beside Theodore Roosevelt's bedside plotting the destruction of Woodrow Wilson's dream for humanity and turning America back from the world, unto herself.

361

Bibliography

Abbott, Lawrence F., *The Letters of Archie Butt*. 1924

Abbott, Lyman, *Silhouettes of My Contemporaries*. 1921

Adams, Henry, *The Education of Henry Adams, An Autobiography*. 1927

—— *History of the United States of America: 1801–1817*. 1921

—— *Letters of Henry Adams (1858–1891)*. Edited by Worthington Chauncey Ford. 1930

—— *Letters of Henry Adams (1892–1918)*. Edited by Worthington Chauncey Ford. 1938

—— *The Life of George Cabot Lodge*. 1911

Adams, James Truslow, *The History of New England*. 3 vols. 1927

—— *The March of Democracy*. Vol. II. 1933

Adams, Randolph G., "Henry White." *Current History*. Vol. 33, No. 4. January 1931

American Historical Review, articles and reviews, especially Vol. XIX, p. 691, and Vol. XXXI, pp. 555–557

Arena Magazine, unsigned articles: "Battle Between Plutocracy and Democracy," October 1906; "Leading Citizens Denounce Machine Rule" and "Opposition of the Boss and Corporate Agencies to Popular Government," June 1907; "Apostle of the Autocratic Money-Controlled Machine," November 1906

Bailey, Thomas A., "The Lodge Corollary to the Monroe Doctrine." *Political Science Quarterly*, June 1933. Vol. 48, No. 2, pp. 220–229

Baker, Ray Stannard, *Woodrow Wilson, Life and Letters*. 8 vols. 1927–1939

Barnes, James A., *John G. Carlisle, Financial Statesman*. 1931

Bates, Ernest Sutherland, *The Story of Congress, 1789–1935*. 1936

Beard, Charles A., *The Idea of National Interest*. 1934

Bemis, Samuel Flagg, *American Secretaries of State and Their Diplomacy*. 10 vols. 1927–1929

Bemis, Samuel Flagg, *A Diplomatic History of the United States.* Revised ed. 1942

Bishop,. Joseph Bucklin, *Presidential Nominations and Elections.* 1916

Bonsal, Stephen, *Unfinished Business.* 1944

Boston. *Fifty Years of Boston, a Memorial Volume.* 1930

Boston Advertiser, files

Boston Evening Transcript, files

Boston Globe, files

Boston Herald, files

Boston Journal, files

Boston Post, files

Bowers, Claude G., *Beveridge and the Progressive Era.* 1932

Bridgman, R. L., "Who Runs Massachusetts?" *New England Magazine,* November 1906. N.S. 35, pp. 285–290

Briggs, L. Vernon, *History and Genealogy of the Cabot Family, 1475–1927.* 2 vols. 1927

Brooks, Van Wyck, *The Flowering of New England.* 1936

—— *New England's Indian Summer.* 1940

—— *Opinions of Oliver Alston.* 1941

Burdette, Franklin L., *Filibustering in the Senate.* 1940

Butler, Nicholas Murray, *Across the Busy Years.* 1939

—— "Herbert Spencer's 'The Great Political Superstition.'" *Forum.* Vol. LV, pp. 81–108

Butt, Archie, *Taft and Roosevelt, the Intimate Papers of Archie Butt, Military Aide.* 1930

Clark, Champ, *My Quarter Century of American Politics.* 1920

Cochran, Thomas C., and Miller, William, *The Age of Enterprise: a Social Study of Industrial America.* 1942

Cohalan, Daniel F., *Senator Lodge Past and Present.* 1922

Colgrove, Kenneth, *The American Senate and World Peace.* 1944

Congressional Directory, 1887–1925

Congressional Record, 1887–1925

Coolidge, Harold Jefferson (and Robert H. Lord), *Life and Letters of Archibald Cary Coolidge.* 1932

Coolidge, Louis A., "Henry Cabot Lodge." *New England Historical and Genealogical Register.* Vol. LXXIX, pp. 227–243

Council on Foreign Relations Survey of American Foreign Relations. 1928

Cowles, Anna Roosevelt, *Letters of Theodore Roosevelt to Anna Roosevelt Cowles, 1870–1891.* 1924

Crapo, Henry Howland, *The Story of William Wallace Crapo, 1830–1926.* 1942

Cullom, Shelby Moore, *Fifty Years of Public Service.* 1911

Curtis, Francis, *The Republican Party.* 2 vols. 1904

Darling, H. Maurice, "Who Kept the United States Out of the League of Nations?" *Canadian National Review.* Vol. 10, pp. 196–211. 1929

Davis, Oscar King, *Released for Publication.* 1925

Dennis, A. L. P., *Adventures of American Diplomacy, 1896–1906.* 1928

Dictionary of American Biography, ed. Allen Johnson and Dumas Malone. 20 vols. 1928–1936. Article by William B. Munro on Henry Cabot Lodge, Vol. XI

Dodd, William E., *Woodrow Wilson and His Work.* 1921

Dunn, Arthur Wallace, *From Harrison to Harding.* 1922

Evans, Lawrence Boyd, *Samuel W. McCall.* 1916

Fleming, Denna F., *The Treaty Veto of the American Senate.* 1930

—— *The United States and the League of Nations, 1918–1920.* 1932

—— *United States and World Organization, 1920–1933.* 1938

Foraker, Joseph B., *Notes of a Busy Life.* 1926

Ford, Worthington Chauncey, ed. *See* Adams, Henry

Fuess, Claude Moore, *Calvin Coolidge, the Man from Vermont.* 1940

—— *Carl Schurz.* 1932

—— "Carl Schurz, Henry Cabot Lodge, and the Campaign of 1884: A Study in Temperament and Political Philosophy." *New England Quarterly.* Vol. V, No. 3, pp. 453–482. 1932

—— Unpublished address to the Massachusetts Historical Society: "Henry Cabot Lodge as Man of Letters"

Gardner, Augustus P., *Letters.* 1918

Gosnall, Harold F., *Boss Platt and the New York Machine.* 1924

Griffin, Solomon B., *W. Murray Crane, a Man and Brother.* 1926

Groves, Charles S., *Henry Cabot Lodge the Statesman.* 1925

Gwynn, Stephen, ed., *Letters and Friendships of Sir Cecil Spring-Rice*. 2 vols. 1929

Haines, Lynn, *The Senate from 1907 to 1912*. 1912

Hammond, John Hays, *The Autobiography of John Hays Hammond*. 2 vols. 1935

Handlin, Oscar R., *Boston's Immigrants, 1790–1865, A Study in Acculturation*. 1941

Harvey, George, *Henry Clay Frick the Man*. 1928

Heaton, John L., ed. *Cobb of "The World."* 1924

Hendrick, Burton J., *The Life and Letters of Walter Hines Page*. 1927

Hennessy, Michael E., "Social and Political Readjustments, 1889–1929." *Commonwealth History of Massachusetts*. Vol. V, Ch. VI, pp. 168–196

—— *Twenty-five Years of Massachusetts Politics*. 1917

Hill, H. C., *Roosevelt and the Caribbean*. 1927

Hoar, George Frisbie, *Autobiography of 75 Years*. 1903

House, E. M., and Seymour, Charles, *What Really Happened at Paris*. 1921

Howden-Smith, Arthur D., *Mr. House of Texas*. 1940

Howe, M. A. De W., *Boston: The Place and People*. 1903.

—— *George von Lengerke Meyer, His Life and Public Service*. 1920

—— *Portrait of an Independent: Moorfield Storey, 1845–1929*. 1932

Independent, files

James, Henry, *Charles W. Eliot*. 1930

Jessup, Philip C., *Elihu Root*. 1938

Johnson, Willis Fletcher, *George Harvey, a Passionate Portrait*. 1929

Josephson, Matthew, *The President Makers, Culture and Politics in the Age of Enlightenment*. 1940

Journal of the House of Representatives of the Commonwealth of Massachusetts for 1880 and 1881

Kerney, James, *The Political Education of Woodrow Wilson*. 1926

King, E. M., "The Spotlight Beats on Lodge." *New York Evening Post,* July 5, 1919

Kohlsaat, H. H., *From McKinley to Harding.* 1923

Laferriere, J., *"La Résolution Lodge et la Doctrine Monroe."
Revue Générale de Droit International Politique.* Vol. XX.
1913

La Follette, Robert, *La Follette's Autobiography.* 1913

Lansing, Robert, *The Peace Negotiations, a Personal Narrative.*
1921. "War Memories"

Lawrence, David, *The True Story of Woodrow Wilson.* 1924

Lawrence, William, *Henry Cabot Lodge.* 1925

Lippmann, Walter, *U. S. Foreign Policy: Shield of the Republic.*
1943

Literary Digest, files

Living Age, files

Lodge, Henry Cabot, *Alexander Hamilton.* 1882

—— *Ballads and Lyrics.* 1881

—— *Boston.* 1891

—— *Certain Accepted Heroes* (with Theodore Roosevelt). 1897

—— Commencement Addresses, Two. 1915

—— *The Compulsory Initiative and Referendum and Recall of
Judges.* 1912

—— "The Constitution and Its Makers" (Address). 1911

—— *The Constitution of the United States.* 1911

—— *Daniel Webster.* 1883

—— *Democracy of Abraham Lincoln.* 1913

—— *Democracy of the Constitution and Other Addresses.* 1915

—— *Early Memories.* 1913

—— *A Fighting Frigate.* 1906

—— "Francis Parkman" (Essay). 1903

—— *A Frontier Town and Other Essays.* 1906

—— *General Arbitration Treaties with Great Britain and
France.* 1912

—— "Gold Policy" (Speech). 1895

—— *The Life of George Washington.* 1889

—— *Hero Tales* (with Theodore Roosevelt). 1895

—— *Historical and Political Essays.* 1892

—— "Immigration" (Speech). 1891

—— "Immigration" (Speech). 1908

—— "Intervention in Cuba" (Speech). 1898

—— "The Last of the Puritans" (Essay). 1878

Lodge, Henry Cabot, *The Leather Industry and Free Hides.* 1909
—— *The Life and Letters of George Cabot.* 1877
—— *A Memoir of Caleb Strong.* 1897
—— "Monroe Doctrine" (Speech). 1895
—— "National Supervision of National Elections" (Speech). 1890
—— "Obstruction in the Senate." *North American Review,* November 1893. Vol. CLVII, p. 253 ff.
—— *One Hundred Years of Peace.* 1913
—— *Oration Before Boston City Council.* 1879
—— "Our Blundering Foreign Policy." *Forum,* March 1895. Vol. XIX, pp. 8–17
—— "The Pilgrims of Plymouth" (Address). 1920
—— *Poems and Dramas of George Cabot Lodge* (Ed.). 1911
—— "Protection of American Citizens" (Speech). 1897
—— "Protection and Free Trade" (Speech). 1894
—— "The Question of Canal Tolls" (Speech). 1914
—— "Reciprocity with Canada and Affairs in the Philippines" (Speeches). 1903
—— "Restriction of Immigration" (Speech). 1896
—— *The Senate and the League of Nations.* 1925
—— *A Short History of the English Colonies in America.* 1881
—— Speeches. 1895
—— Speeches and Addresses. 1909
—— Speech at Symphony Hall. 1911
—— *The Story of the Revolution.* 1898
—— *Studies in History.* 1884
—— "The Sugar Schedule" (Speech). 1912
—— "Theodore Roosevelt" (Memorial Address). 1919
—— "Timothy Pickering" (Essay). 1878
—— War Addresses. 1917
—— "War Revenue" (Speech). 1912
—— *The War with Spain.* 1899
—— "Washington's Principles of Neutrality" (Speech). 1916
—— "Charles Francis Adams" (Address). 1916
—— *André's Journal* (Ed.). 1903
—— *Essays in Anglo-Saxon Law* (Contributor). 1876
—— *The Federalist* (Ed.). 1907
—— *Works of Alexander Hamilton* (Ed.). 9 vols. 1884–1885

—— *Selections from the Correspondence of Theodore Roosevelt and Henry Cabot Lodge* (Ed.). 1925

Lodge, Henry Cabot, Jr., "Lessons from a Historic Debate." *The New York Times Magazine*, January 30, 1944

Longworth, Alice Roosevelt, *Crowded Hours.* 1933

Loth, David, *Woodrow Wilson, the Fifteenth Point.* 1941

Lynn Item, files

McAdoo, William G., *Crowded Years.* 1931

McCall, Samuel W., *The Life of Thomas B. Reed.* 1914

McElroy, R. L., *Grover Cleveland, the Man and the Statesman.* 1923

Mahan, Alfred Thayer, *Armaments and Arbitration.* 1912

Matthews, Brander, "Henry Cabot Lodge as a Man of Letters." *New York Times Book Review*, June 19, 1921, p. 17

Millis, Walter, *The Martial Spirit*, 1931

—— *The Road to War, 1914–1917.* 1935.

Moors, John F., "President Wilson and Senator Lodge." *The Public*, September 6, 1919

Morison, Samuel Eliot, *The Development of Harvard University, 1869–1929.* 1929

—— "Memoir of Edward H. Clement." *Massachusetts Historical Society Proceedings.* Vol. LVI, p. 64

Morse, John Torrey, Jr., "Henry Cabot Lodge." *Harvard Graduates Magazine.* Vol. XXXIII, pp. 439–455. 1925

—— "Henry Cabot Lodge." *Massachusetts Historical Society Proceedings.* Vol. LVIII, pp. 99–110. 1925

Mott, F. L., "History of the North American Review." *North American Review.* Vol. 240, No. 1, pp. 162–165. 1935

Muzzey, David S., *James G. Blaine.* 1934

Myers, William Starr, *The Republican Party, a History.* 1928

Nevins, Allan, "Henry Cabot Lodge as Historian." *New York Times Magazine*, December 20, 1919

—— *Henry White, Thirty Years of American Diplomacy.* 1930

New York Herald, files

New York Post, files

New York Sun, files

New York Times, files

New York Tribune, files

Nichols, Jeannette Paddock, "The Politics and Personalities of Silver Repeal in the U. S." *American Historical Review,* October 1925. Vol. XLI, pp. 26–53

Norton, Charles Eliot, "The Public Life and Services of William Eustis Russell." *Harvard Graduates Magazine.* Vol. V, pp. 177–194. 1896

Notter, Harley, *The Origins of the Foreign Policy of Woodrow Wilson.* 1937

Outlook, files, especially November 19 and December 20, 1924

Pepper, Claude, "A Summons Against the 'Kiss of Death.'" *The New York Times Magazine,* December 12, 1943

Perkins, Dexter, *The Monroe Doctrine, 1867–1907.* 1937

—— *Hands Off, a History of the Monroe Doctrine.* 1941

Phillips, David Graham, "Menace of Plutocracy." *Arena Magazine,* March 1906. Vol. 35, pp. 258–264

—— "Treason of the Senate." *Cosmopolitan,* September 1906. Vol. 41, pp. 528–533

Political Science Quarterly, articles and reviews

Pratt, Julian W., *Expansionists of 1898, the Acquisition of Hawaii and the Spanish Islands.* 1936

Pringle, Henry F., *Theodore Roosevelt, a Biography.* 1931

—— *The Life and Times of William Howard Taft.* 2 vols. 1939

Robinson, Corinne Roosevelt, *My Brother, Theodore Roosevelt.* 1921

Roosevelt, Theodore, *Autobiography.* 1913

Russell, Charles Edward, *Blaine of Maine.* 1931

Schriftgiesser, Karl, *The Amazing Roosevelt Family.* 1942

—— *Families.* 1940

Seymour, Charles, *American Diplomacy During the World War.* 1934

—— *American Neutrality, 1914–1917.* 1934

Shibley, G. H., "Lodge as Upholder of Machine Rule." *Atlas Magazine,* November 1907. Vol. 38, pp. 517–519

Sprout, Harold and Margaret, *The Rise of American Naval Power, 1776–1918.* 1939

370

Stein, Charles W., *The Third Term Tradition, Its Rise and Collapse in American Politics*. 1943

Stephenson, N. W., *Nelson W. Aldrich*. 1930

Sullivan, Mark, "Henry Cabot Lodge, a Massachusetts Institution." *World's Work*, September 1922

—— *Our Times*. 6 vols. 1926–1935

—— "America and the League Six Years After." *World's Work*, January 1926

Taylor, Charles Carlisle, *The Life of Admiral Mahan*. 1920

Tumulty, Joseph, *Woodrow Wilson as I Knew Him*. 1921

Van Alstyne, Richard W., *American Diplomacy in Action, a Series of Case Studies*. 1944

Villard, Oswald Garrison, *Prophets True and False*. 1928

Washburn, Charles G., "Henry Cabot Lodge." *Massachusetts Historical Society Proceedings*. Vol. 58, pp. 324–376. 1925

—— *Life of John W. Weeks*. 1928

—— Unpublished notes and papers in the American Antiquarian Society, Worcester, Massachusetts

Watson, James E., *As I Knew Them*. 1936

White, William Allen, *A Puritan in Babylon, the Story of Calvin Coolidge*. 1938

Wilson, Woodrow, *Messages and Papers*. 1924

World Peace Foundation, pamphlets

Index

Hildreth's *History*, 39
Hill, Dr. Thomas, 25
Hindustan, 288
Hitchcock, Gilbert M. (U. S. Senator), 332, 337, 345–346, 348
Hitt, Robert P., 144
Hoar, George Frisbie (U. S. Senator), 81, 83, 87, 90, 106 n., 125, 153, 158, 171, 181, 182, 210, 213
Holmes, Oliver Wendell, Sr., 46
Holmes, Oliver Wendell, Jr., 22, 25, 203–204
Holy Alliance, 338
Holy Cross College, 200 n.
Home Market Club, 118
Hong Kong, 176
Hoover, Herbert, 310
Horticultural Society of Boston, 13
House, Col. Edward Mandell, 299, 301, 304, 344–345
House of Representatives, U. S., 97, 112, 125, 143, 144
Howard Athenaeum, Boston, 26
Howells, William Dean, 36, 44, 95
Huerta, Victoriano, 262–266
Hughes, Charles Evans, 232, 278, 281–282, 325
Hull, Commodore Isaac, 28
Hungary, 336

ILLINOIS, 67
Immigration, 110, 114–117, 245, 237, 290, 323, 325
Immigration Commission, 223–224
Income tax, 239
Independent Party, 53
Interior, Department of the, 55
International Copyright Law, 131
International Review, 43, 57, 71, 259
Interstate Commerce Commission, 215
Ireland, 336
Irish vote, 127, 336 n., 348 n., 358
Irreconcilables (Versailles Treaty), 320, 349

JACKSON, ANDREW, 76
Jackson, Charles Cabot, 47, 212
Jamaica, 179
James, Henry, 30, 36
James River, 6

Japan, 172, 173, 202, 223–224, 247, 252, 253, 335
Japanese Exclusion Act, 360
Jefferson, Thomas (U. S. President), 10, 38, 96, 137, 147, 277 n., 291
Jersey, Isles of, 4
Jetté, Sir Louis, 209
Johns Hopkins University, 43
Johnson, Andrew (U. S. President), 46
Johnson, Hiram W. (U. S. Senator), 318, 320, 324, 330, 331, 333 f., 344, 353

KANSAS CITY STOCKYARDS (pfd.), 218 n.
Kelley, Florence, 226
Kemble, Fanny, 19
Key West, 174
Keyes, Lorrin P., 61
King, E. M., 200 n.
Kipling, Rudyard, 181
Kirkland, Elizabeth Cabot, 17
Kirkland, John Thornton, 17
Knights of Labor, 98, 121
Knox, Philander C. (U. S. Senator), 306, 314–318, 328, 331, 333
Knox treaties, 256
Kohlsaat, H. H., 157 and n.
Korea, 288
Kruger, President, 148

LA FOLLETTE, ROBERT M. (U. S. Senator), 217, 232, 238
Lane, Gardiner, 212
Langdon, Samuel, 12
Lansdowne, Marquis of, 139, 201
Lansing, Robert (U. S. Secretary of State), 299, 337
Laughlin, J. Laurence, 38
Laurier, Sir Wilfrid, 207
Lawrence, Mass., 16
Lawrence, William (Bishop of Mass.), 90, 219 n., 273
League of Nations, seed sown, 276–277, 279; Lodge on, 303; discussed by Roosevelt and Lodge, 304; Lodge speaks on, in Senate, 306–307; first draft of Covenant, 307–308; Lodge says it cannot pass, 311; "round robin" against, 317–319; debate in Boston on,

321–324; new covenant framed, 324–325; Monroe Doctrine incorporated, 325; Article Ten attacked, 327; offered "pitiless publicity," 328–329; delivered to Senate, 331; attacked by Lodge, 338 ff.; discussed by Lodge and Wilson, 340; amendments adopted, 340; committee reports on, 341–342; reservations attached, 342; the Lodge Reservations, 344–346; compromise fails, 349–350; defeated, 350–351; endorsed by Republican Convention, 352, 356

League to Enforce Peace, 276, 287

Lee, Fitzhugh, 174

Lee, George Cabot, 80

Lee, Henry, 20

Lee, Col. Henry, 40, 41

Lee, Joseph, 9

Lee, Gen. Robert E., 76

Leland Hotel, Chicago, 65

Lenroot, Irvine (U. S. Senator), 357

Liberal Party, 69

Liberal Republicans, 41

Life of Alexander Hamilton (Morse), 36 and *n.*

Life and Letters of George Cabot Lodge, 41–42

Lincoln, Abraham, 23, 50, 108

Lincoln, Robert Todd, 80

Lippmann, Jonas, 284 *n.*

Lippmann, Walter, 284

Liverpool, 12

Lodge, Constance (Mrs. Constance Gardner Williams), 31, 130, 351

Lodge, Elizabeth Cabot (sister of Henry Cabot Lodge, Mrs. James), 18, 21, 24

Lodge, Henry Cabot, ancestry, 3–12; birth, 13; childhood, 18; early schooling, 18–19; moves to Beacon Street, 19; at Mr. Sullivan's school, 19–20; at Dixwell's School, 21; death of father, 21–22; Civil War, 23–24; first European trip, 24; enters Harvard, 25; meets Henry Adams, 26; engaged to Miss Davis, 27–28; graduated from Harvard, married, 30; spends year abroad, 30–33; daughter Con-

stance born, 31; advised by Henry Adams, 33; assistant editor of *North American Review*, 35; enters Harvard Law School, 35; resigns from *Review*, 37; studies Anglo-Saxon Land Law, 37–38; receives doctorate, 38; teaches history at Harvard, 38–39; publishes *Life of George Cabot*, 40–41; birth of sons, 42; Lowell lecturer, 42; co-edits *International Review*, 43; writes for *Atlantic Monthly*, 44; meets Carl Schurz, 45; associated with Boston reformers, 46–47; founds Commonwealth Club, 47; supports Bristow, 49–50; attends New York reform convention, 51; stand on political independence, 54; appointed to State Board of Library Trustees, 56; resigns from Harvard, 57; nominated to Massachusetts House of Representatives, 58; supported by Lynn liquor dealers, 59; elected, 60; legislative career, 60–63; delegate to Republican National Convention, 1880, 65–69; re-elected to House, 70; writes *Alexander Hamilton*, 71; nominated to State Senate, campaign, defeat, 72–73; elected chairman Republican State Committee, 75; leads anti-Ben Butler campaign, 76–77; against Blaine's nomination, delegate to convention, 1884, 79–82; goes over to Blaine, 83–92; elected Overseer of Harvard, 88; nominated for Congress, defeated, 90–92; edits Hamilton's papers, writes Webster's and Washington's biographies, 93–96; writes Republican state platform, 96; elected to Congress, 97; defends Thobe in election case, 98–100; early legislative record, 100; attacks Cleveland's foreign policy, 100–101; re-elected, 101; Navy Yard charges, 102; advocates post office reform, 102–103; puts 1890 Force Bill through House, 104–108; advocates big navy, 110–114; advocates immigration restriction, 114–117; perfects "Lodge machine," 118–119; elected to U. S. Senate, 119–120; stand on silver, tariff, and the British, 123–127; as "scholar in politics," 120–122; 129–131; "rediscovers" Monroe Doctrine, 132 ff.; urges annexation of Hawaii, 133, 134; speech in favor of expansion, 134–136; part in "Venezuela Affair," 136–144; attacks England, 141; foreign-policy speech in Senate, 146–148; urges purchase of Danish West Indies and Greenland, 149–151; introduces coastal defense bill, discusses Cuban situation, 151–152; backs Tom Reed for President, 139, 153–159; forces Republican "gold plank," 156–158; writes party platform, 159; stumps for McKinley, 160; backs Roosevelt for Navy post, 162–165; against Olney-Pauncefote Treaty, 166–168; works with Roosevelt for Big Navy, 169 ff.; plots seizure of Philippines, 175–176; leads Peace Treaty ratification, 179–181; re-elected to Senate, 184, 240–246, 285, 358–359; seeks Vice Presidency for Roosevelt, 185–188; writings, 188; fights with Henry Adams, 188–190; European trip, 190; death of mother, 190; against Hay-Pauncefote Treaty, 190–192; mentioned for cabinet, 196; defends Senate's treaty rights, 201; "investigates" Philippines, 202; suggests O. W. Holmes, Jr., for Supreme Court, 203–204; on "trusts" and coal strike, 204–206; attacked by Eugene Foss, 206; on Alaska Boundary Commission, 207–210; receives honorary Harvard degree, 211; campaigns for Roosevelt, 211 ff.; disagrees with Roosevelt on arbitration and railroad rates, 214–218; his wealth explained, 218–219 and *n.*; on Algeciras convention, 221; forces through Japanese "passport clause," 223–224; advocates child labor law, 225–227; meets Taft, 227; sup-

ports Taft's candidacy, 228–233; suspected by Taft, 235; on Payne-Aldrich tariff, 237–239; opposes income tax, 239; death of his poet son, 239; against arbitration treaties, 246–251; his Monroe Doctrine "corollary," 252–254; "breaks" with Roosevelt, supports Taft, 255–258; early liking for Woodrow Wilson, 258–259; illness, 259; against New Freedom domestic legislation, 259 ff.; opposes Mexican policy, 262–266; attacks Ship Purchase Bill, 266; resorts to filibuster, 267; for large standing army, 268–269; his dual stand on Presidency, 270; advocates a league of nations (Union College speech), 271–273; death of Mrs. Lodge, 273; assails Wilson's "meaningless words," 275; speaks with Wilson for a league, 276–277; at 1916 convention, 278–282; attacks Wilson on *Lusitania* note, apologizes to Wilson, 282–284; enmity for Wilson grows, attacks him in Senate, 287–288; warns of "amblings to disaster," 293; meets Calvin Coolidge, 295; joins Roosevelt's anti-Wilson cabal, 296–298; disapproves Peace Commission, 299; meets with dying Roosevelt, 304–305; attacks League in Senate speech, 306–307; "evil thing with holy name," 311; White House parley, 312, 314–315; Republican "round robin," 317–319; debates with A. Lawrence Lowell on League, 322–324; assumes anti-League leadership in Senate, 326; attacks Article Ten, 327; warns of "pitiless publicity," 328–329; attacks Shantung settlement, 336; seeks Irish vote, 336 *n.*; cheered in Senate, 338–339; conference with Wilson, 339–340; Lodge reservations, 344–349; Treaty fails, 350; rebuked by Murray Crane, 352; favors Harding, 353 ff.; seventieth birthday, 354; 1920 keynote speech, 354–355; described by

294, 295, 298, 301, 304–305, 306, 324, 361
Roosevelt, Mrs. Theodore, 185, 187, 200
Root, Elihu, 121, 148, 196, 202, 208, 215, 235, 253, 255, 267, 275, 276, 301, 324, 325, 330
Ropes & Gray, law firm, 35
Rough Riders, 184, 193, 293
"Round Robin," 317–320, 332
Rowell, Jonathan H., 105
Roxbury Latin School, 18
Russell, Charles Edward, 79
Russell, William Eustis, 109
Russia, 221; Russian Revolution, 294–295; treaty with, 207

St. Louis, Mo., 64, 156, 159
St. Nicholas Hotel, N. Y., 24
Salisbury, Lord, 138
Saltonstall, Leverett, 89
Samoa, 112, 129, 136
Sandwich Islands, 135 f.
Sanguilly, Julio, 171
Santa Cruz, 12
Santo Domingo, 12, 129
Saturday Evening Post, 157 n.
Saugus, Mass., 72, 73
Schurz, Carl, 45 ff., 55, 56, 64, 79, 83, 85–86, 89, 132, 172
Schurz, Mrs. Carl, 46
Scribner's Magazine, 188, 201
Senate and the League of Nations, The (Lodge), 259, 268, 317 n.
Senate committees of H. C. Lodge, listed, 129, 169 n., 237 n.
Seward, William (U. S. Secretary of State), 149–150, 190
Shakespeare, William, 20, 90, 198 and n.
Shantung Settlement, 335–336, 343
Shaw, Robert Gould, 23
Sherman, John (U. S. Senator), 66, 67, 145, 317
Sherman, William, 66
Shields, John K. (U. S. Senator), 332
Ship Purchase Bill, 266–268
Shipping Board Act, 268 n.
Short History of English Colonies (Lodge), 42
Silver Purchase Act of 1890, 122 ff.

Simpson, "Jerry," 78
Simpson, Michael Henry, 31–32, 35
Slav provinces of Austria, 288
Smalley, George W., 140
Smith, Adam, 126
Smith, Marcus A. (U. S. Senator), 332
Smoot, Reed (U. S. Senator), 267, 278–279, 314, 356
Socialism, 216, 266
Soldiers' Bonus Act, 359–360
Southern Hotel, St. Louis, 156, 159
Sovereignty, 249 ff.
Spain, 141, 170, 269
Spanish-American War, 188, 196
Spanish Main, 147
Speeches and Addresses (Lodge), 220 n.
Spenser, Edmund, 20
Springfield Republican, 55, 89, 101, 184, 275
Spring-Rice, Sir Cecil, 121
Sprout, Harold and Margaret, 113 n.
State Street, Boston, 15, 211
Stearns, Frank, 353
Stetson, Cushing, 131
Stevenson, Adlai E. (U. S. Vice President), 123
Stewart, William (U. S. Senator), 125
Stimson, Henry L., 258
Stoddard, Henry L., 356
Stone, William J. (U. S. Senator), 107–108, 107 n., 269
Storey, Moorfield, 46, 50, 80, 86
Story, William Wetmore, 71
Studies in History (Lodge), 96
Submarine warfare, 274 f.
Sullivan, Mark, 218, 351, 354
Sullivan, Thomas Russell, 19–21
Summer Street, Boston, 13, 15, 17
Sumner, Charles (U. S. Senator), 21, 22, 46, 105, 108, 120, 245
Sutherland, Duke of, 139
Swampscott, Mass., 72
Swanson, Claude (U. S. Senator), 319, 332, 346
Swift, Jonathan, 37
Symphony Hall, Boston, 244, 246

Taft, William Howard, 202, 216, 227–229, 232, 235, 241, 244, 248,

"White slave" act, 280 *n.*
Whittier, John Greenleaf, 108
Wilde, Oscar, 108
Wilhelm, Kaiser, of Germany, 148, 220
Williams, Mrs. Constance Gardner. See Lodge, Constance
Williams, John Sharp, 309, 329, 332, 334, 339
Wilson, Joseph Thomas, 56, 58, 65, 84
Wilson, (Thomas) Woodrow (U. S. President), 43, 148; elected President, 243; 258, 259, 260, 264, 265, 266, 267, 269, 270 and *n.*, 271, 274, 275; addresses League to Enforce Peace, 276–277, 279 *n.*; sends *Lusitania* note, 283–285; speech to Senate, 286–287; severs relations with Germany, 291–292; war message, 292; asks return of Democratic Congress, 297; appoints Peace Commission, 299; sails for Paris, 300; drafts League Covenant, 307–

308; invites Congressional interrogation, 312; arrives in Boston, 312; address in Boston, 313–314; returns to Paris, 320; frames new covenant, 324 ff.; wins over French, 325; Fiume issue, 327; calls special session of Congress, 328 ff.; sails for home, 330; delivers treaty to Senate, 331; Congressional conference, 339; continental tour, 341; illness, 343; message, 348; funeral, 361
Wilson, Mrs. Woodrow, 315, 344
Winchester, Mass., 91, 103
Wingate, Charles F., 36
Winthrop Place, Boston, 18–19
Winthrop Square, Boston, 13
Wolcott, Huntington, 22
Wolcott, Roger, 22, 53, 54, 80
Woman suffrage, 279–280, 280 *n.*
Wood, Leonard, 276, 353, 356
Woolsey, Theodore Dwight, 50
World Court, 279, 358, 360
Wright, Chauncey, 36
Wright, Silas, 188